Business Opportunities in India

THE BOOK, A remarkable effort on the part of the Business Study Mission of Nanyang University Business School, provides a comprehensive Environment Scan of the Indian Industry- and Macro-Environment. The Resource based view of the economy combining the external analysis of the industry and competitive environment with the internal analysis viz. core competence of India in various industries could be of interest to policy planners and business groups interested in the investment opportunities offered by the Indian economy. The refreshing change in the book is the use of Porter's approach built on an analysis of factor conditions, demand conditions, related and supporting industries to analyse the competitiveness of Indian firms relative to others in the global context. The industry analysis of the Indian software, telecom and tourism sectors provides useful insights into the concerned areas.

R. Venkatesan (Chief of Industry and Infrastructure Division, National Council of Applied Economic Research, New Delhi, India)

THIS AUTHORITATIVE BOOK on business opportunities in India is essential reading for investors who want to explore the vast potential for business in and with India.

The book's methodology of research, interviews and discussions with top Indian officials and businessmen bring out the "real" India that shows that "India is indeed on the move".

Tan Sri Dato' R. V. Navaratnam (Corporate Advisor, The Sungei Way Group of Companies, Petaling Jaya, Malaysia)

Titles in the Nanyang Business Report Series

Business Opportunities in Penang, Malaysia

Business Opportunities in Sichuan Province, China

Business Opportunities in India

Business Opportunities in the Philippines

Business Opportunities in Myanmar

Business Opportunities in the Yangtze River Delta, China

For further enquiries, information or feedback on the series, please write to the Editor at e-mail: prenhall@singnet.com.sg or Simon & Schuster (Asia) Pte Ltd, 317 Alexandra Road, #04-01 IKEA Building, Singapore 159965.

NANYANG BUSINESS REPORT SERIES

Business Opportunities in India

Edited by

Tan Teck Meng (Dean)
Low Aik Meng (Vice Dean and Director of MBA Programme)
John J. Williams (Chief Coordinator, Business Study Mission)
Ravinder Zutshi (Coordinator, Business Study Mission)

Nanyang Technological University
Singapore

Prentice Hall
Singapore New York London Toronto Sydney Tokyo

First published 1996 by
Prentice Hall
Simon & Schuster (Asia) Pte Ltd
317 Alexandra Road
#04-01 IKEA Building
Singapore 159965

Printed in Singapore

1 2 3 4 5   00 99 98 97 96

ISBN 0-13-713363-4
ISBN 0-13-267899-3 (pbk)

Prentice Hall International (UK) Limited, *London*
Prentice Hall of Australia Pty. Limited, *Sydney*
Prentice Hall Canada Inc., *Toronto*
Prentice Hall Hispanoamericana, *S.A., Mexico*
Prentice Hall of India Private Limited, *New Delhi*
Prentice Hall of Japan, Inc., *Tokyo*
Editora Prentice Hall do Brasil, Ltda., *Rio de Janeiro*
Prentice Hall, Inc., *Upper Saddle River, New Jersey*

CONTENTS

LOCATION

INDUSTRY ANALYSES

ABOUT THE EDITORS

TAN TECK MENG is Professor and Dean at the Nanyang Business School. Since joining academia in the early 1970s, Professor Tan has combined his university responsibilities with extensive consultancy work, largely in the field of accountancy. He holds senior positions on a number of institutional boards and committees in Singapore including the Accounting and Auditing Services Working Group of the Economic Committee, the Public Accountants Board, the Board of Directors of Singapore Reinsurance Corporation Limited, the Institute of Certified Public Accountants of Singapore (ICPAS) Annual Report Award Competition Committee and the Income Tax Board of Review. Professor Tan is founding Director of the Entrepreneurship Development Centre (ENDEC) and in 1992 was elected to the Board of Governors of the MIT Sloan School of Management Society for Senior Executives. He is a council member of the ICPAS.

LOW AIK MENG is Associate Professor and Director of the MBA programme at the Nanyang Business School. He worked for five years as an accountant and an internal auditor before joining academia in 1975. He was Vice Dean of the Faculty of Accountancy and Business Administration at the National University of Singapore until he joined the Nanyang Technological University in 1987. He is currently Vice Dean at the Nanyang Business School and has been the Director of its very successful MBA Programme since its inception in 1991. Under his leadership, the MBA Programme has been building a network of contacts with businesses and government bodies in Singapore and overseas. He spearheads the thrice-yearly Business Study Missions which are an integral part of the MBA Programme. Associate Professor Low continues to be active in the accountancy profession and serves on several committees in the Institute of Certified Public Accountants of Singapore.

JOHN J. WILLIAMS is Associate Professor at the Nanyang Business School and Chief Coordinator of the MBA Business Study Mission programme. He has taught and carried out research projects in several countries including Canada, the U.S., Kenya, and Singapore. Throughout the latter part of the 1980s, Dr. Williams served as Vice-Chairman and Chairman of the Final Accreditation Exam Board for the Society of Management Accountants of Canada, which admitted him as a Fellow in the Society in 1992. Although active in consulting for government agencies in the U.S. and Canada during this period, he has published extensively in leading academic and professional journals and he continues to pursue the study of emerging regional economies in the Asean region.

RAVI K. ZUTSHI is a Senior Fellow at the Nanyang Business School. Previously, he was Professor of Strategic Management at the Indian Institute of Management, Lucknow. Dr. Zutshi received his PhD degree from the University of Pittsburgh where he was also the Assistant Director of the Small Business Development Centre. In India, he was Director of the Operations Research Group for a major marketing research consultancy company in the mid-1970s. After returning to India from the U.S. in the early 1980s, he became Advisor to the Planning Commission, Government of India, and was responsible for planning and review of public enterprise policy. He has consulted for the Industrial Development Bank of India and Singapore Technologies Industrial Corporation. In addition, he has been a consultant to the Ministry of Science and Technology, Ministry of Water Resources, Ministry of Labour, Ministry of Industry, and the Department of Electronics for the Government of India. He is a founding member of the Professional Association for Development Action in India as well as Policy Alternatives, a non-profit society for policy research. He is presently the Vice-President of the Entrepreneurship Forum in Singapore.

PREFACE

The Master of Business Administration (MBA) programme of the Nanyang Business School at Nanyang Technological University requires participants to complete a Business Study Mission (BSM) before graduation. The purpose of these visits to other countries is to expose MBA participants to business opportunities and the realities of doing business in cultural environments different from Singapore.

This book presents the business reports emanating from the MBA Business Study Mission to India in December 1994. The capital city, New Delhi, and Bangalore and Madras, India's two largest southern cities, were the focus of the BSM which spanned ten days. These three business and investment centres are of paramount importance to India's new reform policies and they are the driving engines of much of India's growth potential. More importantly, the areas of economic development and opportunity envisioned for these three centres have definite complementarities with many economies in the Asean region as well as other trade linkages worldwide. This theme was echoed time and again in seminars, discussions and personal interviews provided by top government officials, local academics, prominent business leaders and entrepreneurs.

In New Delhi, two half-days were devoted to seminars. At the Management Development Institute, a seminar was held on the Indian financial and service industries while the Federation of Indian Chamber of Commerce and Industry hosted a seminar on the business opportunities and investment environment in India. Our delegation was privileged by the presence of some of the leading authorities on investment and reform developments in India, including Professor A. M. Khusro, Chancellor of Aligarh Muslim University and Editor-in-Chief of the Financial Express; Mr. Salman Khursheed, Minister of State for External Affairs; and Professor Mukhi, Finance Minister of the National Capital Territory of Delhi. A member of our delegation, nominated Member of Parliament, Dr. Lee Tsao Yuan, also addressed the Indian representatives.

In Bangalore, we were received by the Greater Mysore Chamber of Industry and the Karnataka Investment and Industrial Development Corporation, both of which are leading trade organisations in the state of Karnataka. Some very influential and knowledgeable speakers, including directors from the Karnataka State Industrial Investment and Development Corporation, Karnataka State Finance Corporation, Indian Institute of Management, and the Indian Institute of Science, shared invaluable knowledge with us. Also, the CEO of the Singapore-Bangalore IT Park Project discussed the inception and development of the park. In Madras, the Tamil Nadu Industrial Development Corporation hosted our visit.

Of course, a number of very impressive site visits to various companies and investment projects were a part of our itinerary to gather information about investment opportunities and critical success factors. Together with the seminars and the interaction with leading government and industrial representatives, the real momentum of India's reforms triggered a new understanding for our delegation, something worthy of sharing with a much larger audience. The editors hope that the rich set of information in this book will benefit any potential investor, not just Singaporean, in evaluating the burgeoning opportunities springing from India's new economic reform initiatives.

Editors:
TAN Teck Meng
LOW Aik Meng
John J. WILLIAMS
Ravinder K. ZUTSHI

ACKNOWLEDGEMENTS

A number of institutions and individuals contributed enormously to make this Business Study Mission a great learning experience. In Delhi, we were fortunate to have the support and effort of the Federation of Indian Chamber of Commerce and Industry and, in particular, the President of FICCI, Mr. Rungta, who organised the seminar on The Business Opportunities and Investment Environment in India. Indeed, we thank the Honourable Mr. Salman Khursheed, Minister of State for External Affairs, for a comprehensive overview of reform policies in India. Thanks also to the speakers, Dr. Amit Mitra, Secretary General, FICCI; Mr. Ashok Mahindra, Partner, A. F. Fergueson and Co.; Dr. Rakesh Mohan, Adviser, Ministry of Industry; Dr. Lee Tsao Yuan, Nominated Member of Parliament, Singapore; Professor A. M. Khusro, Chancellor of Aligarh Muslim University; and to Professor Abad Ahmad, Executive Director of the Management Development Institute, for organising the introductory seminar on the Indian economy; and all of the speakers and invited guests at the opening seminar.

For hosting our sojourn to Bangalore, thanks to Ms. Laxam Sankaran, President, and Mr. S. K. Alagh, Vice President, of The Greater Mysore Chamber of Industry; and to the insightful speakers at the seminar, Mr. J. C. Lynn, Chief Secretary, Government of Karnataka; and the Directors from the Indian Institute of Management and the Indian Institute of Science. Thanks also to the Tamil Nadu Industrial Development Corporation and Mr. Ramachandran, Principal Secretary of Industries, for the briefing on economic developments in Tamil Nadu.

Thanks as well to the many organisations and firms which hosted site visits, lunches and tours of their plant facilities, including DCM Daewoo Motors Ltd., Hindustan Computers Ltd., the India International Centre, Allen Bradley (Delhi), the PHD Chamber of Commerce, Infosys Technologies Ltd., Tamil Nadu Industrial Development Corporation, and Nucleus Software Systems.

Many thanks go to the wonderful media coverage, including the televised "A.M. Singapore" programme, *The Straits Times*, *Lianhe Zaobao* and *Tamil Murasu* before the trip and to the media in India, including the national newspapers *Hindustan Times* and *Economic Times,* the feature on BBC World Service, the national television Doordarshan and the Jain television network.

Appreciation is extended to the many pre-trip seminar speakers in Singapore in preparation for the BSM to India, including the Deputy High Commissioner of India to Singapore, Mr. Shetty; the Director of the Confederation of Indian Industries (Singapore), Mr. Zubin Kabraji; and the Executive Director of the Singapore Indian Chamber of Commerce, Mr. George Abraham.

We are particularly grateful to the tireless efforts of Mr. Anil Dang, Managing Director of Networks Ltd.; Mr. Vishnu Dusad, Director of Nucleus Software Systems; and Mr. M. K. Zutshi, Director of International Business Consultants, for all of the networking arrangements on the trip. Finally, thanks to all of our MBA participants for their diligent efforts in gathering information, to the MBA Office, to Grace Cheng and Adelene Ang for attending to all of the administrative and operational details, to our publisher Prentice Hall for their guidance, and to Alison Soo for her patience in bringing this book to fruition.

INTRODUCTION

Chapter 1

Investment Potential in India: An Overview

BY
TAN Teck Meng
LOW Aik Meng
John J. WILLIAMS
Ravinder K. ZUTSHI

INTRODUCTION

IN JANUARY 1994, when Singapore Prime Minister Goh Chok Tong took his place as the guest of honour at India's Republic Day celebration, it was a tribute to Singapore's leadership, its pragmatic policies and its economic success. It was also an affirmation of India's keen desire to strengthen its economic and cultural ties with East Asia, and recognition that Singapore was well-placed to play a vital role in India's search for capital and markets.

Singapore and India nurture a very special relationship. Singapore, once an uninhabited island on the southern tip of Malaysia, was acquired by the East India Company in 1819 from the Temengong of Johor, the local ruler, to protect its trade routes from India to China. Singapore, thereby, effectively became a part of British India. For almost half a century, Singapore was administered from India and its civil service was manned mostly by Indians. During this period, not only did it inherit the administrative and legal systems from India, but it also became home to some Indian cultural traditions.

Therefore, it is not surprising that when the Government of India initiated economic liberalisation, and decided to broaden its trade and investment linkages with East Asia, that it should turn to Singapore as a strategic ally. Immediately after announcing the new policies, Singapore was the destination of India's leaders. The architect of the new economic policies, Dr. Manmohan Singh, India's former Finance Minister, acknowledged Singapore's relevance to India and, in October 1991, at the joint conference organised by the Indian Government and hosted by the Trade Development Board of Singapore, the Finance Minister commented that "We, in the Government of India thought, that if we have to market India, we have to begin with Singapore".

India holds many attractions. It has the world's second largest population, is fifth largest in land size and, if we consider income parity, is sixth largest in GDP. It is the largest democracy in the world and, militarily, has the third largest standing army. From the geo-political perspective, India is a regional military power and can play an important role in maintaining regional stability. It is also an economy with a large home market and tremendous market potential.[1] All these indicators suggest that it is a country that is hard to ignore.

India's initiatives towards externalising its economy have attracted the interest of the investment community around the world. During 1993–94, portfolio investments reached Rs 3.5 billion as compared to Rs 8 million in 1991–92. The policy changes have been well received by the international business community and, from their pronouncements, economic analysts seem convinced that India offers tremendous opportunities. Even within the country, three decades of meagre 2.5% per capita income growth have left many convinced that change is needed. There is now a new optimism that the reforms will create a conducive climate for growth (Wadhva, 1994).

Singapore has taken cognizance of the reforms in India, as evidenced by the visits of high level business delegations between the two countries during the last three years. In March 1992, Singapore's Deputy Prime Minister and Minister for Trade and Industry led a large delegation of businessmen to India. This was followed by the visit of Singapore's Minister of Information and the Arts to India in February 1993. The Prime Minister of Singapore visited India in January 1994, and again in January 1995, as the chief guest of the Confederation of Indian

---

[1] Indian middle class is supposed to be around 200 million (McDonald, 1994), but only one in 30 owns a TV and there are 100 people per telephone as compared to two per telephone in Singapore.

Industry. From India, there has also been a steady stream of visitors to Singapore including Mr. P.V. Narasimha Rao, former Prime Minister of India, his cabinet colleagues and the Chief Ministers of major Indian States. These exchanges have helped increase general awareness and interest about India among Singapore's business community. And, the business community has taken the cue from the government. Singapore companies have actively searched for opportunities in the country and, today, are the largest group of ASEAN investors in India.

However, to many, India still remains an enigma. Ask a Singapore businessman who has dealings with India and he is more likely to say that Indians are complicated. What complicates the understanding of India is not only its cultural, religious, ethnic and linguistic diversity but, also, the nature of the Hindu world view which stands in contrast to the Western, or more specifically, American concept of civilisation. Therefore, for those who view the world through the American prism, the perception of India and the Indians can be unflattering.

In spite of its ancient cultural ties with the region, and with Singapore in particular, independent India has paid little attention to South-east Asia. This could partly be attributed to India's preoccupation with the security of its borders, and partly due to the Indian elite's Eurocentricity. The Indian business community in South-east Asia might have played a catalytic role in building business linkages, and dispelling negative perceptions. But, unfortunately, and for a variety of reasons which we will comment on later, their contributions and, hence, influence in the communities in which they live, including India, have been marginal.

Therefore, it is not surprising that the business community in Singapore continues to wonder whether India's economic reforms are sustainable and whether India will continue to welcome foreign investments. There is also the underlying fear of the unknown. In spite of the changes and a liberalised economic regime, investment flows into India from this region are still minuscule compared to investments that have poured into China, Malaysia or Indonesia. Considering its proximity to India, Singapore is well-placed to be a window to India, just as Hong Kong is to China. The question is whether Singapore business is positioned to take advantage of these circumstances.

Given India's importance to Singapore's regionalisation strategy, it is imperative for Singapore businessmen to understand the socio-political dynamics of that country. One recognises that in a democracy the economic policy is dictated by the socio-political realities. In India, this reality is embedded in its historical and cultural past. The intent of the MBA Business Study Mission is to expose the participants to the cultural setting and, thus, to provide the contextual framework for the economic data to add depth and enrich the analysis. To add perspective to the contents of this book, it is important to understand what prompted India to initiate economic reforms.

LOGIC OF REFORMS

It is argued that the economic policy changes were dictated by circumstances rather than by economic logic or by changes in leadership. In 1991, when the Congress Party was returned to power under Prime Minister Rao, India was facing a precarious economic situation. The GNP in the previous year had grown by only 1%, and foreign exchange reserves had declined to tenuous levels. At one point, the reserves were equivalent to three weeks of imports. To overcome the balance of payment crisis, the government had to initiate negotiations with multilateral agencies for long-term loans. The IMF came to its rescue but it committed the Government of India to structural adjustments leading to economic reforms. To this extent, reforms were externally driven.

To understand the genesis of the reforms, one has to go a step back and try to understand why India had earlier adopted the Soviet model of planned economic development. After independence, India's political leaders, drawn mainly from the intellectual and professional elite, were committed to rapid industrialisation of the country. Nehru, India's first Prime Minister and architect of its economic policy, had been greatly impressed by the strides made by the Soviet Union in achieving rapid industrialisation and tremendous technological mastery. Faced with problems of poverty, scarcities, and unemployment, planned economic development was unavoidable. India was also committed to democratic ideals and free enterprise, as it had a well entrenched business class. It was these circumstances that underpinned India's adoption of a planned economic development strategy and mixed economy.

But the Indian elite was also conscious of the dehumanising influences of modernity and materialism. In his autobiography, Nehru (1962, p. 500) enumerated on the dilemmas facing Indian policy makers:

> ... right through history the old Indian ideal did not glorify political and military triumph, and it looked down upon money and the professional money-making class. Honour and wealth did not go together, and honour was meant to go, at least in theory, to the men who served the community with little in the shape of financial reward. Today (the old culture) is fighting silently and desperately against a new all-powerful opponent – the bania (Vaishya) civilisation of the West. It will succumb to the newcomer ... But the West also brings an antidote to the evils of this cut-throat civilisation – the principle of socialism, of cooperation, and service to the community for the common good. This is not so unlike the old Brahmin ideal of service, but the Brahmanisation – not in the religious sense, of course – of all classes and groups and the abolition of class distinction.

Colonisation had reinforced the Indian elite's perception of the business class as an exploiter of resources rather than creator of wealth. Two hundred years of British rule had left a legacy of poverty and economic stagnation. From 1860 to 1911, subsequent to the British takeover, India's per capita income had grown at the rate of 0.5%. In the period after 1911, the per capita income, in fact, remained unchanged. While Europe and the U.S. were going through the industrial revolution, the colonial policies had the effect of retarding growth of indigenous industries in India. Indigenous industries in India suffered greatly during the British rule. In Uttar Pradesh, which had expanding silk, cotton, textile and metal working industries, the percentage of the population working in the secondary sector suffered a decline.

India, therefore, adopted an economic framework which accepted private enterprise but assigned to the state a central role in planning and directing the economy. The core sectors of the economy were reserved for the public sector. The industrial policy stipulated that the public sector would attain the "commanding heights" of the economy.

In the decades following independence, protectionism and state control over a large part of the industrial sector have led to the growth of an inefficient and globally uncompetitive industrial sector. But growth of indigenous industries and investments in technology and institutions also have created a large pool of world class scientists, technologists and administrators, well positioned to take advantage of economic opportunities.

More important, during these years, there has been a silent revolution in the country and political power has gradually shifted from the upper castes to the lower castes. Many of the state governments today are headed by the lower castes.

It has been said that with the shifting of political power, economic liberalisation and privatisation have been adopted by the high castes to protect their economic interest (McDonald, 1994). India has met its Nehruvian economic agenda with political stability. The income distribution in India today is not very different from that in communist China (Wadhva, 1994). As long as infusion of private capital and foreign enterprise does not drastically curtail the socio-economic evolution taking place in the country, the economic reforms will endure.

A SYNOPSIS OF THEMES

Given the rationale for emerging reforms in India discussed earlier, this volume pursues a selective menu of initiatives for investment in India. Several topics, of commonality to any investment strategy, are addressed at a macro level of analysis. At the same time, particular emphasis is accorded to investment opportunities in New Delhi, Bangalore and Madras, and necessarily follows a more regional and micro level orientation. This mix of analyses produced ten chapters which have been divided into the following four categories: (1) new policies and emerging reforms aimed at enhancing foreign investment and growth; (2) human resource development, wage issues, and the legal framework appropriate to business investments; (3) regional investment opportunities in New Delhi, Bangalore, Madras and southern India; and (4) industry analysis centred on tourism, telecommunications and software as three rapidly expanding sectors of the Indian economy, plus the important issue of technology transfer.

Chapter 2 evaluates India's achievements in terms of trade policy reforms. Specifically, it reviews several major policy changes spanning industrial licensing, foreign investment, foreign technology agreements and overall public sector policy. Empirical data, based on personal interviews with prominent corporate directors and government officials, evaluates the impact of these policy changes. The authors then extend this data to an assessment of future development trends and conclude the chapter with a number of specific suggestions for investment linkages between Singapore and India.

Chapter 3 deals with India's financial and capital market reforms. In particular, the nature of financial institutions, banks and capital institutions are described and forms the basis for understanding the nature and impact of financial reforms. These include the liberalisation of the capital markets, changes to the statutory liquidity ratio, liberalisation of interest rates, formation of new private banks and new powers associated with the stock exchange board. The chapter concludes with several poignant limitations of the reform movement and suggests several viable opportunities for investment based on Singapore's highly developed financial services sector.

Chapter 4 pursues a number of issues relating to the labour force, labour relations, regulations on labour and wages, and demographic profile information. Of course, one of the main investment attractions of India is her highly skilled workforce at relatively low cost. After an analysis of available labour by sectors, the chapter turns to a discussion of labour regulations which must be understood by any investor going into India. A discussion of trade unions and mechanisms for dispute resolution are presented next, followed by empirical data on current wages in different sectors of the economy. The chapter closes with comments on the important area of human resource development, including educational institutes and the caste system.

Chapter 5 adopts a practical perspective in examining the ways of doing business in India and the related business laws. Several forms of indirect investment are discussed followed by an examination of different forms of direct investment available to investors. These investment forms are discussed with the related foreign investment laws, employment laws, tax laws, company law and relevant land laws.

Consistent with the objectives of the Business Study Mission, two chapters deal with regional investment opportunities. Chapter 6 is somewhat broader in perspective and adopts a SWOT analysis in surveying investment potential in southern India. Economic data and demographic information for the southern Indian states of Tamil Nadu, Karnataka, Kerala and Andhra Pradesh are presented. One interesting feature is a comparative profile of state government incentives available to investors across these four states.

Chapter 7 extends the focus of both Chapter 6 and 7 by considering some types of possible collaborative agreements between Singapore and the economic zones of New Delhi, Bangalore and Madras. In addition, several types of alliances promoted by the Indian government *vis-à-vis* specific industrial sectors, or products, are discussed. Finally, the authors recommend alternative investment opportunities in the various zones that would complement the strengths of Singapore businesses.

The last four chapters focus on specific industry sectors in the Indian economy. Chapter 8 takes a comprehensive look at opportunities in the tourism industry. A macro model of a tourism system in supply and demand terms is presented. This is applied to six areas including the development and management of attractions and the development of airports, hotels and beach resorts. A strategic positioning matrix is used to present recommendations by investment size and type of investors.

The telecommunications sector is the focus of Chapter 9. It includes a brief summary on government initiatives to attract foreign direct investment, a macro overview of opportunities for investments, and the types of entry strategies that potential investors might consider. The chapter concludes with several concerns, such as tendering and exit policies, which need careful evaluation prior to any investment decision.

Chapter 10 addresses the giant software industry in India which has proliferated in recent years. Trend and SWOT analyses are used to assess industry potential followed by a specific case example in the industry. In concluding, the authors present a general theme of "opportunity or competition" to business people in Singapore's software industry.

In Chapter 11, the authors address the important issue of technology transfer into India. They point out that there is a delicate balance required between foreign direct investment and technology transfer in order to accommodate planned expansion of the Indian economy. The economic reforms are, in large measure, an urgent attempt by the government to acquire massive infusions of technology in order to bolster exports and sustain a positive growth trend in India's balance of payments. After discussing several incentive mechanisms to encourage new technology agreements, the chapter focuses on the relationship between technological knowledge and manufacturing, followed by a look at the market for technology. Among the areas of opportunity are the engineering goods, the electronics, and the food processing sectors.

REFERENCES

McDonald M., "Pride and Prejudice", *Far Eastern Economic Review*, November 1994, p. 25.

Nehru J., *An Autobiography*, Allied Publishers, Delhi, 1962.

Wadhva C. D., *Economic Reforms in India and the Market Economy*, Allied Publishers, Delhi, 1994.

POLICY AND REFORMS

Chapter 2

Industrial Policy and Foreign Investment Reforms

BY

Kala ANANDARAJAH

Guillermo GRANADOS

INTRODUCTION

TRADE POLICY REFORMS constituted a major platform of the new industrial policy announced in July 1991. The objective was to create a liberal environment for trade, simplify and streamline procedures for import and export, and to facilitate production for export; in short, to open up the Indian economy to the dynamic forces of foreign trade.

The new industrial policy, and the subsequent policy changes, have introduced wide-ranging measures aimed at delicensing and deregulation. In turn, they have opened up the economy to foreign investments. The new business environment in India allows a greater role for the private sector and encourages direct foreign investments. The private sector can now operate in all areas except those of strategic concerns such as defence, railway, transport and atomic energy.[1] Even the latter areas have been expanded to permit private initiative in mining, oil exploration, refining and marketing, and parts of the railway transport sectors.

[1] See Appendix 2-1 for a list of the areas where private sector intervention is still not allowed.

Likewise, the requirement of obtaining an industrial license for manufacturing activity is now limited to only 15 industries of strategic, social or environmental importance.[2]

This chapter assesses the extent to which the objectives stated above have been achieved. It begins by setting out the various reforms that have been undertaken, including the various stages of the process. Next, it examines where India stands at this point in time. It is important to note that the dynamics of an opening economy are such that nothing is static. Hence, the position today may very well be changed by tomorrow. The magnitude of these potential changes are highlighted accordingly. Finally, Singapore's role in India is assessed.

BACKGROUND

The process of liberalisation in industrial and trade policy was first initiated in the early 1980s by Mrs. Indira Gandhi, who was then Prime Minister. Mr. Rajiv Gandhi who succeeded her urged the process on. Liberalisation was gradually intensified in the mid-1980s so that for the first time the economy attained a growth rate of 5.5%. Even then, the process of deregulation was not undertaken with the fervor that underpinned business in India in the 1990s. It was only in 1991 that a comprehensive review of the policies was undertaken and the new industrial policy was tabled.

The circumstances that led to the introduction of the new industrial policy had much to do with the problems concerning India's foreign reserves.[3] The elements of the industrial policy are:

(i) Trade and commerce will be free.
(ii) Industrial licensing will be virtually eliminated.
(iii) The government will lay down a transparent set of rules and will provide for a level playing field.
(iv) Competition will promote the efficient use of resources and will produce better goods and services.
(v) The flow of capital, information and technology into India will benefit the Indian economy and the Indian people.

---

[2] See Appendix 2-2 for the list of industries that requires an industrial licence.

[3] Much has already been said on this elsewhere so it will not be dealt with here.

(vi) India cannot remain isolated from the rest of the world, and it is necessary and desirable that her economy becomes integrated with the world's economy.

(vii) In order to become a major player in world trade, India must be a willing and active member of international organisations, and must abide by internationally accepted rules of business, trade and commerce.

(viii) Amendments and deletions will be made to the *Foreign Exchange Regulation Act* and the *Monopolies and Restrictive Trade Practice Act*.

One of the main objectives of the new industrial policy was to build on the gains already made, correct distortions or the weaknesses that may have crept in, maintain and improve growth in productivity and gainful employment and attain international competitiveness for the Indian industry, eventually paving the way for global integration of the Indian economy. Market forces were given a progressively greater role in efficient allocation and performance of resources. These measures (were expected to) complement the other measures taken by the government in the areas of trade policy, exchange rate management, fiscal policy, financial sector reforms, and macro economic management (Vaish Associates, 1994). The question, then, is to what extent have the objectives of the economic policy been achieved?

METHOD

The literature on the status of the reforms in India is not consistent. This can be attributed to the different perceptions of different writers. In this paper, an attempt was made to gather information that enabled some conclusive statements about the status of the developments and progress in India. To achieve this end, the following steps were undertaken:

(i) Data was collected on the actual status of development and progress in India. Furthermore, depending on the sources of individual communication, conflicting data was obtained.

(ii) Significant literature was reviewed and substantiated by actual data.

(iii) First-hand information was obtained from: (a) policy makers in India and in Singapore; and (b) retailers, businessmen, and manufac-

FIGURE 2–1
Foreign Collaboration Approvals (in Rs Billion)

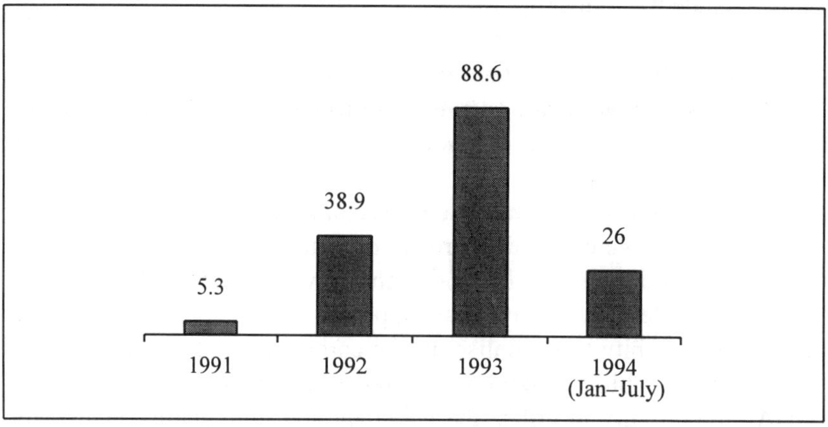

FIGURE 2–2
Actual Inflow of Direct Foreign Investment (In Rs Crores)

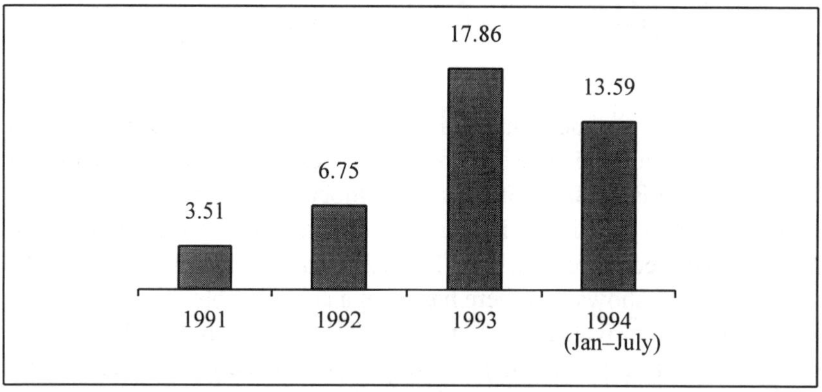

A breakdown of foreign investment by state is presented in Table 2–2 and Figures 2–4 and 2–5. It can be seen that the states of Maharashtra (where Bombay is situated), Delhi, and Tamil Nadu (where Madras is situated), together make up almost 40% of India's foreign investment.

In addition to this data, Appendix 2–7 provides further economic data on GDP, agricultural production, industrial production, the capital goods industry, electrical machinery, transport equipment and proposed industrial investment by state.

TABLE 2–1
Foreign Collaboration Approvals[5]

	1991	1992	1993	1994 (up to July)
1. Total number of foreign collaboration approvals by:				
(i) Secretariat for Industrial Approvals	760	585	307	233
(ii) Reserve Bank of India	188	736	676	354
(iii) Foreign Investment Promotion Board	2	199	493	355
TOTAL	**950**	**1,520**	**1,476**	**942**
2. Number of foreign collaboration approvals involving foreign investment:				
(i) Secretariat for Industrial Approvals	242	243	59	57
(ii) Reserve Bank of India	41	252	235	99
(iii) Foreign Investment Promotion Board	2	198	491	355
TOTAL	**285**	**693**	**785**	**511**
3. Total amount of foreign investment involved (in Rs Billion)				
(i) Secretariat for Industrial Approvals	3.6	4.2	1.6	1.9
(ii) Reserve Bank of India	1.4	7.8	6.6	1.1
(iii) Foreign Investment Promotion Board	0.3	26.9	80.4	23.0
TOTAL	**5.3**	**38.9**	**88.6**	**26.0**

5 For the most recent investment approvals see Appendix 2–6.

FIGURE 2–3(a)
Number of Foreign Investment Projects

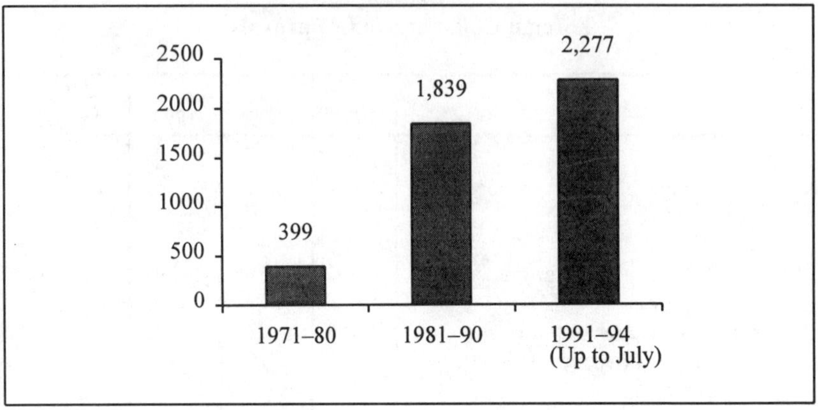

FIGURE 2–3(b)
Amount of Foreign Investment (Rs Billion)

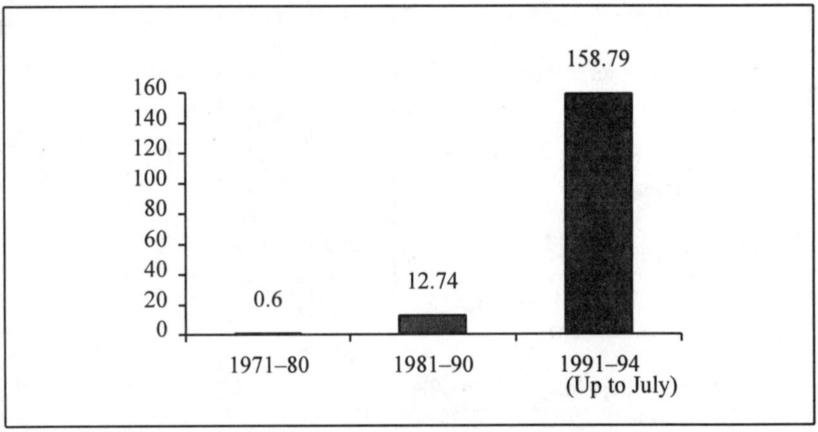

RESISTANCE TO DEVELOPMENTS

As expected in any process of reform, problems emerge which hamper progress. The issue then becomes one of assessing their severity. This section identifies some of the problems and considers their impact on the process of reform. When possible, suggestions are given on how these problems may be reduced or resolved.

TABLE 2–2
Foreign Investment Approvals: January 1993–July 1994

State Name	Total Number of Investment Approvals	Amount Approved (Rs Million)
Maharashtra	202	1,900.39
Delhi	140	1,220.87
Tamil Nadu	136	1,125.13
Gujarat	65	1,123.87
Orissa	14	788.21
Madhya Pradesh	26	770.22
Andhra Pradesh	61	275.86
Haryana	67	186.60
Rajasthan	42	138.34
Karnataka	83	113.38
Uttar Pradesh	49	111.24
Pondicherry	9	108.61
West Bengal	34	86.87
Bihar	5	52.02
Goa	13	36.82
Dadra & Nagar Haveli	5	33.94
Chandigarh	5	29.04
Kerala	13	27.19
Punjab	15	14.47
Himachal Pradesh	5	11.53
Daman & Diu	5	4.08
Andaman & Nicobar	1	0.90
Assam	2	0.27
Others (States not indicated)	299	3,299.19
TOTAL	**1,296**	**11,459.04**

Note: (i) Data prior to 1993 were not maintained. However, action to compile this data has begun.

(ii) The Department of Industrial Development is also undertaking a study through an independent agency to examine various aspects of approved foreign investment and the post-policy period. *Inter alia*, the study will cover information about the locations of projects.

FIGURE 2–4
Foreign Direct Investment Approvals by State: January 1993 – July 1994

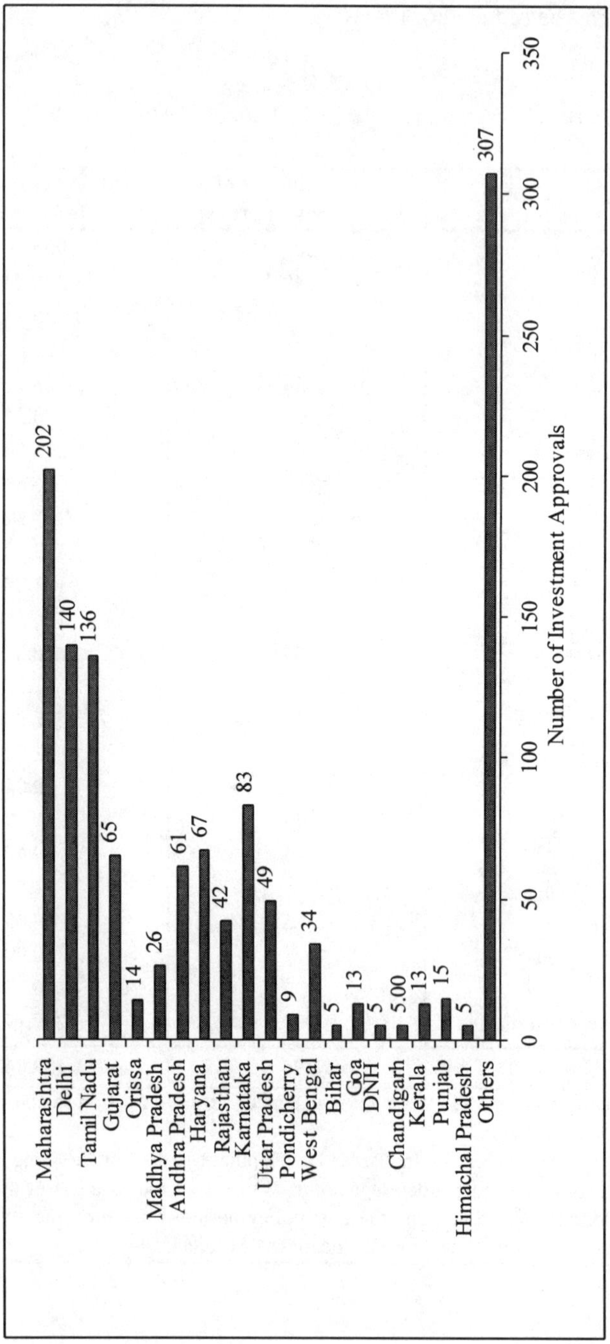

FIGURE 2–5

Foreign Direct Investment by State: January 1993 – July 1994 (Rs Million)

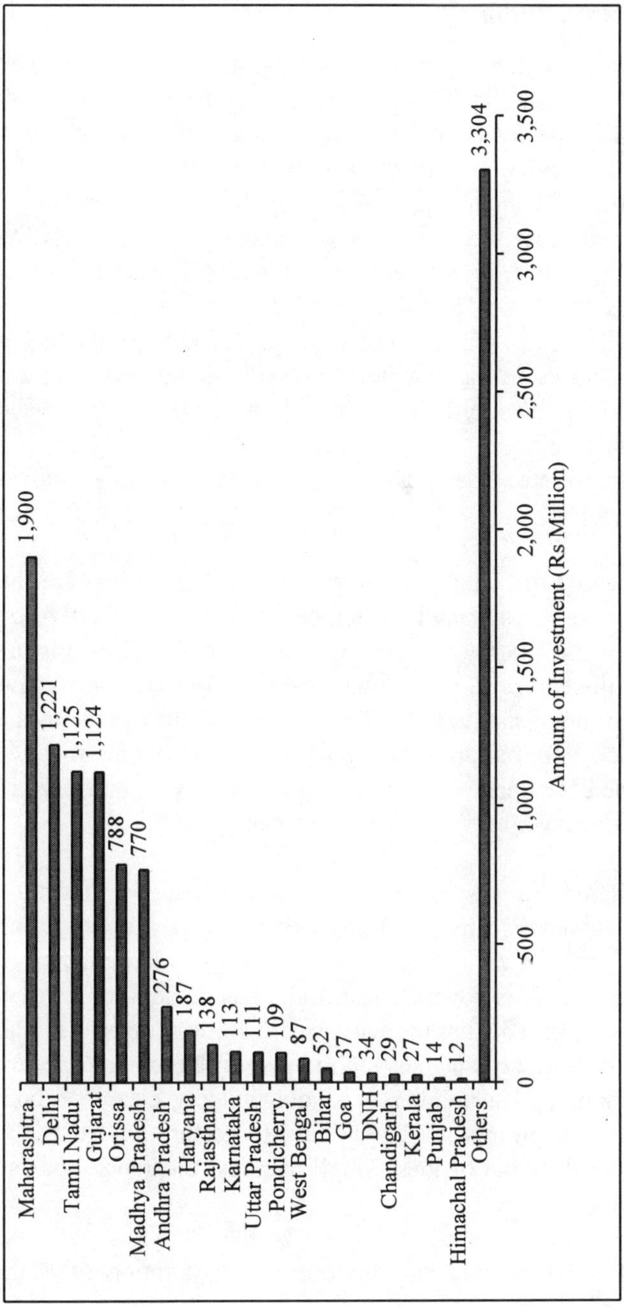

Bureaucracy in India

Perhaps the most starkly perceived restriction is the continuing existence of bureaucracy in India. This primarily arises from the legacy of British rule which lasted for over 200 years. Upon obtaining independence in 1947, the country concentrated on becoming self-sufficient and meeting the economic and social needs of the population. One way of achieving this was to increase the size of the bureaucracy and government participation in the industrial and service sectors. To illustrate, India's public sector employs some 18 million people in government and in public sector undertakings. This compares with the U.S. equivalent of three million. A more startling comparison is with the business sector in India, which employs seven million, the remainder being in small-scale industry and rural workers.

Mr. R. Alletru, Zone Director, Telemecanique — India, Group Schneider notes:

> On account of being isolated for too long, the industry in India is not able to withstand foreign competition particularly on account of the quality and cost. One of the major problems in India is the existence of too many decision centres. The bureaucracy in India is a major hurdle. Absence of clear guidelines and advance information with regard to various permissions to be obtained for opening a branch or setting up an industry is indeed a heavy burden on foreign investors.

To attempt to by-pass any bureaucracy can be difficult. But to change it, which effectively means wrenching power away from older employees with set mentalities (as well as effectively reducing the number of employees), is no small feat. India has come a long way over the last few years in reducing the red tape for foreign investors. This is apparent from the list of changes highlighted in the previous section. With the introduction of a number of single window clearance bodies, the maze that a foreign investor would have to go through has been considerably reduced. Some of these single window clearance bodies include the following:

(i) The State Industrial and Investment Corporation of Maharashtra Ltd.

(ii) The State Industries Promotion Corporation of Tamil Nadu Ltd.
(iii) The Karnataka State Industrial Investment and Development Corporation Ltd.
(iv) Tamil Nadu Industrial Development Corporation Ltd.
(v) Confederation of Indian Industry.
(vi) The Foreign Investment and Trade Promotion Centre.
(vii) Federation of Indian Chambers of Commerce and Industry.

But investors must remember that when investing in any country, the bottom line is that business law is like an iceberg. The small visible tip consists of a few statutes and some subordinate legislation. The much larger invisible portion consists of numerous guidelines, notifications, press notes and other official pronouncements. These bind not only the businessman but, also, the government. If a businessman acts (e.g., invests money) on the basis of a policy or assurance contained in such pronouncements, the government cannot deny him the benefit of that policy or assurance.

Corruption in India

Where there is a bureaucracy there is always an issue of corruption. It has been stated that the degree of corruption experienced is directly related to the number of steps and procedures one has to go through in order to obtain approvals. Mikael Gistern, the Managing Director of GSE Pte. Ltd., a Swedish company which has a software operation in Madras, said that there are two ways of going about obtaining the necessary approvals to commence operations in India namely, the "long" and the "short" way The long way, of course, is to submit the various applications to the relevant bodies. This could take from a few months to much longer.[6]

The short way would involve paying "tea" money to the right person(s) who will then allow you to short circuit the system by placing you first in the queue. Mikael Gistern, however, observed that this is gradually decreasing. In fact, he advised that when a foreign investor is asked

---

[6] We are told that the time period for obtaining various approvals has been considerably shortened in view of the increasing number of single window operations. However, the time period is not certain, and we know of at least one Singapore organisation which has been trying to start operations in Bombay for the last year and one-half.

for "tea" money, he should refuse to pay it. Over time, the officers will stop asking for money. This attitude has developed from the desire to move towards internationalisation. In other words, corruption in India gradually is becoming manageable.

Constitutional Structure of India

A related problem stems from the constitutional structure of India where the regulatory powers are with the central government while the states are responsible for the promotion of industry and infrastructure.[7] India's quasi federal structure means that there are considerable powers vested at the state level, so that apart from any central government involvement in business, state government approvals are also required.

This structure is a facet of India that will not be changed in the near future. The primary reason for this is because of the state governments' power and the popularity that they enjoy among the people. Nevertheless, the individual states in India are totally supportive of the ongoing reforms in India. This is reflected by the fact that they have taken numerous steps to provide incentives in an effort to attract foreign investment.

However, as John M. Golden of House, Golden, Kingsmill & Riess observed, the economic reforms currently underway in India promise fundamental changes in the roles that government and private sector will play in the direction of the Indian economy. The 1991 industrial policy resolution recasts the central government's role in guiding the economy. The government will continue to have a pivotal role in directing development, but through fiscal and monetary means, rather than through direct investment in particular industries.

The view of Sunder N. Bhatia, Vice-President of Commercial Banking of Arab Banking Corporation, is that India cannot be treated strictly as one country. The conditions among states, and among cities, vary considerably so that an investor must study the existing conditions in any one city, or state, and then decide if those conditions fit within his framework of investment. One illustration of the differences that pervade the different cities and states in India relates to tax collection. Over 40% of government revenue comes from the city of Bombay. The cost of living in Bombay is also very high; in fact, it is as high as Hong Kong. In Madras, on the other hand, one can live very comfortably with

---

7 This is to some extent like the system in the United States of America.

Rs 2,000 per month (approximately S$100 per month).

To further illustrate, the Managing Director of GSE Pte. Ltd., Mikael Gistern, indicated that he chose Madras city over the other cities in India primarily because the price of land and labour was one-half of that in Bombay. Also, the employees in Madras tended to be more loyal than those in Bombay where the turnover rate tended to be very high.[8] To establish the whole operation (software) it costs GSE Pte. Ltd. only rupees one crore (which is equivalent to S$500,000).

Continuity of Reforms in India

Another perceived restriction is that the reforms in India are not permanent. Speak to any Indian, however, from a government official or a diplomat, to a businessman or an academician, or even the man in the street, and you will hear a resounding affirmation that the reforms are here to stay. In fact, India has no other choice. If the reformative steps were not taken at this point in time and, if they were not carried through to their positive end, then India would not have any hope of tapping the world market. As Desai (1994) notes it takes a long time for a democratic country to bring about any change, as every change is subject to debate, discussion and sometimes demonstration and protest. Having gone through this process, it takes an equally long time to reverse the change, particularly when it has been so successful.

A related issue is the status of political stability. Of course, as with any other implemented change, there were opponents to the liberalisation policies in India. However, liberalisation remained a general feature. It is not personality driven; and, so, it will not stop merely because there is a change in the ruling government. We take the view that the question of political stability is of no significance. In any case, since India has now taken off, even if an opposition party comes into government, the winds of change will not be affected in any way. This appears to be supported by the fact that Mr. Manmohan Singh has managed to push through four revolutionary budgets since 1991 without encountering serious opposition although he is a finance minister in a minority government.

Further confirmation of political stability comes from the Deputy High Commissioner of India to Singapore. He states in the *Economic*

8 Unfortunately no figure was given.

Bulletin (December 1994)[9] with regard to the impact of the recent ongoing economic reforms that "economic reforms were not an issue during the elections which were fought on local issues ... Indian business leaders too have voiced the opinion that state election results largely reflected a vote for state issues and their significance to industry was minimal".

Exit Policy in India[10]

Perhaps the only serious restriction in India relates to the exit policy and labour laws generally. As a rule, the exit policy for corporations tends to be very difficult. Where a venture becomes non-profitable, it is considered to be sick and will fall under the *Sick Industries Act*. A board is appointed then to try and revive the company. Where the loss is experienced for a continuous period of three years, the board reviews the matter and may allow a certificate to be filed in court allowing the venture to be shut down. Note that these rules are not provided for in the *Companies Act 1956* but, rather, are contained in regulations and circulars issued by the government. Although the legal effect is suspect, the rules are now too ingrained, and they can only be removed by an amendment to the *Companies Act*.[11]

Next, redundancy and factory closures are regulated by the provisions of the *Industrial Disputes Act 1947* and the *Industrial Disputes (Amendment) Act of 1982 and 1984*. Under these *Acts,* any worker who has completed not less than one year of continuous service is entitled to a minimum amount of compensation for retrenchment or factory closure. In businesses employing more than 100 workers, there can be no retrenchment, redundancy, or closure without the prior permission of the appropriate government body.[12] Of course, this issue is easily surmountable. Any large corporation can separate its business operations into several subsidiaries with each employing less than 100 persons at any one time, thereby circumventing this regulation. Or the investor could enter into a technology intensive venture which employs less than 100 people.

---

9 This is published by the Commissioner of India on a monthly basis.

10 As this topic is considered in detail elsewhere in this book, we will only briefly consider the same hereunder.

11 The *Companies Amendment Bill* has been tabled in Parliament.

12 There has been pressure from the business community to have the figure increased to 300. The government is now considering the matter.

Infrastructure in India

Infrastructure, or rather the lack of it, in India is a major problem. Prior to 1991, many of the Indian states pursued a policy of balanced regional development by dispersing industries to the rural and less developed urban areas. While tax breaks, subsidies, and the like, were offered for locating in these areas, the biggest incentive was the grant of an industrial licence since an investor could not get a licence unless he agreed to locate in a backward area. This, however, had a negative effect because of underdeveloped infrastructure in backward areas. In Delhi, travel to factory sites could take as much as one-and-one-half to two hours. The roads are very narrow and extremely dusty. Another example of the lack of infrastructure occurred on our visit to a button factory outside Delhi. It was discovered that there was no telephone and the only means of communication between the factory and head office in Delhi was a messenger-boy on a motorbike. On the other hand, though, good infrastructure exists in the established technology parks and economic zones.

With most industries delicenced, investors now have a free choice in locating ventures in any area in India. The government has now shifted its attention from forcing investors to locate in backward areas to promoting certain areas as "growth centres" and encouraging private investment in infrastructure. New Delhi, itself, has identified 68 centres on the basis of area, population and extent of industrial backwardness. It is spending Rs 250 to Rs 300 million (US$7.8 to US$9.4 million) at each centre to provide basic facilities such as power, telecommunications, water and other services. Also, it is inviting private sector investment for the provision of infrastructure services in these areas.

Joint Ventures, Takeovers, Mergers and Acquisitions

There is also minimal regulation of takeovers, mergers and acquisitions. Foreign investors do not always want to operate with a local partner and, therefore, look to purchasing a company. Until very recently, there was no tradition of company purchases and sales. This means that regulations and practice in this area are very much in their infancy and could have a negative effect on investment. The government has recognised these problems and has introduced regulations pertaining to the substantial acquisition of shares and takeovers. The main objective of these regulations is to provide greater transparency in the acquisition of shares and takeovers of companies through a system of information disclosure.

Understanding the Indian People

This is perhaps the major obstacle to be overcome when investing in India. To illustrate the point, it was observed on some site visits that the concept of "trust", as perceived by the Indian, differed somewhat from the perception of a Singaporean. To the Indian, the word "trust" corresponds exactly with that contained in the Oxford English Dictionary, namely, "a firm belief in the reliability or truth or strength of a person or thing". To the Chinese, however, the word "trust" has a deeper meaning as it also embodies the concept of timeliness including punctuality at meetings and in meeting deadlines and payments. It is thus important when doing business in India not to impose conditions that one is familiar with in Singapore. Allowing for leeway and flexibility is essential when investing in India.

FUTURE DEVELOPMENT TRENDS

Thus far, the changes that have taken place in India to encourage the inflow of foreign investments have been discussed. Some areas of possible resistance to the reform process were also considered. The following sections now focus on future developments in India.

Continued Efforts at Industrial Reform

The 1994–95 budget included a package of measures to boost industrial investment and capital goods production. The then Finance Minister Dr. Singh revealed a vision of India's industrial firms acquiring a global reach and becoming household names in far off lands.

Changes also continue to pervade the realm of India's import and export policies. Although India's trade policy now allows most items to be freely imported and exported, there continues to be a small negative list comprised mainly of consumer goods. The import and export of these goods are prohibited or restricted through licensing, or are channelled through state trading corporations. These restrictions apply to some 1,350 out of the 5,000 items under India's tariff classification system. Plans, have been announced to reduce this list further. It would appear that over time the list may be eliminated completely.

Although export incentives and regulations have been made more flexible, the Finance Minister has recognised in the 1994–95 budget that they remain complex. The government has made a commitment to simplify these over time.

Western versus Eastern Investment

Tables 2–3 and 2–4 show a profile of investment by countries. One observation is that there is a larger proportion of investors in India from the West than from the East. A question constantly asked was why investments from the East were nominal, if not almost non-existent. For instance, Japanese investment in East Asia, and in the West, is extremely high. But their investment in India is nominal. Even recent investments in India tend to come from the West. Recent investment approvals totalling over Rs 5 billion (S$250 million) show a paucity of investment from the East.

TABLE 2–3
Ranking of Approval Foreign Investments: 1991–1994 (in Rs Billion)

Ranking	Name of the Country	Investment
1.	U.S.A.	58.66
2.	Switzerland	11.72
3.	Japan	9.80
4.	U.K.	9.63
5.	Germany	6.25
6.	Netherlands	5.55
7.	Oman	5.45
8.	U.A.E.	4.61
9.	Thailand	3.74
10.	Hong Kong	2.86
11.	Italy	2.81
12.	Mexico	2.44
13.	Singapore	2.05
14.	France	1.98
15.	Mauritius	1.96
16.	Ireland	1.66
17.	Australia	1.41
18.	Russia	1.24
19.	Malaysia	1.05
20.	All countries including above	158.79

TABLE 2–4
Approved Foreign Direct Investments and Foreign Technology Agreements: January 1994 – July 1994

Name of Country	Total Approvals			Amount of Foreign Investments (Rs Million)
	Total	Tech	Fin	
Australia	22	8	14	315.61
Austria	15	12	3	88.86
Argentina	1	1	0	0.00
Bahamas	1	0	1	44.80
Bahrain	2	0	2	17.00
Belgium	4	3	1	0.60
British Virginia	1	1	0	0.00
Canada	12	7	5	407.55
Channel Island	1	0	1	4.00
China	7	3	4	19.67
Cyprus	1	1	0	0.00
Denmark	11	8	3	309.45
Finland	6	4	2	62.20
Chile	1	1	0	0.00
France	31	15	16	203.95
Germany	116	69	47	3,208.07
Hong Kong	15	1	14	1,195.79
Hungary	2	1	1	1.60
Ireland	1	0	1	0.50
Israel	5	4	1	0.71
Italy	49	21	28	560.80
Japan	69	48	21	682.99
Korea (South)	20	7	13	224.39
Kuwait	1	0	1	6.00
Malaysia	3	0	3	218.00
Mauritius	3	0	3	720.75
Netherlands	39	15	24	799.52
New Zealand	5	5	0	0.00
Nigeria	1	0	1	14.15
Norway	3	2	1	3.12
Oman	1	0	1	15.75
Philippines	4	3	1	34.00
Portugal	1	1	0	0.00
Russia	9	2	7	1,014.28
Singapore	29	7	22	771.30
Spain	5	3	2	16.67
Sri Lanka	2	0	2	1.48
Sweden	12	9	3	2.65

TABLE 2–4 (cont'd)

Name of Country	Total Approvals			Amount of Foreign Investments (Rs Million)
	Total	Tech	Fin	
Slovenia	1	1	0	0.00
Switzerland	36	18	18	195.17
Taiwan	6	4	2	18.10
Thailand	8	5	3	29.44
U.A.E.	3	0	3	479.49
U.K.	106	54	52	1,901.09
U.S.A.	184	86	98	9,871.56
Ukraine	1	1	0	0.00
West Indies	1	0	1	0.50
NRI	82	0	82	2,483.09
Unindicated country	3	0	3	27.62
TOTAL	**942**	**431**	**511**	**25,972.27**

A *Business Times* report (22 March 1994) comparing India, Pakistan and Bangladesh with China, states the following:

> Each of them, unlike the other Asian giant, China, has stable, established political, legal and commercial systems with commerce conducted generally through English. Each has a large, articulate consumer-conscious middle class, who are accumulating more wealth and buying power.
>
> Why then, when the Indian sub-continent has so many advantages over China, is everyone rushing to China? The answer is that China commenced market reforms in 1978, throwing off the constraints imposed by socialism in its various forms, but India didn't really start until after the collapse of her main trading partner, Russia, in 1991.

While the answer appears correct, it is incomplete. Of course, a safe answer would be to state that the Eastern countries are, themselves, developing countries. Naturally, investments from these countries would be minimal. But, then, what about Japan, Hong Kong and Taiwan?

We believe that one of the primary reasons for a lower proportion of investment from the East into India can be attributed to the fact that quicker profits can be made in Vietnam and China. For instance, the pay back period is much shorter in China and Vietnam than it is in India.

However, there are no statistics to support these contentions.

A second plausible reason is that the emphasis placed on legal documentation in China and Vietnam is minimal whereas in India, which has an established legal system based upon the English system, the emphasis is on documentation. While this may have some bearing, it does not appear accurate. Red tape continues to abound in China and even in Vietnam. For instance, obtaining a licence to establish a representative office in Vietnam can take up to one year. Moreover, the laws and regulations in the latter two countries are frequently subject to changes as they are still in the process of being established.

Mr. Robert O. Brewis, Associate Director, Credit Lyonnais International Asset Management (Hong Kong) Ltd., sees the presence of a long standing framework of the rule of law in India, which includes an established corporate code, accounting standards that are reassuring to foreign investors, and established and sizeable equity markets, as the major advantage in encouraging investments in India. He states that the advantages are particularly stark when contrasted with conditions existing in China where there is no established corporate code plus the fact that it has a fledging capital market. It is for these reasons that Credit Lyonnais is presently promoting a unit trust scheme in India.

In short, then, although a quicker pay back is possible in China and in Vietnam, greater stability will be found in India. As stated in the *Business Times* (25 October 1994): "India is like a very large ship. It turns slowly. Most emerging markets are like small sail boats. They can make quick turns, but they can also be blown over." India is not for the meek or for those who intend to make a quick return. India is a country where the expected pay back period will probably be longer than in China or Vietnam. Some clients generally prefer to invest in Vietnam for the simple reason that there are no laws in Vietnam, thus making it easier to do business and to make profits. The same reasoning, however, is not valid in India.

Amendments to the Companies Legislation

Amendments have been proposed to the *Companies Act* to bring it in line with contemporary requirements, and to create an environment in which industry can compete effectively in a highly competitive market place.

Promotion of Education

Although India has a very large population which is literate and highly skilled, there are also many people who are not educated. Plans had been undertaken to rectify this problem in the 1994/95 budget, with special efforts being made to strengthen elementary education as well as to make it reachable to everyone.

Infrastructure Services

The 1994/95 budget also noted that efficient and abundant infrastructure services are a necessary precondition for the success of India's economic reforms and especially for international competitiveness. Toward this end, a committee was appointed to look into the reform of the power system. Significant steps were also taken to promote investment in the oil and gas sector.

Amidst the ongoing economic development in India, the government has made it a point to study the impact of the liberalisation process on the poor. Dar (1994) states:

> The government has realised that while we let the budgets of the enterprises swell, we should also not allow the budgets of the individuals to shrink. We cannot have another nation of malcontents and hungry people silently living out an existence under the general ambience of good living in five-star hotels and swimming pools. The government's policy on this, for instance, on rationalization of people working in enterprises has showed that it is concerned about it. True, this may hurt the high fliers of enterprises and even slow down their progress somewhat, but it is something that the government has to be thinking of.

SINGAPORE'S ROLE IN INDIA

Undoubtedly, Singapore is one of the most successful nations in the world in terms of economic development. Its small size, however, necessitates building up investment portfolios in the booming Asia-Pacific region for continued economic success. In 1994, the Singapore government indicated that as much as 30% of reserves will be invested in Asia's booming economies. Table 2–5 (extracted from *Business Times*, 22 December

1994) gives a breakdown of Singapore's investments in Asia in 1993 and up to September 1994.

TABLE 2–5
Going Regional: Singapore Investments in Asia

Country	January–September 1994			1993		
	Value of investments (US$m)	No. of projects	Ranking	Value of investments (US$m)	No. of projects	Ranking
China	1,974*	712*	5	2,950	1,751	5
Myanmar	272**	20**	1	NA	NA	NA
Vietnam	250	22	3	73	27	6
India	27	36	NA	22	42	16
ASEAN						
Indonesia	1,470***	81***	6	1,460	60	1
Thailand	368	41	4	236	33	3
Malaysia	275	119	5	204	150	4
Philippines	52*	5*	6	39	10	3

Note: Ranking among foreign investors in the country
* as at June 1994;
** cumulative committed figure as at September 1994;
***as at 15 November 1994.

Tables 2–6, 2–7 and 2–8 give a breakdown of the bilateral trade between India and Singapore, the number of collaborations Singapore has in India and the quantum of Singapore's investment in India, respectively.

These figures are set to increase. *The Straits Times* (30 December 1994) states that in 1995, the Trade Development Board, the Economic Development Board and the Singapore Tourist Promotion Board intend to:

(i) Encourage Indian companies to internationalise their operations by setting up trading and operational headquarters in Singapore.
(ii) Promote Singapore investments in India in areas like real estate, in-

frastructure, tourism-related ventures and export-oriented industrial projects.

(iii) Encourage and develop Singapore-India collaboration in third-country markets and projects.

TABLE 2–6

India-Singapore Bilateral Trade (Value in Rs Million)

Year	Exports to Singapore	Imports to Singapore	Balance of Trade	Total Trade
1985–86	1,415.0	3,421.6	-2,006.6	4,836.6
1986–87	2,208.1	3,697.2	-1,489.1	5,905.3
1987–88	2,750.9	4,164.7	-1,413.8	6,915.6
1988–89	3,252.2	6,898.0	-3,645.8	9,450.2
1989–90	4,674.6	8,999.9	-4,352.3	13,674.5
1990–91	6,790.7	14,304.6	-7,513.9	21,095.3
1991–92	9,547.4	17,021.28	-7,473.8	26,568.8
1992–93	17,012.91	18,227.7	-1,214.8	35,240.62

TABLE 2–7

Number of Singapore Collaborations in India (Rs Million)

Year	Technical	Financial	Total
1985	1	2	3
1986	3	2	5
1987	2	1	3
1988	3	2	5
1989	6	5	11
1990	7	4	11
1991	0	0	0
1992	9	7	16
1993	11	24	35
1994*	13	32	45

* 9 months

Apart from direct investments, Singapore can also act as an intermediary or link between India and other countries, particularly in the East. As Jeff Leong in his article "Singapore – Forging Strategic Alliances to Exploit Emerging Markets" states:

> Singapore's credentials and relationships with other Asian governments have resulted in the award of several major infrastruc-

ture projects in Asia to Singapore-led consortiums and Singapore companies. Opportunities for strategic alliances and joint ventures with companies in the West for joint venture investment and participation in business ventures in Asia are in abundance.

TABLE 2–8
Singapore Investment in India (Rs Million)

Year	Foreign Investment		
	All Countries	**Singapore**	**% Share**
1985	1,130.02	2.46	0.2
1986	1,260.66	3.70	0.3
1987	1,069.5	2.50	0.2
1988	1,077.0	8.53	0.8
1989	2,397.5	46.26	1.9
1990	3,166.6	34.87	1.1
1991	1,283.2	–	–
1992	5,166.96	13.73	0.3
1993	38,015.42	602.11	1.6
1994*	91,126.82*	881.94	–

* 9 months

In addition, with East and South-east Asia representing the fastest growing region in the world and protectionist sentiments increasing in the more developed markets, India offers a vast market. As productivity and incomes of Indian people increase, their demand for imports will rise substantially (Singh, 1994). Singapore can be an essential link here.

Singapore can also consider a partnership with India to act jointly as a link between the East and West. An article in the *Business Times* (21 October 1994) notes that "with its historical ties with the West, command of the English language and familiarity with British law and corporate practice, the new India-in-the-making can also be the bridge between Asia and Europe, geographically, culturally and psychologically."

In relation to infrastructure projects, the Singapore Minister of Finance, Dr. Richard Hu, said that "with its extensive links to international financial markets, Singapore is in a good position to develop as a centre for regional infrastructure developers to raise project funds" (*Business Times,* 15 December 1994). Singapore is well-placed to serve the financial needs of large regional companies as the presence of a large number of international fund managers in Singapore would ensure that regional companies have ready access to a large pool of international funds. Also, there is ample liquidity in the Singapore stock market, given the high proportion of international investor participation and the exchange's efficient, and transparent, trading facilities.

To reiterate, India is a country which has tremendous potential for infrastructure developments. Singapore can provide the knowledge and technology for ventures in this area. Other areas of cooperation between India and Singapore could include power generation,[13] public housing, telecommunications, research, development, as well as defence cooperation.

Apart from this, Singapore has taken a bold step in the construction of a technology park in India. The first one situated at Bangalore is known as the Technology Park. Plans are being finalised to build a second park at Haryana in the north.

Another obvious advantage that Singapore has is the ability of her people to speak several different languages. Singapore can be a link between India and the non-English speaking world of the East.

Recognising the increasing role that it can play in India, Singapore has set up an India Business Interaction Group, the role of which is to disseminate information and gather market intelligence about new business opportunities in India. Singapore also has set up Trade Development Board offices in New Delhi, Bombay and Madras, and is thus able to provide India-wide coverage in helping companies do business.

CONCLUSION

This paper has attempted to provide an overview of the changes that have taken place in India. It looked at the investment climate as a whole, identifying possible areas of resistance to developments and suggesting some solutions to circumventing the resistance. Finally, it highlighted the role that Singapore can play in opening up the Indian economy.

In returning to the question posed at the beginning of this chapter namely, whether India has achieved her objectives arising from recent initiatives, it is important to realise that three years is too short to accomplish all of the objectives. It is but a blip in the life of a nation. The important thing is that India has made an about turn during the last three

---

13 See Appendix 2–8 for the potential development of the power sector.

years in her economic policies and, in so doing, has achieved a considerable amount of progress.

APPENDIX 2–1

Industries Reserved for the Public Sector
1. Arms and ammunition and allied items of defence equipment, defence aircraft and warships.
2. Atomic energy.
3. Coal and lignite.
4. Mineral oils.
5. Mining of iron ore, manganese ore, chrome ore, gypsum, sulphur, gold and diamonds.
6. Mining of copper, lead, zinc, tin, molybdenum and wolfram.
7. Minerals specified in the Schedule to the Atomic Energy (Control of Production and Use) Order, 1953.
8. Railway transport.
Note: Private investment is now allowed in mining, oil exploration, refining and marketing and parts of the railway transport sector.

APPENDIX 2–2

Industries for Which Industrial Licensing is Compulsory
1. Coal and lignite.
2. Petroleum (other than crude) and its distillation products.
3. Distillation and brewing of alcoholic drinks.
4. Sugar.
5. Animal fats and oils.
6. Cigars and cigarettes of tobacco and manufactured tobacco substitutes.
7. Asbestos and asbestos-based products.
8. Plywood, decorative veneers and other wood-based products such as particle board, black board.
9. Tanned or dressed fur skins.
10. Paper and newsprint except bagasse-based units.
11. Electronic aerospace and defence equipment, all types.
12. Industrial explosives, including detonating fuse, safety fuse, gun powder, nitrocellulose and matches.
13. Hazardous chemicals.
14. Drugs and pharmaceuticals (according to drug policy).
15. Entertainment electronics (VCRs, colour TVs, CD players, tape recorders).

APPENDIX 2–3

Industries Eligible for Automatic Approval of Foreign Technology Agreements and for 51% Foreign Equity

1. **Metallurgical industries.**
   - Ferro alloys.
   - Castings and forgings.
   - Non-ferrous metals and their alloys.
   - Sponge iron and palletisation.
   - Large diameter steel welded pipes of over 300 mm diameter and stainless steel pipes.
   - Pig iron.

2. **Boilers and steam generating plants.**

3. **Prime movers (other than electrical generators).**
   - Industrial turbines.
   - Internal combustion engines.
   - Alternate energy system like solar, wind, etc. and equipment thereof.
   - Gas/hydro/steam turbines up to 60 mw.

4. **Electrical equipment.**
   - Equipment for transmission and distribution of electricity including power and distribution transformers, power relays, HT-switch gear, synchronous condensers.
   - Electrical motors.
   - Electrical furnaces, industrial furnaces and induction heating equipment.
   - X-ray equipment.
   - Electronic equipment and components, including subscribers' and telecommunication equipment.
   - Component wires for manufacture of lead-in-wires.
   - Hydro/steam/gas generators/ generating sets up to 60 MW.
   - Generating sets and pumping sets based on internal combustion engines.
   - Jelly-filled telecommunication cables.
   - Optic fibre.
   - Energy-efficient lamps.
   - Midget carbon electrodes.

5. **Transportation.**
   - Mechanised sailing vessels up to 10,000 DWT including fishing trawlers.
   - Ship ancillaries.
   - Commercial vehicles, public transport vehicles including automotive commercial three-wheeler jeep type vehicles, industrial locomotives.
   - Automotive two-wheelers and three-wheelers.
   - Automotive components/spares and ancillaries.
   - Shock absorbers for railway equipment.
   - Brake system for railway stock and locomotives.

6. **Industrial machinery.**
   - Industrial machinery and equipment.

7. **Industrial tools.**
   - Machine tools and industrial robots and their controls and accessories.
   - Jigs, fixtures, tools and dies of specialised types and cross land tooling.

APPENDIX 2–3 (cont'd)

- Engineering production aids such as cutting and forming tools, patterns and dies and mining tools.

8. Agricultural machinery.
- Tractors.
- Self-propelled harvester combines.
- Rice transplanters.

9. Earthmoving machinery.
- Earth-moving machinery and construction machinery and components thereof.

10. Industrial instruments.
- Indicating, recording and regulating devices for pressure, temperature, rate of flow, weight levels and the like.

11. Scientific and electromedical instruments and laboratory equipment.

12. Nitrogenous & phosphatic fertilisers
- Inorganic fertiliser under "18–fertilizers" in the First Schedule to Industries (Development and Regulation) Act, 1951.
- Mineral or chemical fertilisers, nitrogenous and phosphatic.

13. Chemicals (other than fertilizers).
- Heavy organic chemicals including petrochemicals.
- Heavy inorganic chemicals.
- Organic fine chemicals.
- Synthetic reins and plastics.
- Man-made fibres.
- Synthetic rubber.
- Industrial explosives.
- Technical grade insecticides, fumigides, weedicides, and the like.
- Synthetic detergents.
- Miscellaneous chemicals (for industrial use only).
  - Catalysts and catalysts supports.
  - Photographic chemicals.
  - Rubber chemicals.
  - Isocyanates, urethanes, etc.
  - Speciality chemicals for enhanced oil recovery.
  - Heating fluids.
  - Coal-tar distillation and products therefrom.
  - Tonnage plants for the manufacture of industrial gases.
  - High altitude breathing oxygen/medical oxygen.
  - Nitrous oxide.
  - Refrigerant gases like liquid nitrogen, carbon dioxide, etc. in large volumes.
  - Argon and other rare gases.
  - Alkali/acid-resisting cement, compounds.
  - Leather chemicals and auxiliaries.

14. Drugs and pharmaceuticals.

15. Paper and pulp including paper products. Industrial laminates.

16. Automobile tyres and tubes.
- Automobile tyres and tubes.

APPENDIX 2–3 (cont'd)

- Rubberised heavy duty industrial beltings of all types.
- Rubberised conveyor beltings.
- Rubber reinforced and lined fire fighting hose pipes.
- High pressure braided hoses.
- Engineering and industrial plastic products.

17. **Plate glass.**
    - Glass shells for television tubes.
    - Float glass and plate glass.
    - HT insulators.
    - Glass fibres of all types.

18. **Ceramics.**
    - Ceramics for industrial uses.

19. **Cement products.**
    - Portland cement.
    - Gypsum boards, wall boards and the like.

20. **High technology reproduction and multiplication equipment.**

21. **Carbon and carbon products.**
    - Graphite electrodes and anodes.
    - Impervious graphite blocks and sheets.

22. **Pretensioned high pressure RCC pipes.**

23. **Rubber machinery.**

24. **Printing machinery.**
    - Web-fed high speed offset rotary printing machine with output of 30,000 or more impressions per hour.
    - Photo composing/typesetting machines.
    - Multi-colour sheet-fed offset printing machines of sizes 18" by 25" and above.
    - High speed rotogravure printing machines with output of 30,000 or more impressions per hour.

25. **Welding electrodes other than those for welding mild steel.**

26. **Industrial synthetic diamonds.**

27. **Photosynthesis improvers.**
    - Generally modified free living-symbiotics nitrogen fixer.
    - Pheromones.
    - Bio-insecticides.

28. **Extraction and upgrading of minor oils.**

29. **Prefabricated building materials.**

30. **Soya products.**
    - Soya texture proteins.
    - Soya protein isolates.
    - Soya protein concentrates.
    - Other specialised products of soyabean.
    - Winterised and deodorised refined soyabean oil.

31. **Certified high yielding hybrid seeds and synthetic seeds and**
    - Certified high yielding plantlets developed through plant tissue culture.

32. **All food processing industries other than milk food, malted foods and flour, but excluding the items reserved for the small-scale sector.**

33. **All items of packaging for food processing industries excluding the items reserved for the small-scale sector.**

34. **Hotels and tourism-related industry.**

35. **Software.**

36. **Shipping, shipbuilding and ship repair.**

APPENDIX 2–4

Consumer Goods Industries Where Dividend Balances are Required

1. Manufacture of food and food products.
2. Manufacture of dairy products.
3. Grain mill products.
4. Manufacture of bakery products.
5. Manufacture and refining of sugar (vacuum pan sugar factories).
6. Production of common salt.
7. Manufacture of hydrogenated oil (vanaspati).
8. Tea processing.
9. Coffee.
10. Manufacture of beverages, tobacco and tobacco products.
11. Distilling, rectifying and blending of spirits, wine industries, malt liquors and malt production of country liquors and toddy.
12. Soft drinks and carbonated water industry.
13. Manufacture of cigars, cigarettes, cheroot and cigarette tobacco.
14. Manufacture of wood and wood products, furniture and fixtures.
15. Manufacture of leather and fur products.
16. Tanning, curing, finishing, embossing and japanning of leather.
17. Manufacture of footwear (excluding repair) except vulcanised or moulded rubber or plastic footwear.
18. Manufacture of footwear made primarily by vulcanized or moulded products.
19. Prophylactics (rubber contraceptive).
20. Motor cars.
21. Entertainment electronics (VCRs, colour TVs, CD players, tape recorders).
22. White goods (domestic refrigerators, domestic dishwashing machines, programmable domestic washing machines, microwave ovens, airconditioners).

APPENDIX 2–5

Fresh Concessions for Exporters

The Government announced on 13 December 1994 fresh concessions for exporters:

(i) Gems and jewellery manufactured by units in export processing zones may be sold to foreign bound passengers as baggage. Such items may also be transferred by such passengers to any retail outlet or showroom in the departure area of any international airport, to the customs warehouse, or handed over to another passenger at the time of departure.

(ii) Infrastructure equipment imported by software exporters in Software Technology Park complexes may be allowed to be linked to research and educational institutes (other than those engaged in commercial activities) for use by those institutes.

(iii) Exporters of computer software in technology parks have been allowed to supply or transfer goods imported by their units to another 100% export-orientated unit (EOU) or to a unit in export processing zone or free trade zone (EPZ/FTZ) for the purpose of exporting software.

(iv) Hundred per cent EOUs have been allowed to re-import goods within three years of export thereof for repairs or reconditioning and ensure better after-sales service to foreign buyers. This also applies to units under the Electronic Hardware Technology Park Scheme (EHTPS).

(v) Exporters of electronic hardware covered by the EHTPS for 100% EOUs have been allowed to send their imported goods or the manufactured goods temporarily outside the unit without payment of duty for the purpose of repairs, processing or display. Such units can also supply or transfer these goods to any other 100% EOU or to a unit in EPZ/FTZ for manufacture and export or for use within the said unit.

APPENDIX 2–6

Recent Investment Approvals

(a) A subsidiary of the Royal Dutch Airlines will be set up in India to carry on transportation, carriage, warehousing, cargo handling and logistic services to customers. Initially, the Indian subsidiary would provide these services at international airports in India and subsequently extend the services to a door-to-door distribution network.

(b) M/s ITC Agro-Tech will set up a joint venture for the development of oil plantations in Andhra Pradesh State in association with two Malaysian companies.

(c) M/s Raisurama PC will establish an integrated coconut processing plant in collaboration with M/s Scrav Development AB of Sweden. The plant, to be set up near Bangalore, will manufacture food products, oil, husk, coir and activated carbon.

(d) M/s Croda International, a global chemical company, will set up 100% owned subsidiary in India to market speciality chemicals as well as establish its manufacturing facilities in India.

(e) M/s Rhone-Poulenc, a pharmaceutical company will set up a joint venture in India to produce pharmaceutical products.

(f) M/s Gateway Distri-Parks Ltd will establish a joint venture in India to set up warehouses. The first would be near Jawaharlal Nehru Port, New Bombay. The proposed warehouses will comprise general and bonded warehousing, container freight station, container yard depot and transportation services.

(g) M/s General Electric Company of the United States will manufacture, design and distribute electric motors and control appliances in India in partnership with M/s DLF, Faridabad. The proposed joint venture expects to serve the export market, especially the Middle East. It will also establish a product development centre for providing engineering and software services related to motor and control systems.

APPENDIX 2–7
Indian Economy at a Glance

Growth in Real GDP (% change over previous year)

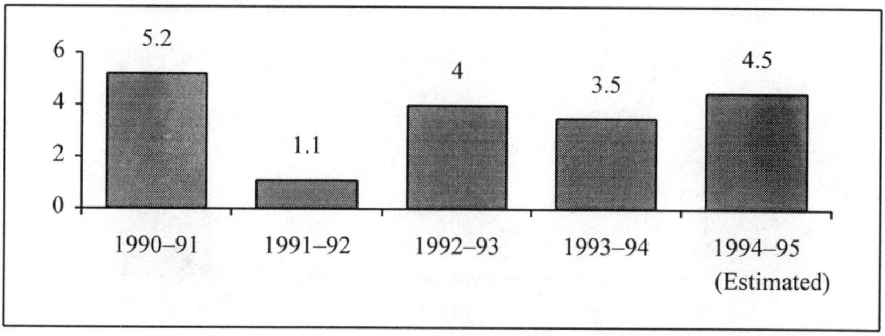

Agricultural Production (% change over previous year)

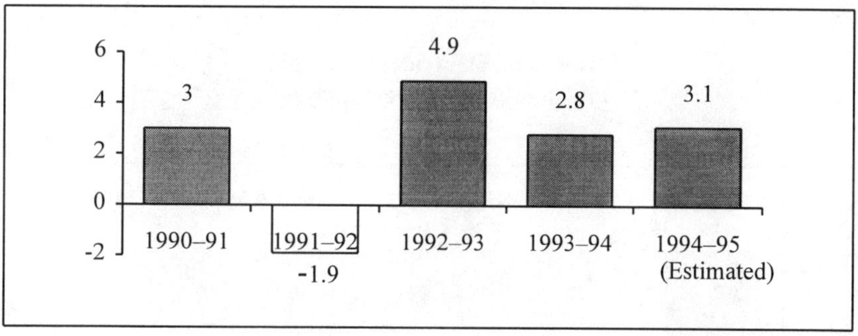

Industrial Production (% change over previous year)

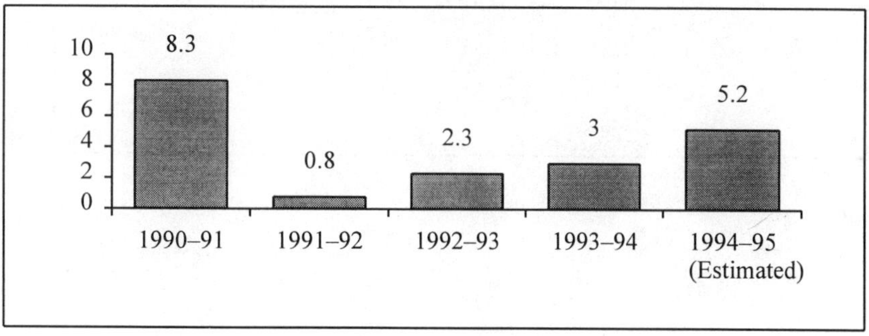

APPENDIX 2–7 (cont'd)

Growth of Capital Goods Industry
(% change over previous year)

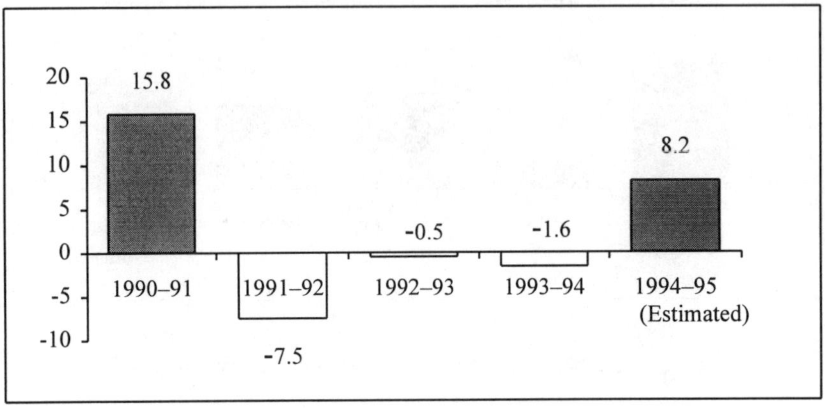

Growth of Electrical Machinery
(% change over previous year)

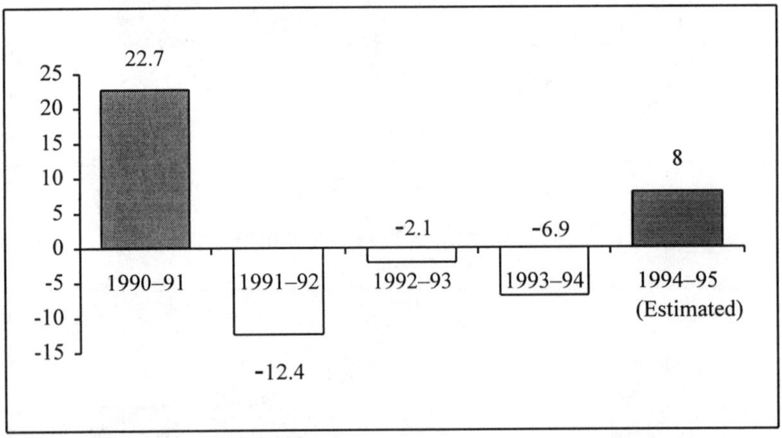

APPENDIX 2–7 (cont'd)

Growth of Non-electrical Machinery
(% change over previous year)

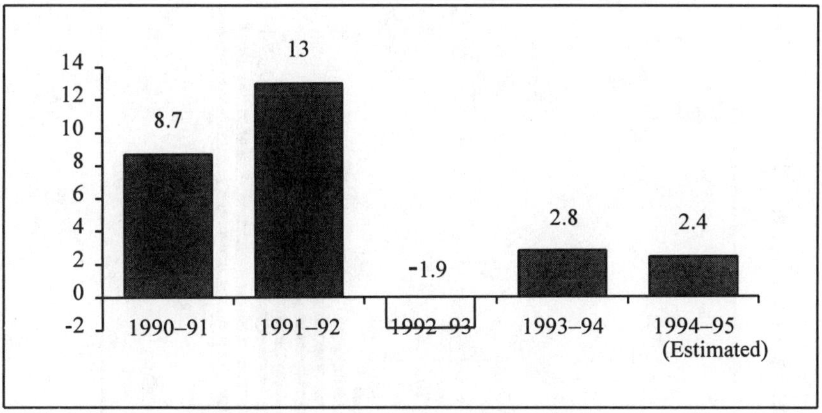

Growth of Transport Equipment
(% change over previous year)

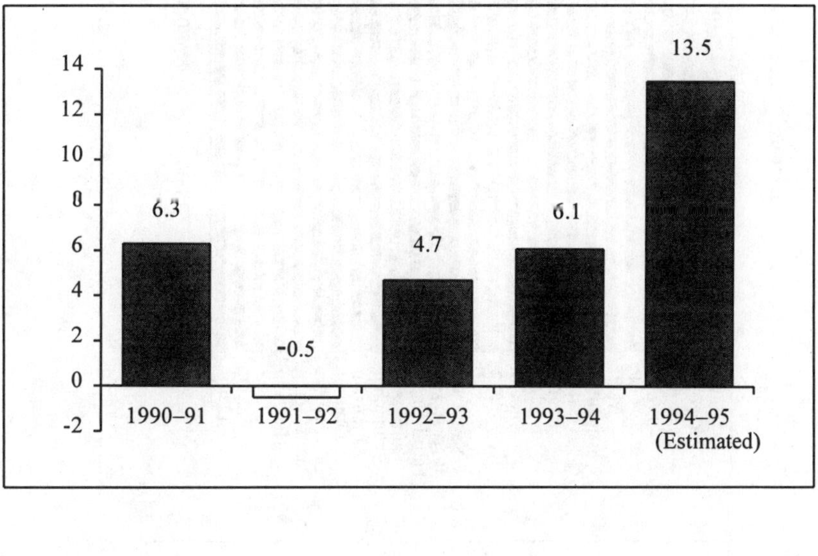

APPENDIX 2–7 (cont'd)

Disparity in Per Capita Income Among Indian States: 1992–1993 (Rs)

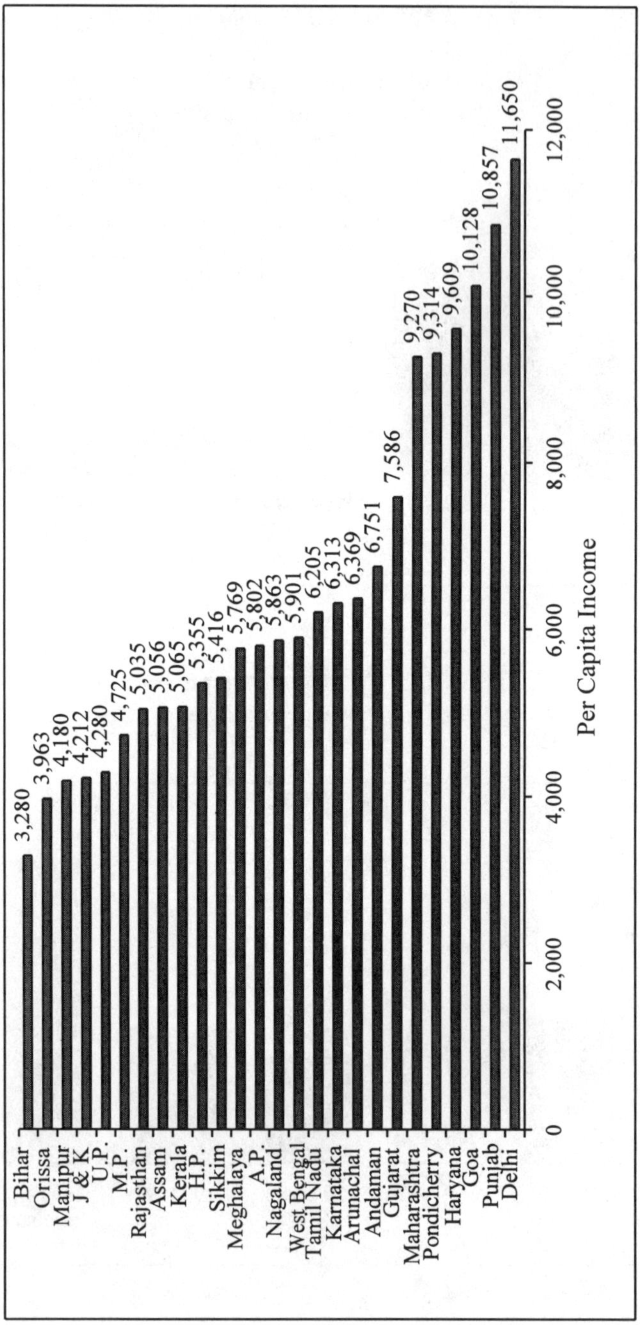

APPENDIX 2–7(cont'd)

Statewise Breakup of Industrial Entrepreneurs Memoranda Filed From August 1991 to July 1994

State Name	Number Filed	Investment Proposed (Rs. in Billion)	Employment Potential
Andhra Pradesh	797	222.27	163,735
Assam	35	4.11	3,195
Bihar	136	39.21	20,436
Gujarat	2,100	506.64	38,184
Haryana	676	117.75	168,704
Himachal Pradesh	149	45.38	47,963
Jammu & Kashmir	23	1.18	6,764
Karnataka	527	114.17	75,776
Kerala	120	28.04	24,346
Madhya Pradesh	945	314.34	241,575
Maharashtra	3,047	617.79	527,844
Meghalaya	3	0.38	482
Nagaland	2	0.53	252
Orissa	95	292.60	40,606
Punjab	888	110.51	258,897
Rajasthan	867	136.85	172,714
Tamil Nadu	1,075	152.65	175,398
Tripura	3	10.38	1,345
Uttar Pradesh	1,597	356.25	294,564
West Bengal	496	76.98	109,699
Sikkim	8	0.22	680
Andaman & Nicobar	4	2.61	2,180
Arunachal Pradesh	1	0.35	23
Chandigarh	12	1.21	3,604
Dadra & Nagar Haveli	266	37.87	323,258
Dolhi	338	52.18	38,644
Goa	91	20.96	11,715
Lakshadweep	1	0.04	278
Pondicherry	102	5.48	10,500
Daman & Diu	160	171.13	14,200
TOTAL	**14,564**	**3,440.06**	**2,777,561**

APPENDIX 2–8
Potential for Developments in the Power Sector

Capacity (MW)

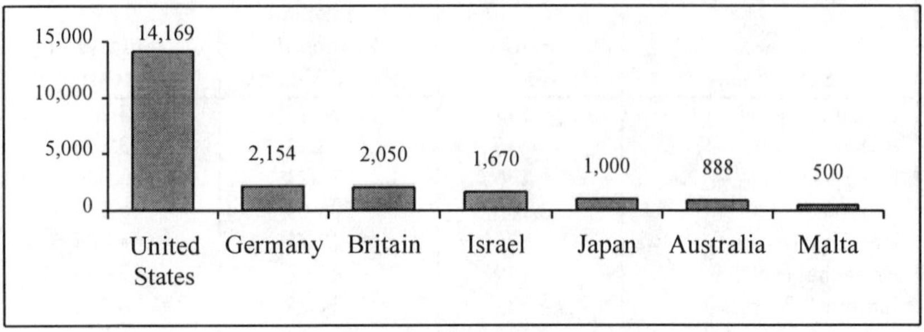

Costs (Rs. crores)

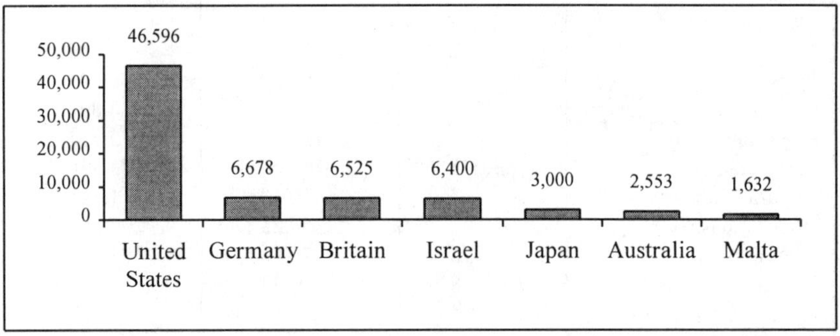

Number of Offers

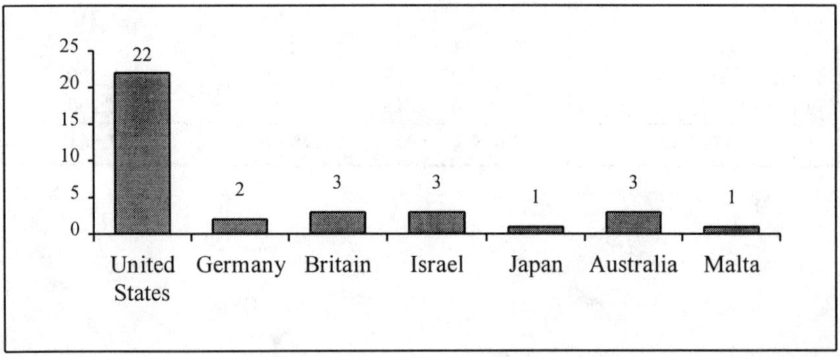

APPENDIX 2–8 (cont'd)

Developments in the Power Sector
Counter-Guarantee Norms for Power Projects: The Government of India have approved the general parameters for counter-guarantee in respect of six private sector power projects. Brief details are as follows: (i) Counter-guarantee will only be extended where the management of the state electricity board (SEBs) is prudent in the opinion of the Government. A rate of return of 3% on fixed assets in the preceding year by the SEBs would be a minimum essential requirement. (ii) The promoter shareholder would need to hold at least 50% of issued share capital until the elapse of 12 months after commencement of commercial operations. Thereafter, until the guarantee remains in force, the promoters' stake shall not fall below 33.33%. (iii) Government of India will adjust outstanding dues from SEBs against Central plan assistance and States' share of Central taxes. (iv) Ministry of Power, Government of India, would need to certify the reasonableness of the cost per MW of electricity generated. (v) Foreign debt guaranteed by the Government of India to be restricted to an amount equivalent to foreign equity. (vi) The maximum annual liability of the Government of India to be fixed at pre-determined level.

REFERENCES

Asher Mukul G., "The 1994–1995 Budget: Implications for India's 'Look East' Policy", National University of Singapore, 1994.

Bradley Edward, "India Woos Investment", *IFLR,* March 1994.

Chadha Chetan, "Foreign Investment: Need for Major Trust".

Chidambaram P., "The Impact of Reforms on Business and Investment Opportunities in India", Public Address, 14 November 1994.

Dar A. N., "Liberalisation: What About the Poor?", *Kaleidoscope*, 14 August 1994.

Desai Nitish M., "India Opens its Doors to Foreign Investors", *Asia Law Journal,* Vol. 3, No. 2, 1994.

Federation of Indian Chambers of Commerce and Industry, *International Business Initiatives* Vol. 1, No. 9, November 1994.

Federation of Indian Chambers of Commerce and Industry, *Economic Trends,* Vol. 23, No. 4, December 1994.

Federation of Indian Chambers of Commerce and Industry, *Business Digest*, Vol. 4, Issue 44–45, 1994.

"Foreign Direct Investment", *Kaleidoscope*, 18 August 1994.

Foreign Investment in India: A Brief Report, PHD Chamber of Commerce, Special Issue, March 1994.

High Commission of India, Singapore, *Economic Bulletin*, December 1994.

"India's 'Big Ship' Economy: Plenty of Room to Grow", *Business Times,* 25 October 1994.

"India's Market-Opening Could be a Boom to Asia and the West", *The Straits Times,* 21 October 1994.

"India to Trim High Import Duties on Foreign Consumer Goods", *The Straits Times*, 15 September 1994.

India-Singapore Trade and Investment: Some Facts, Meeting with Delegation from Nanyang Technological University, Singapore, at PHD House, 14 December 1994.

"Indian Minister Calls for Higher Growth, More Reforms", *Business Times,* 21 September 1994.

Indo-Singapore Bilateral Relations: Trade and Economics, Speech by the High Commissioner of India, Singapore, November 1994.

"Japanese Firms Want More Open Indian Market", *Straits Times,* 20 September 1994.

Kurien and Associates, "Statistics and Leaflets", India, 1994.

Monthly Report Covering India, Pakistan and Sri Lanka, *Business South Asia*, November 1994.

"PM Rao Has a Lot More Reforming to do in India", *Business Times,* 13 September 1994.

"Rao Extends His Hand of Partnership", *The Straits Times,* 9 September 1994.

"Rao's Economic Reforms Compare with Deng's: SM — India's PM Defends Reform Pace, Welcomes Foreign Businessmen", *Business Times*, 9 September 1994.

"Singapore Set to Be India's Gateway to East Asia: TDB", *Business Times*, 7 August 1994.

Singh, Manmohan, *India's Economic Relations With East and South-east Asia*, Meeting of the World Economic Forum, Singapore, 14 October 1994.

"Status of Indian Reforms — Rao Presses on and the Gods are Smiling; India Fever Looks Set to Take Hold Again", *Business Times,* 7 September 1994.

Vaish Associates, *Doing Business in India — Policies and Procedures*, 1994.

Winterbotham James, "Removing the Red Tape — The Reform of Business Regulations in India", *Asia Law Journal,* Vol. 3, No. 2, 1994.

Chapter 3

Financial and Capital Market Reforms

BY
CHONG Boo Chien
WOO Fook Cheong

INTRODUCTION

AS THE SIXTH largest and second most populous country in the world, India has long been considered a country of vast unrealised potential. A new spirit of economic freedom is now stirring in the country, bringing sweeping changes in its wake. A series of ambitious economic reforms aimed at deregulating the economy and stimulating foreign investment have moved India firmly into the front ranks of the rapidly growing Asia-Pacific region.

Since gaining independence, India has made significant social and economic progress.[1] Indian agriculture has progressively modernised and the country is now self-sufficient in food. India has also built up a well-diversified industrial structure and a vast reservoir of scientific, technical and managerial skills. However, the overall pace has fallen short of the potential objectives of the economy as well as the aspirations of people. In order to achieve full employment and remove poverty in a reasonably short period of time, the Indian economy will need to grow at a minimum rate of 7% to 8% during

[1] Extracted from the *World Economic Forum*, 14 October 1994.

the second half of the 1990s. Moreover, the growth pattern will have to be more labour intensive than in the past and, also, greater attention will have to be paid to human resource development and the protection of the environment. This is the basic justification of the wide-ranging programme of economic reforms launched since June 1991. A recent study (Ariff, 1994) of nine Asian countries that reformed their financial systems concluded that financial liberialisation helped to establish their financial system. Hence, this is the rationale for focusing on reforms in the financial sector in this chapter.

The Need for Economic Reforms in the 1990s

India has undertaken a bold programme of market oriented economic reforms to integrate the national economy with the international mainstream. Her economic policies are tailored towards the expansion of mutually beneficial economic cooperation with countries in East and South-east Asia. She is also keen in developing new dynamic links of trade, investment and technology flows with these countries.

The fundamental objective of economic reform is to bring about rapid and sustained improvement in the quality of her residents' life (Government of India, 1994). Central to this goal is a rapid increase in income and productive employment. With hundreds of millions of Indians still trapped in abject poverty, the only durable solution to the curse of poverty is sustained growth of incomes and employment in agriculture, industry and services. Successful and sustained development depends on continued increases in the productivity of capital, land and labour. The obstacle that lies ahead is to change traditional ways of thinking and working efficiency. Tough decisions, which may hurt powerful vested interests are needed; otherwise, reforms of broad policies will not work.

Early Years of Reform

The reforms took place after the government assumed office in June 1991. The country was at a point of unprecedented economic crisis and socio-political turmoil. It was the first time that India was faced with the prospect of defaulting on its international commitments (Government of India, 1994). With the denial of foreign funds and downgrading of credit rating, the country could only resort to borrowing against their gold reserves.

Faced with such a dilemma, the government took immediate and swift action to restore international confidence in the economy and redress the imbalances that had emerged in external and domestic financial conditions. Numerous reforms in the micro as well as the macro economy were prescribed but emphasis was on those in the financial sector. One of the first policies that the government conducted was checking the extent of inflation. Also, the rate of growth of money was checked. The exchange rate of the rupee was adjusted downwards to a level that could be sustained in the light of the country's balance of payments situation and the state of the domestic economy. Emergency financing was mobilised from both multilateral and bilateral sources to relieve the pressure of immediate debt servicing on the balance of payments and to build up foreign exchange reserves.

This chapter explores in more detail the extent of reforms applicable to the financial and capital markets. Next, the effects of these policies on business as well as the general public are illustrated. The chapter will then discuss the effectiveness of India's reforms and compare them with some of the countries in the surrounding region.

INDIA'S FINANCIAL SYSTEM[2]

There are six broad types of institutions in any modern financial system. These are: (1) commercial banks; (2) specialised banking institutions; (3) mutual credit organisations; (4) informal financing organisations; (5) organised securities exchanges; and (6) insurance and pension funds. Figures 3–1 and 3–2 provide an overview of the Indian financial system (see also Appendix 3–3). In this context, we focus mainly on the first five classes and exclude the insurance and pension funds.

All financial institutions are licensed by the central government agencies and, in this regard, India's financial system is similar to those found in most commonwealth countries. Banks are divided into two groups, namely, the more significant public-sector banks and the important private-sector banks. This terminology does not mean that the banks are restricted to transactions within their respective domains. The dominant public-sector banks number about 224 and they have a large number of branches throughout the country. Of the public-sector banks, 196

---

[2] This section is adapted from Ariff (1994).

FINANCIAL REFORMS IN INDIA

Background

An efficient banking system that is capable of mobilizing and deploying national savings is essential for successful economic restructuring. However, prior to 1991, the banking sector suffered from many deficiencies in the efficiency and quality of operations. Multiple regulated interest rates, and the maintenance of huge reserves as a result of the required statutory liquidity ratio, have weakened the financial health of the banking system and forced banks to charge very high interest rates on their commercial advances. The lack of international accounting norms resulted in bank balance sheets which do not reflect financial position accurately. Unless major reforms are initiated, India cannot expect to achieve accelerated growth and increased competitiveness.

Since Rao's government took office in June 1991, the momentum of reforms has been rapid. Interest rates are now freed from administrative control. The Reserve Bank of India (RBI) has prescribed new norms for income recognition according to national standards, and new capital adequacy standards as prescribed by the Basel Committee. In order to introduce competitive elements into the banking sector, which is nationalised to a large degree, guidelines have been issued governing the entry of new private sector banks (see Appendix 3–1). The process of partial disinvestment of government equity in nationalised banks has begun. The rapid reforms in the 1990s will increase the stability of India's financial markets, increase efficiency, and set the trend for higher average growth performance.

Liberalisation of Capital Markets

Foreign Institutional Investors (FIIs) such as pension funds and mutual funds, are permitted to invest in Indian capital markets on registration with the SEBI (Joint Business Council, 1994). Common application forms have been simplified and foreign brokers are also permitted to assist investors. All mutual funds are allowed to apply for firm allotment in public issues. These funds are also exempted from income tax regardless of whether they are in the public or the private sectors.

The procedures for lodgement of securities for transfer were eased considerably for domestic and foreign institutional investors through the introduction of a jumbo transfer deed and consolidated payment of stamp duty. The Securities Contracts (Regulations) Rules have been amended to enable widely held stock broking companies to become members of the stock market. This is expected to encourage the growth of corporate membership in the stock exchange, induce greater professionalism and ensure better services for the investing public.

The amount of capital that was raised as a result of India opening up to international capital markets was a hefty US$9 billion from foreign countries. Almost 70% (US$5 billion) was from GDRs . It should be noted that out of 22 GDRs that were issued in 1994 only six were actually launched in the United States, which is the largest financial centre in the world. Even more interesting, is that all of them were launched in the NASDAQ market instead of the traditional NYSE, despite its liquidity.

The reason why India's companies were deterred from the U.S. market is because of the strict listing regulations that the Securities Exchange Council (SEC) imposed on the listed firms such as the submission of tedious quarterly reports and close scrutiny by the council.[3] In addition, it is almost impossible for foreign firms, once launched, to delist from the stock exchange. This is probably the reason behind the absence of German firms in the New York Stock Exchange too.

Reduction in Statutory Liquidity Ratio (SLR)

As far back as the 1950s, India's central bank imposed a high liquidity requirement on the banking sector such that almost 47% of deposits ended up as reserves with the central bank in the form of bank deposits and government securities. Singapore, by contrast, requires 11% plus 7% as reserves, which totals 18%. A simple arithmetic calculation would show that Singapore's credit multiplier is almost four times the total deposits whereas India's banking system can generate twice its deposit rate at most.

The Narasimahan Committee's recommendation to reduce the SLR has since been adopted. The reduction will provide banks with greater flexibility in the deployment of their resources. They will be able to expand credit to agriculture and industry and, subsequently, reduce the fiscal deficit. As a result of the reduction, the amount of the SLR required to be maintained by banks would be reduced by about Rs 28 billion.[4] The SLR is targeted to be 25% by the end of 1996.

---

[3] Extracted from the *Financial Express*, 12 December 1994.

[4] Extracted from *Economic Bulletin*, October 1994.

One of the steps the government has undertaken is the liberalisation of the restrictive monetary policy. The SLR was 38% in 1994 and it was slated to be reduced to 33% by the end of 1995 (Government of India, 1994). Plans were made to reduce this ratio further to a comfortable level of 25%, which is almost one-half of the 1950s level. With these steps installed, there has been a steady flow of funds into India. The cumulative total has been increasing in the last six years. It was US$3.6 billion in 1990 and reached US$5 billion by 1993.

This fulcrum of increasing liquidity also spells trouble for the funds-starved nationalised companies. These companies have traditionally been acquiring cheap funds out of the central bank's reserves derived from SLR deposits. When the SLR was reduced, the availability of cheap funds diminished exponentially, and companies were forced to approach the capital market for liquidity. In fact, many companies have appealed to overseas sources for global depository receipts (GDRs) over the last few years.

In view of this opportunity, Singapore could be very attractive to Indian companies as a source to raise funds. Moreover, Indian companies could tap into the South-east Asia countries. Singapore, of course, would benefit from the service commissions.

Liberalisation of Interest Rates

The difference between the deposit rate and the minimum lending rate in India is 2.88%. This is very low compared with the 4.4% in Singapore. The lower spread would make Indian banks less profitable and, hence, less able to modernise quickly.

Today, the minimum lending rate for loans above Rs 2 lakhs (Rs 200,000) has been abolished.[5] Banks are now able to set their own prime lending rates. The banks' prime lending rate would need to be declared and be uniformly applicable at all branches. In the aftermath of freeing the lending rates for amounts above Rs 2 lakhs, many banks have decided to reduce the minimum rates to 14%.[6] The lifting of the restriction on interest rates would result in a new realignment among banks because efficiency would become the criterion for survival, thus leading to more mergers and takeovers.

With the banking reform in 1994, the regulated interest rate struc-

---

5 Extracted from FICCI *Economic Trends,* December 1994.

6 Extracted from FICCI *Business Digest*, November 1994.

ture is being rationalised and simplified. Bank deposit rates have been deregulated subject to a ceiling rate. The number of lending rates has been reduced from about 20 before the reforms to three rates today, two concessional and one floor, for all advances above Rs 2 lakhs.[7]

Unified Exchange Rate

A unified market determined exchange rate of the rupee was introduced in March 1993. Foreign exchange controls have been eased significantly and market forces now determine the exchange rate of the rupee. The rupee has shown remarkable stability since it was floated and it has tended to appreciate.

Also, the premium on foreign exchange in the illegal or "hawala" market has dropped to about 8% as compared to 25% earlier. The new system provides a powerful incentive for exports including services, exports and remittances. It has also greatly reduced the incentive for inward remittances flowing to the illegal "hawala" market.

Convertibility of Rupee

The rupee has been made fully convertible on the current account. This assures foreign investors that there will be no impediment in the repatriation of their earnings and other service charges in the coming years. Finally, the government opted for full convertibility of the rupee on the capital account in the 1995–96 budget to complete the process of foreign exchange liberalisation.[8]

New Private Sector Banks

The restrictions on the formation of new banks in the private sector have finally been removed. They are allowed provided that they conform to RBI guidelines for such banks. By October 1994, RBI had issued licences to six new private banks.[9] Also, existing private sector banks are allowed to expand without fear of nationalisation. These banks are allowed to raise capital contributions from foreign institutional investors up to 20%, and up to 40% from non-resident Indians (NRIs). They are

---

7 Extracted from *Economic Reforms,* "Two Years After and the Task Ahead", 1994.

8 Extracted from FICCI *Business Digest*, November 1994.

9 Extracted from *World Economic Forum*, Mr. Manmohan Singh's address, 14 October 1994.

also permitted to close non-viable branches other than in the rural areas.

The introduction of a private sector will inject competition into the financial market. One source states: "Despite the cautious approach followed by banks in reducing their prime lending rates, they may be forced to make further cuts as the competition, especially from foreign banks and private sector banks...".[10] Competition from the entry of new private banks, including joint ventures with foreign banks, in turn, will result in innovative public services.

The approval process for establishment of private banks has been greatly simplified. An example reported in the media in April 1994, indicated that an approval for the establishment of a banking institution by foreign investors was obtained within 69 days.

Elimination of Government Access to RBI

The government's automatic access to RBI to fund its budget deficit has been eliminated so that any increases in the future will have to be made from market borrowings. Government deficits will not be automatically monetised and, as a result, it will be easier to control the growth of the money supply as well as inflation.

Strengthening of SEBI

The CCI has been abolished and control over share prices and premiums was removed in May 1992.[11] Companies are now free to approach the capital market after clearance by the SEBI. The SEBI is armed with the necessary authority, and power, for regulation and reform of the capital market. Rules and regulations governing various aspects of the stock market, and intermediaries operating therein, have been introduced with the aim to improve trading practices, disclosure and investor protection (see Appendix 3–2).

The SEBI has introduced a number of measures for streamlining the secondary market such as reconstitution of the governing board of the stock exchange, capital adequacy norms for brokers and transparency in client/broker relationships. To provide a stimulus to India's financial market growth, the slow and inefficient out-cry system will gradually be abolished and replaced with screen-based trading. This explains the

---

10 Extracted from *Business Digest*, November 1994.

11 Extracted from *Economic Reforms in India*, 1994.

emergence of both the National Stock Exchange of India and the over-the-counter market which both practise the more efficient screen-based trading. All these activities signify the seriousness of the government about the much publicised reforms.[12] Furthermore, companies now are at liberty to price their securities unlike previously, when there was tight control of security issues by the government.

As a result of these deregulations, there has been a massive increase in India's market capitalisation. The amount of capital raised in India during 1992 was 270 billion rupees as compared to less than 1 billion rupees during 1990. The number of investors increased from 2 million to 16 million in 1994 which represents an eight-fold increase. In fact, India has one of the largest capital markets in Asia. These activities led to a multiplication of merchant banks, underwriters and custodians who were almost invisible prior to the pre-1988 era. The Security Exchange Board of India (SEB) was subsequently set up to regulate this growth sector.

As the regional hub for finance and capital movements, Singapore could capitalise on this opportunity in India. There is more than one way to invest in India from Singapore. One can make use of the Indian mutual fund set up by Citibank, or one can approach DBS Securities directly and invest in Indian stocks through a third party (Toh and Low, 1993). The latter route would be slightly more expensive since it entails two services and it is less diversified.

Incorporation of International Accounting Standards

New accounting standards relating to income recognition, provision for bad debts and capital adequacy, in harmony with generally accepted international standards, were implemented in 1992–93.[13] This ensures that the banks' balance sheets reflect an accurate financial position which is prerequisite for effective monitoring and improving performance. Banks are also required to make provisions for doubtful and substandard assets by the end of March 1994. Companies are also required to disclose all material facts and specific risk factors associated with their projects while marketing public issues.

Fifteen accounting standards, which include the consolidation of accounts and funds flow statement requirements, were set up in accordance

---

12 Extracted from a speech by R. N. Malhotra at the FICCI-NTU Symposium, December 1994.

13 Extracted from the *Economic Bulletin*, November 1994.

with generally accepted international accounting standards. Listed firms now are required by legislation to publish financial statements every six months. Plans are also underway to make the listing requirements more stringent by encouraging quarterly reports. This would certainly improve the transparency of the capital markets, thus protecting investors. With increased transparency, greater market efficiency should follow.

DISCUSSION

Comparison with Emerging Markets

Liberalisation of India's US$150 billion capital market is sending shock waves to other parts of Asia especially since the index has a unique negative coefficient of correlation with the South Asian markets (Ariff, 1994). This makes it extremely attractive for diversification. However, the gradual liberalisation process has another repercussion. This unique advantage is fast dissolving because of the advent of GDRs in Asian and European nations by Indian multinational corporations, and its negative coefficient of correlation has fallen to -0.04 in 1994. This effect is inevitable because world capital markets are unifying, and the infrastructure is improving because of technological advancement.

India's credit rating has improved tremendously since its liberalisation. Moody's and Japan have recently upgraded India's credit rating to investment grade. It is simply a matter of time until other major credit rating agencies take similar action.

Further Issues on India's Reforms

The current lack of transparency in India's capital market presents undesirable effects to international institutional investors. Reports on price earnings ratios and earnings per share are not widely practised in India (i.e., fewer than 50% of the listed firms in India have complete reports of their financial ratios in the newspapers). It is also known that one-half of the listed stocks are held by institutional investors. This gives way to market manipulations by the bigger players. One solution is to have a larger holding of shares by investors in the capital market such as Singapore Telecoms did in 1993.

The secondary market is also very weak, particularly bonds, index futures and options trading. This factor might deter many potential investors since they are given limited opportunity to diversify. Although there will be futures trading in the near future, the bureaucratic process in India may hamper the growth of this sector.

Finally, foreign institutional investors might find the seven-year equity policy as somewhat restrictive because of the volatility of the Indian market. An institution is not allowed to transfer dividends out of the country when the quantum is less than its revenue in foreign currencies for the first seven years of operations. This will force institutions to plough their earnings back into the country even though the yields are low.

Singapore's Role in India's Financial Markets

The vast network of financial institutions in India requires some level of modernisation of its technology, management systems, work force and operating procedures at all levels. Given the past, and projected, explosion in the number of transactions handled by banks, it is impossible to provide timely service and to keep track of all the financial flows without widespread computerisation. Singapore's financial institutions have built up considerable knowledge in these areas which, with some modifications, can be applied to the Indian scene. However, there is a strong resistance against computerisation from Indian labour unions (i.e., bank employees). This resistance will need to be removed before mass scale computerisation can take place. The public consumer bodies should mobilise support for reforms aimed at providing better banking, insurance and other financial services to the public. Currently, new branches that are being set up are computerised. Existing ones, however, are rather slow in becoming computerised.

The recent liberalisation allowing the formation of private foreign banks opens another opportunity for Singapore. In fact, one of our local banks (Keppel Bank) has already teamed up with India's Centurion Bank. The formation of branches in India will boost the attractiveness of local companies doing business in India. These companies, until now, have been forced to deal with the host country banks because of the Monetary Authority of Singapore's rule that local credit lines cannot be used for overseas expansion. This has created high exchange risks and interest rates.

The Singapore-based financial institutions can participate with relatively smooth entry into India's financial sector due to their proximity and the existence of similar financial structures. The complementarity between highly developed Singapore financial services and the emerging financial system of India will surely be beneficial to both countries.

CONCLUSION

This chapter initially examined the background to India's four-year old reforms in the financial and capital markets. Next, the current financial structure and the major reforms were reviewed in detail. Finally, India's effort towards reform and the corresponding strengths and weaknesses, including potential opportunities for Singapore were discussed.

The empirical question assessed was whether the closed Indian economy prior to 1992 led to the isolation of its financial markets from international influences. The observations gathered from India suggest that this isolation, indeed, led to slower institutional changes especially because of the inertia in the financial system.

With liberalisation now underway, the markets are likely to gain competition from both the domestic and foreign players. This will lead to greater efficiency and more openness to international influences determining domestic interest rates in the 1990s. Furthermore, there are many opportunities for NIE's, such as Singapore, to join in this growth opportunity in an effort to regionalise their domestic economy.

APPENDIX 3–1 INDIA'S FINANCIAL AND BANKING REFORMS: 1992 TO 1994

(Adapted from "Economic Reforms in India — Highlights and Update", October 1994)

1. Statutory Liquidity Ratio (SLR) on incremental net demand and time liabilities (DTL) reduced from 38.5% to 25% SLR, and on net total DTL, reduced from 38.5% to 34.75%. Expected to fall to 33% by the end of 1995.
2. Incremental Cash Reserve Ratio (ICRR) of 10% removed. One-third of the impounded cash balances under incremental CRR was released, implying a reduction in CRR by 0.6%. CRR on net total

DTL reduced from 15% to 14%.

3. Number of interest rate slabs on bank advances reduced from about 20 in 1989–90 to three in the current financial year. Controlled floor interest rate on bank advances and ceiling interest rate on term deposits reduced by 4% and 3%, respectively.
4. International norms for income recognition, classification of assets and provisioning for bad debts introduced. Banks to complete provisioning for doubtful and substandard assets by the end of March 1994.
5. Introduction of capital adequacy norms requiring 4% to be attained by all banks by 31 March 1993 and 8% by 31 March 1996. Foreign banks operating in India, and Indian banks with branches abroad, must attain 4% by 31 March 1993 and 8% by 31 March 1994, respectively.
6. Budgetary support of Rs 5,700 crore (Rs 57,000 millions) for capitalisation of banks released after the nationalised banks entered into performance agreements with Reserve Bank of India (RBI) for strengthening bank management and ensuring efficiency improvement.
7. *State Bank of India (SBI) Act* amended to enable the bank to access the capital market and allow 10% voting rights to shareholders. SBI raised over Rs 1,400 crores as equity (including premium) and Rs 1,000 crores as bonds through a public issue. The RBI shareholding is now 67% as against 99% earlier.
8. Bill to enable nationalised banks to access the capital market for debt and equity has been introduced in parliament.
9. Banks given freedom to open new branches and upgrade extension counters on attaining capital adequacy norms and prudential accounting standards. They are permitted to close non-viable branches other than in rural areas.
10. New Bank of India merged with Punjab National bank.
11. 'In principle' approval given to seven proposals for setting up of new private sector banks. Banks allowed to raise capital contribution from foreign institutional investors up to 20%, and from Non-Resident Indians (NRIs), up to 40%.
12. A new Board of Financial Supervision is being set up within RBI to strengthen the supervisory system of banks and financial institutions. A new department, viz. Department of Supervision, was established in RBI as an independent unit effective 22 December 1993

for supervision of commercial banks.

13. Recovery of debts due to banks and financial institutions Act, 1993, passed to set up Special Recovery Tribunals to facilitate quicker recoveries of loan arrears.
14. Bank lending norms liberalised, and banks given freedom to decide levels of holding of individual items of inventories and receivables.
15. Ordinance promulgated amending *Banking Regulation Act*, 1949 to enable a banking company to have a non-executive chairman and up to three directors from among the directors of promoting institutions, and to raise the ceiling for the exercise of voting rights for a shareholder up to 10%, and to raise the penalties for contravention of the act.
16. Union agreement in October 1993, paves the way for faster computerisation in banks.
17. Scope of mandatory consortium arrangements narrowed to 76 large accounts in place of 934 accounts hitherto; borrowers allowed to induct new banks into a consortium, and banks permitted to leave consortium after two years.
18. Financial institutions' access to SLR funds reduced and they are encouraged to approach capital market for funds.
19. IFCI converted into a company, and its maiden public issue raised over Rs 600 crore as equity (including premium).
20. Convertibility clause no longer obligatory for assistance sanctioned by the lending institutions.
21. Ceiling on interest rate on debentures and bonds removed except for that on tax-free PSU bonds.

APPENDIX 3–2
INDIA'S CAPITAL MARKET REFORMS: 1992 TO 1994

(Adapted from "Economic Reforms in India — Highlights and Update", October 1994)

1. The *Capital Issues (Control) Act,* 1947 repealed and the Office of the Controller of Capital Issues (CCI) abolished. Control over price and premium of shares removed. Companies are now free to approach capital market after clearance by the Securities and Exchange Board of India (SEBI).

2. SEBI armed with necessary authority and powers for regulation and reform of capital market.
3. Indian companies permitted to access international capital markets through Euro-equity shares.
4. Companies required to disclose all material facts and specific risk factors associated with their projects while making public issues.
5. Merchant banking statutorily brought under the regulatory framework of SEBI and merchant bankers required to abide by a code of conduct.
6. Private mutual funds are permitted and a few have already been set up. All mutual funds are allowed to apply for firm allotment in public issues.
7. Investment norms for NRIs liberalised allowing companies to accept capital contribution, and issue shares or debentures, to NRIs or overseas corporate bodies without prior permission of RBI.
8. Foreign Institutional Investors (FIIs) permitted to invest in Indian capital market on registration with SEBI. Common application forms simplified for them and foreign brokers permitted to assist them.
9. Over-the-Counter Exchange of India (OTCEI) commenced operations and a number of shares already listed with it.
10. SEBI notified several regulations for intermediaries in the secondary market bringing these intermediaries within regularity framework for the first time.
11. SEBI introduced new reforms in the primary market for improving the disclosure standards, introducing prudential norms and simplifying issue procedures.
12. The procedures for lodgement of securities for transfer was considerably eased for domestic and foreign institutional investors through the introduction of a jumbo transfer deed and consolidated payment of stamp duty.
13. SEBI introduced a number of measures for streamlining the functioning of the secondary market, such as reconstitution of the governing boards of the stock exchanges, capital adequacy norms for brokers and for providing transparency in client/broker relationships.
14. National Stock Exchange of India with nationwide stock trading facilities, electronic display, clearing and settlement facilities being set up by financial institutions and banks.

15. The nationalised banks have been allowed to raise 49% of their equity from the market.
16. SEBI introduced a code of advertisement for public issues for ensuring fair and truthful disclosures.

APPENDIX 3–3
INDIA'S FINANCIAL SYSTEM AT MID-1993

Financial Institution Types	Remarks
Banks:	
Reserve Bank of India (RBI)	Central Bank
State Bank of India & Affiliates (SBIA)	Largest Bank
Nationalised Banks	20 Significant Banks
Rural Banks	Many
Other Scheduled Commercial Banks	Not Nationalized
Foreign Banks with Off-shore Origin	24 Banks
Specialised banks, Development:	
Industrial Development Bank of India	Term Lending
EXIMBANK	Trade Finance
NABARD	Agriculture
Industrial Finance Corporation India	Industrial
Industrial Credit & Investment Corp of India	Industrial
Small Industries Development Bank	Industrial
Shipping Credit and Investment Company	Shipping
Technology Development & Information Company	Venture Capital
Tourism Finance Corp of India	Tourism
Risk Capital & Technology Finance Corp	Risk Capital
National Housing Bank	Housing
Industrial Restructuring Bank of India	Industrial
Mutual Credit Organisations:	
Cooperative Rural Banks	Credit Co-ops
Unit Trusts of India (UTI)	Small Investors
Non-Banking Finance Companies	Mortgage Finance
Informal Financing Enterprises:	
Informal Finance (NIDHIS, Chit Funds ...)	Informal
Securities Exchanges:	
Organised Securities Markets	Stock Exchanges
Insurance & Pension Enterprises:	
Life Insurance Corporation of India	Insurance
General Insurance Corporation	Insurance
Public Provident Funds (Public Sector)	Not Significant
Export Credit Guarantee Corp of India	Export Credit Insurance

REFERENCES

Ariff Mohamed, "Indian Financial System: Developments And Opportunities", National University of Singapore, September 1994.

Federation of Indian Chambers of Commerce and Industry, *Business Digest*, Vol. 4, No. 44–45, November 1994.

Federation of Indian Chambers of Commerce and Industry, *Economic Trends*, December 1994.

Government of India, "India Means Business: An Economic Profile", Ministry of External Affair's Economic Coordination Unit, September 1994.

High Commission of India (Singapore), *Economic Bulletin*, October 1994.

High Commission of India (Singapore), *Economic Bulletin*, November 1994.

Joint Business Council, *Economic Reforms in India*, October 1994.

Malhotra R. N., Speech presented at the Federation of Indian Chambers of Commerce and Industry and Nanyang Technological University Symposium, New Delhi, 9 December 1994.

Manmohan Singh, "India's Economic Relations With East and Southeast Asia", Address in *World Economic Forum*, 14 October 1994.

Toh Mun Heng and Low Linda, "Singapore's Rationale For Tapping Emerging Markets", Conference on Singapore-India Emerging Linkages, 24 November 1993.

LABOUR AND LEGAL

Chapter 4

Labour Issues and Human Resource Development

BY
Sarah CHNG
Ricky CHEUNG

INTRODUCTION

THE PURPOSE OF this chapter is to discuss some interesting and crucial issues relating to human resource development in India. Particular emphasis is on the labour force and wage levels in India. For completeness, this chapter provides information relating to the general demographic profile of India and the educational composition within the country. The chapter may be useful to researchers, students, and those who simply want to know more about a country that is becoming important in the global economy.

THE LABOUR FORCE

The labour force has been a selling point used by the government to draw investors to India. One brochure[1] asserted that in India there are "immense pools of inexpensive, skilled workers and technical staff, as well as highly capable senior managers".

A survey to determine reasons for investing

[1] "India Means Business, An Economic Profile", printed by the Director, Economic Coordination Unit, Ministry of External Affairs, Government of India, 1994.

in India and overseas was reported on 29 and 30 December 1994, in *The Straits Times.* It was conducted by former member of parliament, and veteran diplomat, Chiang Hai Ding, now Senior Visiting Fellow at the Institute of Southeast Asian Studies. The single most attractive reason, by far, for investing in India is the large domestic market represented by a significant middle class. Other attractive reasons mentioned for companies are the low costs and the abundance of factors of production in India. These latter characteristics ranked second and fourth, respectively. In the survey, Singaporean companies pointed out that the high cost of factors of production (i.e., land, labour and materials) in Singapore, government encouragement, and limited investment opportunities in Singapore are the reasons for investing overseas.

In Mr. Chiang's survey, the quality of India's information technology (IT) expertise was the attraction for two companies, one a government-linked company (GLC) and the other a small and medium-sized enterprise (SME), to invest in India. A further attraction was India's English-speaking work force, computer literacy and labour supply.

Size and Sectoral Distribution of the Labour Force

The Ministry of External Affairs reported that the total labour force was estimated at 315 million in 1991, representing roughly 38% of the Indian population. Approximately 58% of the population was in the 15 to 59 age group and about 36% of the population was under 15 years of age. Nearly 65% of the labour force was employed in the agriculture sector while the industrial and services sectors accounted for 12.5% and 22.5%, respectively. Growth in employment in the agricultural sector has been less than 1% per annum. Hence, despite fairly rapid growth in employment in the manufacturing and services sectors, growth in overall employment has been restricted to around 1.9% per annum.

The National Sample Survey Organisation (NSSO) figures show that the "usually" unemployed numbered 10.5 million in 1977–78, 7.7 million in 1983, and 11.6 million in 1987–88. The overall unemployment rates were 3.8% in 1977–78, 2.5% in 1983 and 3.5% in 1987–88, respectively.

Before one decides to invest in India, it is important to examine the size and sufficiency of the labour force, and its sectoral contributions in India. Table 4–1 shows the number of households and workers by sector while Table 4–2 shows the sectoral distribution of workers. Table 4–3 shows labour force estimates by age group.[2] The number of professional and service institutions are shown in Table 4–4, and the profile of scientific and technical personnel in India is noted in Table 4–5.

TABLE 4–1
Households and Workers by Sector (1987 to 1988)

Sector	Rural			Urban		
	House-holds (million)	Workers (million)	Ave no. of Workers per House-hold	House-holds (million)	Workers (million)	Ave no. of Workers per Household
Agriculture	78.4	197.7	2.5	3.3	9.3	2.8
Mining, Manufac-turing, Utilities	9.3	20.2	2.2	11.4	19.7	1.7
Construction	4.2	8.4	2.0	2.2	3.8	1.7
Services	22.7	26.2	1.2	26.8	36.9	1.4
Total	114.6	252.5	2.2	43.7	69.7	1.6

Households & Workers by Sector, 1987–88.
Source: NSS (National Sample Survey) 43rd Round Report.

TABLE 4–2
Sectoral Distribution of Workers

Sector	Census 1991 (%)	Census 1981 (%)
Agriculture, Livestock, Forestry, Fishery	71.7	68.8
Mining, Manufacturing, Utility	11.8	11.9
Other Services	8.5	8.8
Trade, Transport, Communication	7.2	8.9
Construction	0.8	1.6

Source: NSS (National Sample Survey) 43rd Round Report.

2 Tables 4–1, 4–2, and 4–3 are adapted from Rao (1993).

TABLE 4–3
Labour Force Estimates

Age Group	Labour Force Participation Rates 1985 (%)	1990 (%)	2001 (%)	2001 (million)	Population 2001 (million)
15–59	65.2	64.8	63.9	383	599
5–14 & 60+	15.6	15.9	15.0	44	296
Total Population	41.0	42.0	42.3	427	1,009

Source: NSS (National Sample Survey) 43rd Round Report.

TABLE 4–4
Number of Professionals and Service Institutions (1993)

Chartered Accountants	65,191
Cost Accountants	11,200
Company Secretaries	9,442
Number of recognised MBA programmes	4,000
Registered Computer Institutes	150
Number of Advertising Agencies	116

Source: NCAER (National Council of Applied Economic Research).

TABLE 4–5
Scientific and Technical Personnel (1990)

	(in thousands)
Engineering & Technology	1,189
Science	2,105
Medicine	320
Agriculture	196
Total	3,810

Source: NCAER (National Council of Applied Economic Research).

It can be seen from Tables 4–1 and 4–2 that the most active, and biggest, labour sector in India is agriculture, livestock, forestry and fishery. As Mr. Chiang stated, a foreign company in commodity trading indicated that it was in India because it was an agricultural country.

Education and Unemployment

According to the 1981 census, 57.5% of the workers were illiterate, and another 9.6% were literate but without formal education. Those with primary education constituted 13.4%, junior and senior secondary education 14.4%, while higher secondary and college graduates made up 5.1% of the workforce.

It might be expected that with such a low educational profile of workers, the educated ones would find employment. However, as reported by Nanda (1991), this is not true. The Council for Scientific and Industrial Research took a sample of 2.5 million graduates from the 1981 census and studied their employment experience. The sample comprised holders of bachelor, master and doctorate degrees in arts, social sciences, education, law, commerce, and business management. The proportion of unemployment in the sample was 24%. Only 53% of the sample was employed; self-employed (7%) and regular employees (46%). Students, trainees and apprentices were 7% of the total sample while 16% were "others" which included those not trying for a job, the retired and those of unknown status. According to Rao (1993), part of these "others" probably would have opted for a job if employment opportunities were available.

Even though the proportion of educated unemployed is high, there appears to be shortages in at least two areas of the labour force in India. These are the managerial sector and the software industry. They are more fully discussed in the following sections.

The Supply of Managers

Each year India's educational institutions train about 5,000 managers for the local market. However, an estimated 30,000 managers are required annually to meet the needs of industry because of the influx of foreign investment.

The shortage of managers has been severe because of the increase of multinational corporations (MNCs) in India. Trained personnel are in short supply, prompting MNCs to poach from the public service units (PSUs). MNCs reportedly pay salaries closer to those "back home". The movement of managerial personnel from the public to the private sector has been so significant that the functioning of the public sector has been threatened. In fact, an editorial in the New Delhi *Financial Express* (14 December 1994) expressed concern, and suggested some measures that the government should take to ease the problem.

To solve the problem of shortage of middle managers, many large firms provide in-house management training for their employees. Mr. Yalaguresh Yalaear, Executive Director of Karnataka State Financial Corporation, commented that some professional bodies, such as the Institute of Chartered Accountants, the Institute of Management Accountants, the Institute of Chartered Secretaries and the Institute of Financial Analysis, have been training middle managers through their professional accreditation process.

Labour in the Software Industry

The technical competence of India's software industry is well known. India's high quality information technology expertise was the attraction for two Singapore companies, one a GLC and the other a SME, in their investment decision. In September 1994, Mani Shankar Aiyar, Member of Parliament, led 22 members of an Indian business delegation to Singapore to attract Tamil businessmen to be partners in Tamil Nadu State. One attraction of this state is that it produces a large number of computer specialists whose services can be tapped at a fraction of international costs. Mr. Aiyar also said that these specialists could handle data processing on a real-time basis through international linkages. Our field visits to software companies HCL-Hewlett Packard in Delhi, and Infosys Technologies in Bangalore, also indicated high levels of professionalism and quality workmanship in the software industry.

However, in an industry that employs some 120,000 professionals and grows at an annual rate of 50%, conserving or retaining software professionals has been a problem. According to figures compiled by the National Association of Software and Service Companies (NASSCOM), the average personnel attrition rate in the top 25 software companies in 1991–1992 was an astounding 19%. The strict immigration laws of the United States and increased focus on off-shore development has reduced the personnel attrition rate but it was still 9.5% in 1993–1994. Other than the attraction of money, the Executive Director of NASSCOM, Dewang Behta, offered another reason for the existing problem. The average age of a professional in the software industry is below 30. And, at that age, young professionals would be looking for opportunities to build up a career and, hence, perpetuating the job hopping trend.

Some companies have devised personnel schemes to retain talent.

For instance, incentives have included yearly salary upgrades, soft loans, medicare benefits, and project completion bonuses. N.R. Narayanamurthy, Chairman and Managing Director of Infosys Technologies, indicated that they had worked out a package of both learning opportunities and profit sharing to attract and retain employees. Up to 6% of Infosys' revenue was budgeted for employee training. Since 1993, an education and research department has been set up to monitor and upgrade employees on technological developments. It also has an employee stock option plan offering 750,000 warrants. The offer to the employees was based on transparent appraisal criteria. Each warrant has a lock-in period of five years after which it can be traded for Rs 425 per share on a 1:1 basis.

With close to 4,000 employed professionals and being one of the largest employers in the industry, Tata Consultancy Services (TCS), on the other hand, was not so optimistic about the lure of incentive schemes. The Vice-President of TCS, S. Mahalingam, perceived that an attrition rate of 10% was inevitable, and attempted to combat the high turnover rate by breaking up projects into incremental processes to ensure that the loss of employees would not stop the continuity of projects.

Quality of the Labour Force

President and Chief Executive Officer of General Electric (India), Scott R. Bayman, stated that Indian labour has enabled GE to become a low cost global manufacturer with world class production. He also said that the technological capabilities of Indian labour are quite high. GE has been importing training programmes and, together with those developed locally, some 20 courses were conducted involving 400 employees in 1994. Thirty courses involving 600 employees were conducted in 1995. Similarly, as reported in the *Asian Wall Street Journal* (12 January 1995), a representative from Motorola Inc. (India), K. Gopalkrishnan, said that "Indians can be amongst the most efficient people in the world, if properly guided".

LABOUR REGULATIONS

In a government move to protect the labour force, companies in India are not allowed to close down factories or to sack their workers without the permission of the government. This is one of the chief concerns for Singapore investors. S. Dhanabalan, Chairman of Parameswara Holdings, which recently entered into a joint venture to build an IT park in Bangalore, said that they remained optimistic about investing in India although investors should be wary about the impact of Indian laws. The difficulty of dismissal of workers is a major concern.

Singapore's Senior Minister, Lee Kuan Yew, in his introductory remarks at the Singapore lecture delivered by Indian Prime Minister, P.V. Narasimha Rao in September 1994 in Singapore, cited the difficulties mentioned in some publications. According to an article in the *Economist* (8 August 1994), reform was continuing but in haphazard fashion. It recommended changes in labour and company laws to make it possible to wind up companies in India. Another article in the 11 June 1994 issue, indicated that approval was rarely given for the closure of factories and the dismissal of workers. Consequently, the assets of a company could not be sold to meet the claims of creditors.

Companies, of course, can circumvent the system by offering monetary incentives for workers to leave voluntarily. An industrialist revealed that when his company closed down two units, it entered into a voluntary separation/retirement scheme with its employees. The scheme was accepted by 99% of the employees to be laid off. The *ex gratia* payment amounted to 60% of the basic wages that would have been earned by the worker from the time of retrenchment until retirement.

In *Economic Trends*, a FICCI survey reported that the total assets including plant, machinery and outstanding bank loans locked up in sick or weak industrial units as of March 1994, was estimated at Rs 50,000 crores (1 Crore = Rs 10 million). Of these, 99% were small-scale companies.

The situation may worsen. A Division Bench of the Supreme Court recently allowed an appeal by a labour union upholding the validity of Section 25-M of the *Industrial Disputes Act* which mandated that prior permission must be obtained by an employer from the appropriate governmental authority before laying off any workers. Setting aside the judgement of the Madras High Court, the Supreme Court held that the underlying requirement of Section 25-M was to "prevent avoidable hardships to the employees by protecting employment of those who were already employed and to maintain a higher tempo of production and productivity by preserving industrial peace and harmony" (*Financial Express*; 13 December 1994).

So workers continue to get paid even if the company is sick and non-operational. Trade unions oppose the change in the law fearing that it would cause mass closures. And, given that every political party in India has a vociferous trade-union wing and the state and general elections held in 1996, it appears that reforms will not be forthcoming.

Other labour legislation to note are the *Factories Act 1948* and the *Workmen's Compensation Act*. The *Factories Act 1948* provides for the welfare and personal security of labour including:

(i) legal minimum age for employment being 15 years;
(ii) a standard working week of 48 hours or nine hours /day;
(iii) overtime at twice the hourly rate;
(iv) leave of one day for every 20 days of work performed. Such leave can be accumulated and carried forward subject to a maximum of 30 days;
(v) protection for workers against health hazards and industrial safety; and
(vi) welfare facilities including washrooms, canteens and first aid.

The *Workmen's Compensation Act 1923* deals with the payment of compensation to the workman, or his dependants, on the death or injury of the workman arising in the course of employment.

TRADE UNIONS, LABOUR RELATIONS AND INDUSTRIAL DISPUTE RESOLUTION

The *Trade Union Act 1926* provides for the registration and operations of trade unions. It provides that seven or more persons may seek registration. A trade union is defined to include "any combination ... for the purposes of regulating the relation between the workmen and employers". Trade unions in India possess significant power because of the *locus standi* for collective bargaining, and immunity from civil suits and prosecution for criminal conspiracy for officials and members.

The *Industrial Disputes Act 1947* provides the machinery for the settlement of industrial disputes which are defined as "any dispute or difference between employers and employers, employers and workmen, and workmen and workmen connected with the employment, non-employment or the terms of employment, or the conditions of labour". In the event that the employer and employees cannot come to a settlement, a government conciliation officer steps in. And, only if the conciliation cannot be reached, can the matter be brought to the labour courts, a long and tedious process in practice.

Rao (1993) observes that a tragic feature of the employment scenario is the man-days lost due to industrial disputes which have increased substantially since independence. Figures show that in 1961, 4.9 million man-days were lost. The figure rises to a peak level of 74.6 million man-days lost in 1982, but the situation improved in 1990 with only 10.6 million man-days lost, and further dropped to 4.3 million in 1991. Rao (1993) warned, however, that this trend should not be interpreted as a change of heart among trade union leaders and employers in preventing industrial disputes and loss of man-days; the situation could easily deteriorate. For instance, on 16 June 1992, several million man-days were lost on that day alone because of the nationwide strike called by trade unions against the process of economic liberalisation and the new economic policies.

Other than nationwide strikes, whether or not individual companies suffer strikes depends very much on the management style adopted by individual companies. When DCM-Daewoo, New Delhi, started its operations (under DCM-Toyota), it was stated that the management actually helped the trade union register themselves with the relevant government body. Also, DCM-Daewoo adopted a policy of sharing all information with the trade union and getting them involved in all company activities. As a result, they have not suffered any strike or loss of labour.

A. K. Rungta, President of the FICCI, which has regular interactions with the trade unions, said that the trade unions were accepting the changes brought by the economic reforms. And some local industrialists in India have remarked that employees were beginning to understand that wages and benefits were linked to productivity instead of outright increments. Lock-outs (i.e., no work, no pay), instead of strikes, seem to be more readily accepted as the norm.

WAGES AND WAGE COMPETITIVENESS

The general wage level in India has been viewed as moderate compared to more developed countries. At the senior management level, according to the brochure "India Means Business, An Economic Profile", wages are about one-fifth to one-tenth the salary levels in Western countries. During our visit to India, we obtained figures of the average salaries of various staff levels at the organisations through discussions with management. Our findings are summarised in Table 4–6.

TABLE 4–6
Wage Level of Selected Industries in Selected States

Company, State	Nature of Operations	Skill Level	Monthly Salary Rs	S$ Equiv.
DCM Daewoo, Uttar Pradesh	Motor car manufacturing	Skilled worker	5,000	250
Allen Bradley, Sahibabad, Uttar Pradesh	Manufacturing of automation control devices	Worker	2,500	125
		Engineer	6,000	300
		Junior manager & senior engineer	8,000	400
		Manager	14,000	700
Zaffiro Fashions Pte. Ltd., Haryana	Manufacturing of fashion accessories	Skilled worker	1,500	75
Tamil Nadu	General	Supervisor	11,500	575
		Skilled worker	7,000	350
Infosys, Bangalore	Software programming	Fresh software engineer	6,500	325
HCL Hewlett-Packard Ltd., Uttar Pradesh	Information technology business	Programming staff	15,000	750
		Engineering staff	19,000	950

Wage Level of Workers

From Table 4–6, the salary range is from Rs 1,500 to Rs 7,000 for workers and Rs 8,000 to Rs 14,000 for supervisors and managers. The range of salaries varies as the organisations are located in different states and in different industries. The minimum wage levels of four prominent manufacturing organisations in India are summarised in Table 4–7.

Based on the information in Tables 4–6 and 4–7, the average monthly salary of workers in the manufacturing sector is about Rs 4,000 to Rs 5,000 (S$200 to S$250). This wage level is not considered very competitive when compared to those in developing countries in Asia. For example, in Indonesia the minimum wage rate is approximately S$70 per month. In the southern provinces of the PRC, the rate is about S$120 per month. Nevertheless, it is suggested that more indepth research should be carried out when comparing wages, given the significant variation in wage levels across India.

TABLE 4–7
Minimum Wages of Selected Enterprises in Private Sector

Company	Number of Workers	Minimum Wage	
		Rs	S$ equiv.
Tata Engineering & Locomotive Company	12,000	5,100	255
Philips India Ltd.	3,000	4,000	200
Bajaj Auto Ltd.	13,000	4,500	225
David Brown Ltd.	700	4,000	200

Source: *Financial Express*, New Delhi, 13 December 1994.

Wage Levels of Professionals and Graduates

From Table 4–6 it appears that graduates receive very good pay, as high as Rs 19,000 per month in HCL. However, it should be noted that the software industry in India is a rising star and HCL is seen as one of the most generous in the industry. Some recruitment advertisements in the *Indian Express*, Bangalore on 15 December 1994, listed in Table 4–8, give a better idea of the graduates' general wage level.

From Table 4–8 it appears that the wages of graduates, especially those from the science disciplines, are even lower than those of ordinary workers. Nevertheless, care must be taken in interpreting these data because of certain factors such as the variation of price levels in different states, and the demand and supply in different industries. For example, the job market in the commercial sector is especially tight, and some benefits are not counted as salary. This is elaborated upon in the following sections.

Managers and Executives

The demand for managers in India far exceeds the supply. A report in the New Delhi's *Financial Express* on 13 December 1994, revealed that over the period 1989 to 1994, the salary of corporate executives increased by a minimum of 25% for junior executives and a maximum of 225% for senior executives. A summary is reproduced in Figure 4–1.

TABLE 4–8
Salary Scale of Professionals and Graduates: Bangalore

Company	Position	Required Qualifications	Salary Scale (Rs)(S$ Equiv.)
Hindustan Aeronautics Limited	Finance/ Accounts Officer	University degree with a pass in the final examination of Institute of Chartered Accountants or/ Institute of Cost and Works Accountants or/MBA (Finance) from reputed institutes	2,500–4,300 (125–215)
Nuclear Science Centre	Scientists	PhD in experimental atomic physics/ material science, 4 years experience	3,700–5,000 (185–250)
	Research Scientist	PhD with 2 years experience	2,400–3,500 (120–175)
	Research Associates	PhD in experimental physics with experience in technical developments with accelerators	2,800–5,000 (140–250) plus HRA

Source: *Indian Express,* Bangalore, 15 December 1994.

FIGURE 4–1
Percentage Increase in Corporate Executive's Salary 1989 to 1994

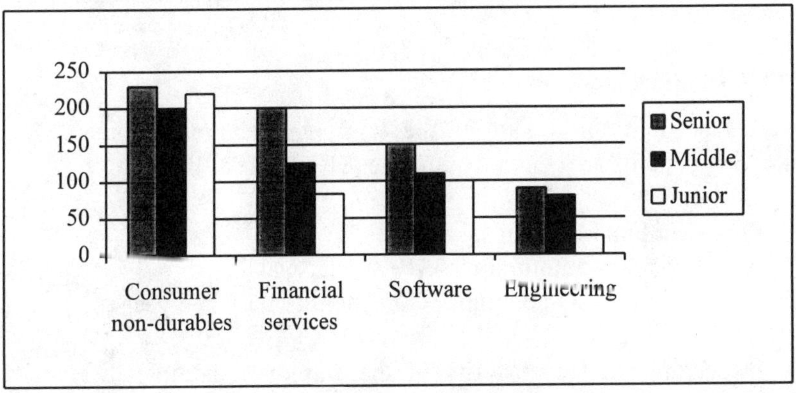

Source: *Financial Express*, New Delhi, 13 December 1994.

Based on the average salary range for managers in 1989 (SICCC, 1989) and the percentage increase over the period, the 1994 salary level for managers in the industries mentioned above are estimated to range from Rs 2,650 to Rs 42,000 (S$130 to S$2,100) per month. More details on these salaries are presented in Table 4–9. The overall salary structure is considered very attractive by international standards given that the general level of education of executives is relatively high. The salaries do not include fringe benefits which, in some cases, may be more than the basic salary.

TABLE 4–9
Estimated 1994 Salary Level of Managers and Executives of Selected Industries (Per Month)

	Junior Manager		Manager		Top Executives	
	From	To	From	To	From	To
1989 salary range (US$)*	125	130	250	450	500	750
1989 salary range (Rs)	2,125	2,210	4,250	7,650	8,500	12,750
Estimated 1994 level based on reported percentage increase during the period Rs (S$ equiv.)						
Consumer non-durables	6,800 (340)	7,072 (350)	12,750 (640)	22,950 (1,150)	28,050 (1,400)	42,075 (2,100)
Financial services	3,889 (190)	4,044 (200)	9,562 (480)	17,212 (860)	25,500 (1,275)	38,250 (1,900)
Software	4,250 (210)	4,420 (220)	8,925 (450)	16,065 (800)	21,250 (1,060)	31,875 (1,600)
Engineering	2,656 (130)	2,762 (140)	7,650 (380)	13,770 (690)	16,150 (800)	24,225 (1,200)

* Source: SICCC, 1989.

Fringe Benefits

Salaries account for a part of the total remuneration package. The following benefits are generally payable (SICCC, 1989):

(i) Provident Fund – 8% of salary;
(ii) Annual bonus – minimum 8.33% of salary; and
(iii) Medical – up to a maximum of one month salary in a year.

Depending on the seniority of the employee, additional benefits such as discretionary bonuses, accommodation, driver and car, annual family trip, etc., may also be payable. For example, the finance/accounting officer position mentioned in Table 4–8 attracts "dearness allowance, HRA, CCA, group insurance, leave travel concession, leave encashment, conveyance reimbursement, gratuity, provident fund, free medical facilities, etc.". In another recruitment notice in the *Indian Express*, Bangalore on 15 December 1994, the package for various positions ranging from vice principal to steno-typist by the Indian

School Al Wadi Al Kabir included "...perks like allowance, furnished accommodation, air passage, medical expenses, gratuity etc.". In another advertisement, the Orissa Minerals Development Company Ltd. & Associates, which was looking for senior mechanical engineers and senior personnel manager, offered "...fringe benefits include attractive superannuation fund, free housing, medical, electricity, CPF, LTA, etc.".

In general, such benefits account for approximately 30% of a worker's total compensation package.[3] For a CEO in the private sector, such benefits may be as high as 80% of the total compensation package. Figure 4–2 shows a typical pay package of a CEO in the private sector.

FIGURE 4–2
Corporate CEO's Pay Package

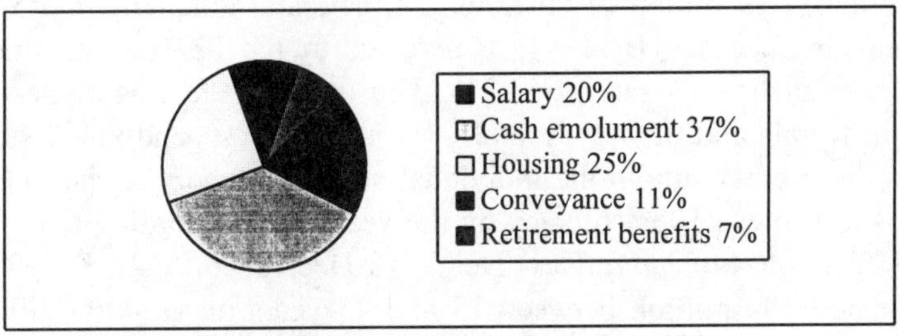

Source: Financial Express, New Delhi, 13 December 1994.

Statutory Regulation

A number of statutory acts relate to wages of employees. The *Payment of Wages Act 1948* requires wages to be paid regularly, the forms of payment, and the types of deductions permissible. The *Minimum Wage Act 1948* provides for minimum wages to be paid for certain classes of labour. Appendix 4–1 provides some salient points concerning the *Minimum Wage Act.* The *Payment of Bonus Act* imposes a minimum bonus of 8.33% even in non-profit situations. The *Provident Fund (and Miscellaneous Provisions) Act*, the *Family Pension Scheme*, the *Deposit Linked Scheme* and the *Employee State Insurance Scheme 1948* govern the retirement benefits.

---

[3] Mr. Alan Yeo, CEO of Information Technology Park Pte. Ltd., Bangalore.

HUMAN RESOURCE DEVELOPMENT

To a potential investor, the quality of local human resources is as important as other considerations such as market potential and cost competitiveness. This section gives an overview of the general literacy rate of India, the difference in levels of education between men and women, and some of the human resources problems associated with scheduled castes and scheduled tribes. This section also briefly identifies certain higher educational institutions which play an important role in ensuring an adequate supply of qualified professionals, managers and researchers.

Literacy Rate

According to figures provided in Rao (1993), in 1901 only 5.3% of the population of 238 million was literate. Literacy rates gradually improved in the ensuing decades. By 1991, as revealed by the 1991 census, India had an overall literacy rate of 52.2%. The literacy rate was highest at 89.8% in Kerala and the lowest at 38.5% in Bihar. Appendix 4–2 summarises the literacy rate in the individual states. The goal of the Indian nation is to achieve 100% literacy by the year 2000, according to an article in *The Times of India*, New Delhi (10 December 1994). By 1997, an estimated 100 million between 15 and 35 years of age will still be illiterate.

Although it is claimed that the average literacy rate was 52.2% in 1991, the 1981 census and the 1987–88 national sample survey (NSS) (see Table 4–10), showed that the average number of years of schooling of the population as at 1981 and 1987–88 was 2 and 2.4 years, respectively. Experts maintain that to achieve 100% literacy, the average number of years of schooling should be 6.5 years, and this can only be achieved beyond the year 2040. We also should be cautious when interpreting the "literacy rate". Literacy may be gained without going to school and the literate may degenerate if there is no daily practice (Bose, 1991).

Education of Gender

It is well recognised that Indian females enjoy a lower social status as compared to their male counterparts. The claim is reflected in the higher literacy rate of the Indian male, which is 64%, as compared to 39% for females. The 1991 census also revealed significant variations in the female literacy rates across the country ranging from a high of 86.1% in Kerala to a low of 20.4% in Rajasthan. Some of the major highlights of the 1991 census are summarised in Table 4–11.

TABLE 4–10
Educational Composition of Population

Level of Education	1981 Census	1987–88 NSS	Assumed Average No. of Years of Schooling
Illiterate	64.8%	55.5%	0
Literate and Primary	21.9%	28.4%	3
Secondary	11.9%	14.1%	9
Tertiary	1.4%	2.4%	14
Average no. of years of schooling	2 years	2.4 years	

Source: Rao (1993).

TABLE 4–11
Educational Composition by Gender

	Males		Females	
Level of education	1981 Census (%)	1987–88 NSS (%)	1981 Census (%)	1987–88 NSS (%)
Illiterate	54.3	45.2	76.0	66.5
Literate and Primary	27.3	33.4	16.2	23.0
Secondary	16.4	18.7	7.1	9.2
Graduate & above	2.0	2.7	0.7	1.3

Source: Rao (1993).

Table 4–11 shows that Indian women attempted to improve their education levels from 1981 to 1987–88. It has also been reported that women's share in enrolments in higher education was 14% in 1950–51 and increased to 46% in 1987–88. Significant improvements can be seen in the following faculties when the enrolment rates in 1971–72 and 1987–88 academic sessions are compared: teachers' training, 28% to 52%; arts, 33% to 43%; science, 20% to 32%; medicine, 22% to 31%; and commerce, 4% to 20%. However, women's share in the enrolments in Engineering, Technology, Agriculture and Veterinary (5% to 6%) and Law (9%) are still significantly lower than their male counterparts.

Scheduled Castes, Tribes and Backward Classes

The caste system originated in ancient India when the roles of people began to be defined. Six castes can be identified under the caste system: the nobility, the agriculturists and merchants, the learned ones, the service communities, the out-castes or untouchables, and outsiders or foreigners. By 1984, it was estimated that the population of the scheduled caste (SC) amounted to 15.8% of the total population. As noted by Bose (1991), the caste system, language, and religion remain as sensitive issues in India today. To add further to the problem, new classes have emerged such as the "socially and economically backward classes" (SEBCs). By 1980, the population of SEBCs accounted for 52% of the total population.

To foreigners, the caste system smacks of "unfairness". Articles 14, 15 and 16 of the Constitution of India, and their subsequent amendments, attempt to alleviate the problem. The spirit behind the statutes is to lift those at the lower end of the caste system and not to pull down those at the top. As such, in education and employment, a system of reservation has been provided for the SC and scheduled tribes (ST).

The literacy rate among SCs improved from 10.3% in 1961 to 21.4% in 1981. Despite the marked improvement, the levels remain low when compared to the national average. In employment, SC's and ST's share of government jobs increased significantly during the period from 1960 to 1980. For example, their share in class 3 jobs increased from 7.2% to 14% during the period.

To tackle the problems of the SEBCs in 1990, the government decided to implement the recommendations of the second Backward Classes Commission of 1980. In November 1992, this decision was upheld by the Supreme Court which specified that 27% of the jobs of the central government services and public undertakings were to be reserved for the SEBCs on top of the 22.5% reservation for the SC and ST. The decision implied that caste is no longer the exclusive factor in classifying the population. However, to remove the caste system, education that imparts human value is the ultimate answer.

Higher Education

It often has been claimed that India has an abundant resource of top engineers and computer technologists. According to "Doing Business with India" (Singapore-Indian Chamber of Commerce, 1989), there were 160 engineering colleges offering courses leading to Bachelor's Degrees in Engineering and Technology, with an annual admission capacity of 25,000 participants. In addition, there were more than 356 industrial training institutes, with an overall capacity of 158,000 in various parts of the country, providing training in 32 engineering and 21 non-engineering trades. According to "An Economic Profile, India Means Business, 1994", India had over 207 universities in a wide range of disciplines. The annual output of scientific and technical (S&T) graduates from the universities has been around 200,000 in recent years. As of 1990, the total stock of S&T manpower (graduates and postgraduates) was estimated at around 3 million. In addition, there were also 800,000 diploma holders and 2 million trained technicians.

Indian Institutes of Technology

According to an article by the Indian High Commission, and published in *The Straits Times* (8 September 1994), there were five national institutions known as the Indian Institute of Technology (IIT) which offered engineering-related training, and admitted 1,500 participants annually. These IITs are located in Bombay, Delhi, Kanpur, Kharagpur and Madras. They were set up under an Act of Parliament during the period from 1951 to 1963. The IITs provide two critical ingredients for industrial growth, namely creative people and fundamental knowledge. While the academic programmes offered by the individual IITs differ in detail, the following features are common:

(i) An undergraduate programme consisting of courses in the sciences, humanities, social sciences, technical arts and engineering sciences;
(ii) A postgraduate programme distinguished by its interdisciplinary approach and emphasis on research; and
(iii) An environment for research permeating both the undergraduate and postgraduate programmes.

The undergraduate programmes in engineering, technology and sciences lead to the B.Tech and MSc. degrees. The postgraduate programmes include three-semester M.Tech programmes and PhD programmes in a large number of specialisations in engineering and technology, sciences, management, humanities and social sciences. The total number of postgraduate students in the IITs is roughly one and one-half times the number in the undergraduate programme. Nearly 400 students receive the PhD degrees and about 2,500 students receive the master's degrees each year. The IITs have established a memoranda of understanding with several overseas institutions which provide opportunities for faculty to do postgraduate work and participate in short-term courses, curriculum development, and joint programmes for industry. All the IITs have established formal mechanisms for interaction with industry, which include science and technology parks, industrial foundations and corporate membership for industry.

Indian Institute of Management

The Indian Institute of Management (IIM) is a major source of supply of managers in India. According to Mr. K.R.S. Murthy, Director of Indian Institute of Management, Bangalore (IIMB), there are four IIMs in India. Annually, 30,000 applicants compete for 800 seats by taking an entrance examination which is similar to the GMAT. The IIMs and some 70 other universities which have departments of management studies offer MBA programmes. These institutions supply about 5,000 managers annually. The IIM also offer PhD and short-term programmes. Individual courses last from two weeks to four months duration.

To meet the increasing demand for managers in India, IIMs also provide technical people with management training. For example, IIMB offers a programme for technologists with the objective of turning technical people into managers.

Indian Institute of Science

The Indian Institute of Science (IIS) is another higher degree institution that offers courses mainly in science and engineering. It is the headquarters of space science. It has 1,100 students which comprised 500 undergraduates and 600 master degree students supported by 400 faculty members.

Problems with Human Resources Development

As indicated in Table 4–10, although one-half of the population is classified as literate, the average number of years of schooling was less than three years as of 1988. According to an article by the Department of Economic Affairs, Ministry of Finance in India, past policies had devoted disproportionate resources to subsidising the education and health care of the better-off sections of society. Higher education was heavily subsidised while primary education and literacy programmes were neglected. Social returns from primary education had been overlooked. India managed to achieve a primary school enrolment rate of 98% only by 1987–88, a rate achieved by other developed countries, such as Japan, a century ago. The Department of Economic Affairs has recommended that more resources be oriented to primary education. Others have cautioned that "to prevent illiteracy from recurring as quickly as literacy is achieved, about six years of continuing education is needed to consolidate the gains of the literacy programmes".

Another serious concern is that even though the IIS trains excellent scientists, many graduates have chosen to work overseas. Graduates also prefer to join the private sector when in fact the IIS, IIM and IITs are actually heavily subsidised by the government.

GENERAL DEMOGRAPHIC DATA

The demographic data included in this section is mainly for additional background information about India.

Population

The 1991 census counted some 840 million people. Based on the population growth rate from 1981 to 1991 of 2.11% per annum, it is estimated that the population of India may surpass the one billion mark by the year 2000. The population trends from 1951 to 1991 are summarised in Table 4–12.

There has been a dramatic impact in the death rate. The average life span is 57 years as compared to a life span of 32 years during the period from 1941 to 1951.

TABLE 4–12
Population Trends: 1951 to 1991

Year	Population (Million)	Density Per Sq Km	Female (%)	Inter-censual Average			Inter-censual Life Expectancy (Years)	
				Birth Rate	Death Rate	Annual Growth Rate of Population (%)	Male	Female
1951	361	110	48.5	39.9	27.4	1.24	32	32
1961	439	134	48.5	41.7	22.8	1.98	42	41
1971	548	167	48.2	41.1	18.9	2.24	46	45
1981	685	208	48.3	37.2	15.0	2.26	51	50
1991	844	257	48.1	32.6	11.5	2.11	56	57

Source: Rao (1993).

One peculiarity of the Indian population is the declining proportion of females which is currently slightly less than 50% of the population. This is due in part to the higher mortality of female children and the impact of relatively high maternal mortality.

Age Structure

The relatively stable birth rate, and a rapidly declining death rate, have produced an age structure that has far too many young persons below the working age thus increasing the dependency burden. The high dependency burden of 2.7 as of 1991, cuts deeply into domestic savings, and increases the private and public burdens of providing various basic human needs such as education, health, sanitation and housing. It is estimated that by 1996 the population below the age of 15 will account for 33.6% of the population. These trends are summarised in Table 4–13. Only an effective birth control programme can solve the social and human resource development problems.

Urban Population

Since 1980, there has been a trend of migration of population from rural to urban areas, as indicated by Table 4–14. By 1991, the most densely populated state was Delhi which accounted for 1.1% of the total population and had 6,319 persons per square kilometre. This contrasts sharply with Uttar Pradesh which accounted for 16.4% of the population and had a density of only 471 persons per square kilometre. The population density of different states can be found in Appendix 4–3.

TABLE 4–13
Age Structure of Indian Population: 1980 to 1986

Age Group	1980	1985	1990*	1996*
	Percentage of Total Population			
0–4	14.08	12.91	11.96	11.18
5–14	25.59	24.33	22.78	21.32
15–59	54.85	56.92	58.94	60.59
60 and above	5.48	5.84	6.32	6.91
Total	100.00	100.00	100.00	100.00

* Projection made in 1988–1989.
Source: Kothari's Industrial Directory of India 1988–1989.

TABLE 4–14
Urban to Total Population Percentage: 1980–1986

Year	Urban Population	Total Population	Percentage of Urban Population
1980	143.81	659.39	21.81
1985	165.65	722.42	22.93
1990*	189.36	786.05	24.09
1996*	220.73	869.00	25.40

* Projection made in 1988–1989.
Source: Kothari's Industrial Directory of India 1988–1989.

Such migration trends have created problems for the big cities such as Delhi, Bombay and Calcutta. Prices of properties have risen significantly in these big cities and the problem of inadequate housing has been accentuated.

Per Capita Income

The per capita income of Indians vary across the country. According to "An Economic Profile – India Means Business" (1994), in 1991 the highest per capita income was Rs 10,638 in Delhi and the lowest was

Rs 2,643 in Lakshadweep. Appendix 4–3 gives an analysis of the per capita income by states, and the value of industrial production in 1988–89.

CONCLUSION

The Indian labour force is large. It is important, however, for an investor to note a few points. A large portion of the labour force is unskilled and competition for managerial and IT expertise is intense. Cognisance must be given to the strict labour regulations in India. Investors must also be aware of the rigid policies relating to the winding up of businesses. As trade unions remain strong and strikes are not exactly rare, concerted efforts are needed to maintain good labour relations. Concerted efforts are needed by the Indian government and its institutions of higher learning, in particular, to provide adequate educational/industrial training to ensure a steady supply of expertise to meet the increasing needs of potential investors. This will also serve the Indian economic reforms to a great extent.

APPENDIX 4–1
Important Points of the *Minimum Wage Act*

1. Definition of wages – "wages" means all remuneration capable of being expressed in terms of money ... but exclude value of accommodation, supply of light, water, medical attendance or any other amenity for any service excluded by general or special order of the appropriate government; employer's contribution to retirement benefits; and gratuity payable on discharge.
2. Weekly holiday (Section 13, Rule 23) – there should be at least one paid weekly holiday.
3. Hours of work (Section 13, Rule 24) – Working hours should include rest time, which should be more than half an hour.
4. Wage of an employee who works for less than normal working day (Section 1) – full day's wage is payable if the reason for failure to work is other than the employee's unwillingness to work.
5. Wage or piece work (Section 17) – minimum piece rate be fixed by the employer not less than the minimum time rate.

6. Fixation of minimum rate of wage (Sections 3 and 5) – to be announced in the official Gazette by the appropriate government.
7. Payment of wage and deduction permissible – (Section 2 Rule 21) – the employer cannot make any deduction from salary except allowed by the *Payment of Wages Act 1936*.

APPENDIX 4–2
Key Demographic Data Analysed by States

	Population (Million)	Density (No. of Persons Per Sq. Km.)	Literacy Rate (%)			Work Participation Rate (%) (Total Workers as Percentage of Total Population)		
			Persons	Male	Female	Persons	Male	Female
India	**846.3**	**NA**	**52.2**	**63.9**	**39.3**	**37.5**	**51.6**	**22.6**
States								
Andhra Pradesh	66.5	241	44.1	55.1	32.7	45.1	55.5	34.3
Arunachal Pradesh	0.9	10	41.6	51.5	29.7	46.2	53.8	37.5
Assam	22.4	284	52.9	61.9	43.0	36.1	49.5	21.6
Bihar	86.4	497	38.5	52.5	22.9	32.2	47.9	14.9
Delhi	9.4	6,319	75.3	82.0	67.0	31.6	51.7	7.4
Goa	1.2	316	75.5	83.6	67.1	35.8	49.6	20.5
Gujarat	41.3	210	61.3	73.1	48.7	40.2	53.6	26.0
Haryana	16.5	369	55.9	69.1	40.5	31.0	48.5	10.8
Himachal Pradesh	5.2	92	63.9	73.4	52.1	42.8	50.6	34.8
Jammu & Kashmir	7.7	76	NA	NA	NA	NA	NA	NA
Karnataka	45.0	234	56.0	67.3	44.3	42.0	54.1	29.4
Kerala	29.1	747	89.8	93.6	86.1	31.4	47.6	15.9
Madhya Pradesh	66.2	149	44.2	58.4	28.9	42.8	52.3	32.7
Maharashtra	78.9	256	64.9	76.6	52.3	43.0	52.2	33.1
Manipur	1.8	82	59.9	71.6	47.6	42.2	45.3	39.0
Meghalaya	1.8	78	49.1	53.1	44.9	42.7	50.1	34.9
Mizoram	0.7	33	82.3	85.6	78.6	48.9	53.9	43.5
Nagaland	1.2	73	61.7	67.6	54.8	42.7	46.9	38.0

APPENDIX 4–2 (cont'd)

	Population (Million)	Density (No. of Persons Per Sq. Km.)	Literacy Rate (%)			Work Participation Rate (%) (Total Workers as Percentage of Total Population)		
			Persons	Male	Female	Persons	Male	Female
Orissa	31.7	202	49.1	63.1	34.7	37.5	53.8	20.8
Punjab	20.3	401	58.5	65.7	50.4	30.9	54.2	4.4
Rajasthan	44.0	128	38.6	55.0	20.4	38.9	49.3	27.4
Sikkim	0.4	57	56.9	65.7	46.7	41.5	51.3	30.4
Tamil Nadu	55.9	428	62.7	73.8	51.3	43.3	56.4	29.9
Tripura	2 8	262	60.4	70.6	49.7	31.1	47.6	13.8
Uttar Pradesh	139.1	471	41.1	55.7	25.3	32.2	49.7	12.3
West Bengal	68.1	766	57.7	67.8	46.6	32.2	51.4	11.3
Union Territories								
Andaman & Nicobar Islands	0.3	34	73.0	79.0	65.5	35.2	53.3	13.1
Chandigarh	0.6	5,620	77.8	82.0	72.3	34.9	54.3	10.3
Dadra & Nagar Haveli	0.1	282	40.7	53.6	27.0	53.3	57.5	48.8
Daman & Diu	0.1	906	71.2	82.7	59.4	37.6	51.6	23.2
Lakshadweep	0.1	1,615	81.8	90.2	72.9	26.4	44.2	7.6
Pondicherry	0.8	1,605	74.7	83.7	65.6	33.1	50.6	15.2
NA: not available								

Source of data: CMIE, extracted from "An Economic Profile, India Means Business", 1991 Census, and from "Population of India", 1991 Census Results and Methodology.

APPENDIX 4–3
Key Economic Data Analysed by States

	Industrial Production 1988–89 (Rs Billion)	Per Capita Income (Rs)		
		1991	1992–93	Percentage Increase
India	**1,843.50**	**3,746**	**6,249**	**66.8**
States				
Andhra Pradesh	114.5	4,731	5,802	22.6
Arunachal Pradesh	NA	5,046	6,369	26.2
Assam	21.7	3,932	5,056	28.6
Bihar	99.6	2,650	3,280	23.8
Delhi	37.8	10,638	11,650**	9.5
Goa	7.5*	7,890	10,128	28.4
Gujarat	201.2	5,850	7,586	29.7
Haryana	64.7	7,516	9,609	27.8
Himachal Pradesh	8.1	4,790	5,355**	11.8
Jammu & Kashmir	3.4	3,872	4,212	8.8
Karnataka	80.0	4,631	6,313	36.3
Kerala	48.6	4,032	5,065	25.6
Madhya Pradesh	87.8	4,021	4,725	17.5
Maharashtra	390.4	7,598	9,270	22.0
Manipur	0.1	3,893	4,180**	7.4
Meghalaya	0.1	4,190	5,769	37.7
Mizoram	NA	NA	NA	NA
Nagaland	NA	4,977	5,863**	17.8
Orissa	43.8	3,596	3,963	10.2
Punjab	84.0	8,423	10,857	28.9
Rajasthan	55.1	4,035	5,035	24.8
Sikkim	NA	5,063	5,416**	7.0
Tamil Nadu	195.5	4,619	6,205	34.3
Tripura	0.5	3,569	NA	NA
Uttar Pradesh	167.0	3,557	4,280	20.3
West Bengal	122.6	4,794	5,901	23.1
Union Territories				
Andaman & Nicobar Islands	0.3	3,524	6,751	91.6
Chandigarh	3.0	5,434	NA	NA
Dadra & Nagar Haveli	3.7	5,325	NA	NA
Daman & Diu	NA	3,763	NA	NA
Lakshadweep	NA	2,643	NA	NA
Pondicherry	2.6	3,308	9,314	181.6

* Includes Daman & Diu.

** Data for Delhi, Himachal Pradesh, Nagaland, Sikkim & Manipur relate to 1991–92.

Source of data: Economic Survey and CMIE extracted from "An Economic Profile, India Means Business".

Source: *Economic Trends,* quarterly journal of Federation of Indian Chambers of Commerce and Industry, Vol. 23, No. 4, December 1994, p. 8.

REFERENCES

An Economic Profile, India Means Business, Economic Coordination Unit, Ministry of External Affairs, Government of India, 1994.

Bose Ashish, *Population of India 1991 Census Results and Methodology*, B. R. Publishing Corporation, New Delhi, 1991.

Federation of Indian Chambers of Commerce and Industry, *Economic Trends,* Vol. 23, December 1994.

"How To Keep Investors Out", *Economist,* 11 June 1994.

"Kothari's Industrial Directory of India 1988–1989", Kothari Enterprise, 1991.

Menon Vijay, "Conserving Manpower", *India Today,* 15 December 1994.

Nanda A. R., "The Inevitable Billion Plus an Exploration of Interconnectivities and Action Possibilities in India", in *India 1991 Population — Some Basic Data*, Vichar Dhara Publications, 1992, pp. 243–52.

Rao Bhanoji V. V., "Human Resource Utilisation and Development", *India's Economic Future Government, People and Attitudes*, 1993.

Singapore–Indian Chamber of Commerce and Citibank, *Doing Business with India*, Singapore, 1989, pp. 31–3.

Chapter 5

The Legal Environment and Types of Investment

BY
Vita SUROWIDJOJO
June OEI

INTRODUCTION

THE SUCCESS OF any foreign investment policy of a country is dependent on the environment within which the investor is expected to work. While the initial decision on whether or not to invest in a foreign country might be made by considering market and cost factors, which can be made more attractive by different kinds of incentive schemes offered, the legal environment is the final determinant of the length of stay of a foreign investor.

Most of the time, the legal environment is not taken into consideration by an eager investor who is attracted only to the potential profitability of the foreign venture. It is only after the decision to invest has been made, and the business has been set up or running, that an investor realises that the legal policies often do not support the economic policies. However, at this stage, time and finances would have already been incurred, and a retraction of the decision would only mean a loss to an investor.

This chapter takes a look at the business related laws of India which a potential investor from Singapore should be aware of. Foreign investment laws, employment laws, tax laws, company laws and relevant land laws are discussed. Business methods and vehicles available to the investor are mentioned at some length and recommendations are offered. Finally, dispute resolution methods are outlined. Singapore business law will be used for comparison, where relevant, for the purpose of highlighting to the reader particularities of the Indian system despite its having the same common law roots as Singapore.

INDO-SINGAPORE BUSINESS COOPERATION

Although the largest democracy in the world, India's economic policy was, until three and a-half years ago, very restrictive to foreign investment. The era of the "licence raj", where constraints and restrictions of every conceivable nature abounded, proved too daunting even for the bravest of investors including Singapore. The economic reform package introduced in 1991 ended this close-door policy and, instead, focused on opening up the economy to the world. Even today, we are witnessing reforms which bear testimony to the commitment of this reform package.

Singapore, prior to India's reform programme, had already embarked on a policy of regionalisation. Entrepreneurs of all sizes and magnitudes were encouraged to extend the boundaries of their business outside the limited market of Singapore. The first visit of Singapore's Prime Minister, Goh Chok Tong, to India in 1994 sparked off a mild "India fever" which soared to new levels after the Indian Prime Minister, P.V. Narasimha Rao, returned the visit in September 1994, and Prime Minister Goh Chok Tong's return visit to India in January 1995.

India is, without doubt, a very attractive new market for Singapore from many perspectives. These include India's relatively close physical proximity, potentially large domestic market and large labour pool, cultural and language similarities, the presence in Singapore of non-resident Indians (NRIs) and the sharing of the same roots in the common law system.

INDIA'S LEGAL BACKGROUND

Before we enter into a discussion of the ways of doing business in India, it is important for a potential investor, legally trained or otherwise, to understand the legal framework within which India functions, and to have an insight into this legal mind set.

India is a federal union comprising 26 states and six union territories. Sovereign power is not held solely by the centre but is divided between the centre and the states. This means that reforms initiated by the centre require the cooperation and commitment of the different states if prompt and successful implementation is to be achieved. Being a functioning democracy also means that no action can be taken, either by the centre or the state, without the majority consent of the representatives of the people.

In terms of legal roots, the colonialisation of India by the British left its legacy in the form of the British common law system. However, as noted in the following discussion, some of the laws originating from the British have evolved to an almost unrecognisable form through decades of close-door policies.

TYPES OF INVESTMENT

The potential foreign investor has two ways of doing business in India: indirect and direct investment. We consider each in detail, and outline the advantages and disadvantages of each type of investment.

Indirect Investment

The different forms of indirect investment available in Singapore are also available in India. These include the following six forms:

(i) ***Direct Export:*** Under this form of indirect investment, the exporter sells goods to a contact in the target market country. This involves the standard sales contract to be signed between the parties involved (the Singaporean exporter and the Indian importer), and payment is usually made through letters of credit.

(ii) ***Distributorship:*** This is based on a distributorship agreement whereby the distributor purchases the product from the manufacturer and sells it at his own risk in the target market. The distributor usually has an obligation for product warranty and service.

(iii) ***Agency:*** The principal-agent relationship can take the form of an exclusive or a non-exclusive agency, and the standard principal-agent rights and obligations apply. In a non-exclusive agency, income earned from business generated by the agent is not subject to Indian income tax. However, if the agency is exclusive, and a permanent establishment is set up by the principal in India, then income generated is subject to Indian income tax.

The trade policy launched in 1991, in particular the Indian Export-Import Policy, has been successful in reducing tariff barriers and almost bringing to extinction the system of import and export licences that prevailed during the days of the licence raj. However, import tax, especially for finished products, remains relatively high at an average of 65%.[1] In addition, it is interesting to note that a negative list of disallowable imports still stands, although this has been substantially pruned since 1991. The most reluctant deletion from the negative list is importing consumer durables.

(iv) ***Licensing:*** Procedures for automatic approvals for licensor-licensee arrangements have been introduced. They are now given for agreements involving a lump sum payment of up to Rs 10 million, and royalty of up to 5% on domestic sales and 8% on exports (net of taxes).

(v) ***Franchising:*** Given the need for production and service expertise in India, franchising is a viable option now open to investors. Under this arrangement, whether it is a production or a service franchise, the franchisor franchises his brand name, and/or production and service methods, to the franchisor for a royalty or like payment. Prior to the reform package, use of foreign brand names and trade marks for the sale of goods into India was not allowed. Licensing and franchising are attractive ways of indirect investment because of the ability to enter the foreign market place without the associated financial investment risks.

(vi) ***Liaison Office:*** This has been categorised under indirect investment by virtue of the fact that all expenditures for the liaison office are remitted from abroad. A liaison office is not allowed to earn income and, therefore, is not subject to income tax. Because the investor is present in the foreign country, contacts can be made more easily. This

---

1 Prior to the reform package of 1991, import taxes averaged 165%. The plan by the Indian government is to bring import taxes in line with international tariff rates, that is, tax rates of 20% to 25% by 1996.

form of presence is especially useful if heavy investments, in the form of a branch or a wholly-owned subsidiary, are planned for the future.

Direct Investment

(i) ***Foreign Direct Investment Policy:*** Under the liberalisation of the foreign investment policy in 1991, India opened itself up to almost every kind of investment. In order to encourage foreign investment, procedures were simplified and made more transparent, and automatic approvals for certain industries will be granted.

Prior to the liberalisation, most investments had to be approved by the Reserve Bank of India (RBI). However, since the liberalisation, few RBI approvals are required either for direct, or indirect, investment.

(ii) ***Branches:*** RBI permission is not required for establishing a branch. However, except for banks, it is not advantageous to set up a branch in India where there is no separate legal entity, and the parent company is fully liable for the actions of the branch subject to Indian jurisdiction for these actions. In addition, the company would be subject to tax on profits both in India and the home country.

(iii) ***Acquisitions:*** The *Foreign Exchange Regulation Act* (FERA) requires the RBI's permission prior to the acquisition of shares in an Indian company by a foreign investor. The advantages of acquiring an existing business include: lower start-up costs, an in-place network of distribution or retail outlets, an experienced local workforce and the goodwill of the existing business.

It is recommended that thorough research be undertaken of the Indian company to be acquired. This is especially necessary in India where, due to the past emphasis on the government sector and de-emphasis to the extent of stunting the growth of the private sector, there are very few pure private sector companies in good business condition.

(iv) ***Equity Joint Ventures:*** Currently, automatic approval for 51% foreign equity is granted in 36 industries in the manufacturing sector. For units set up in export processing zones (EPZs), or units that are 100% export-oriented units (EOUs), 100% foreign equity participation is permitted.

One of the more significant moves has been the establishment of the Foreign Investment Promotion Board (FIPB) which is composed of four senior secretaries in the office of the Prime Minister. The FIPB is empowered to take up any case on a case-by-case basis and grant approvals accordingly. Over the last three years, 90% of the investing companies entered India through this route. The approval period ranges between two to six weeks from the time of submission of the application.

The foreign investor who holds equity in a company, regardless of the percentage holding, enjoys equity in perpetuity, and there is no requirement for the foreign company to divest its equity holding in favour of the local partner. This is unlike the situation in many developing countries, such as Indonesia for example.

The advantage of an equity joint venture is obviously the lower financial risk since it is shared with a local partner. In situations where the local partner is experienced and established in the industry, much benefit can be obtained from the goodwill and market penetration built up by the local partner.

(v) ***Wholly-owned Subsidiaries:*** Wholly-owned subsidiaries must receive the approval of the FIPB, and this approval will only be granted if certain criteria are satisfied.[2] If approval is given, then the business must be incorporated under Indian company law (*Indian Companies Act*, 1956), and it is considered a domestic company. As a separate legal entity, the wholly-owned subsidiary enjoys equity in perpetuity, just as in the case of equity joint ventures.

The advantage of a wholly-owned subsidiary is that the company, incorporated under Indian Company Law, can be fully controlled by the parent company, with the parent company not having to be liable for the actions of the subsidiary. In addition, unlike joint ventures, the subsidiary does not have to share the profits with the local partner.

---

[2] In most cases such approvals are granted if: the business is in a high priority or a high technology area; it is to be located in an economically backward area; or it intends to export all production, as in the case of EPZs.

OTHER BUSINESS LAWS RELEVANT TO A FOREIGN INVESTOR

Company Law

The amendment to the *Companies Act* (1956) was tabled in Parliament in 1994 and was brought into legislation in 1995. The current *Companies Act* reflects India's democracy very poorly. As a result of a close-door policy for decades, the *Companies Act* is very restrictive, not only to the foreign investor, but to private local companies as well. Government intervention in the running of public companies is still high, especially where the appointment of directors is concerned.

Labour Law

Indian labour law, and labour-related laws, still lag behind the economic reforms that have taken place, and this would be a point of concern especially for investors who want to invest directly in India. No exit policy exists and sick companies are not allowed to retrench employees without government approval.

Labour legislation in India aims towards catering for all sections of the workforce. This can be seen from the legislations that are in place. Some of these include:

(i) *Factories Act*, which requires all factories to be licenced and empowers the government to regulate working conditions in terms of health, safety, welfare, payment of wages, etc.;
(ii) *Industrial Disputes Act*, which is the main legislation for the settlement of industrial disputes;
(iii) *Minimum Wages Act*, which empowers the government to stipulate minimum wages; and
(iv) *Trade Unions Act*, which provides for the recognition of trade unions.

Trade unions remain very strong and resistant to change. Given that employment is such a politically sensitive issue, the government is taking a very cautious stand on the situation, and while the assurance has been given to foreign investor that the laws will change, it will be slow to materialise.

Land Law

As Indian law stands currently, although foreign companies can obtain land for their own business use, the *Indian Urban Land Ceiling Act* does not allow foreign companies to buy land to develop and sell.[3] This limits the scope of the property developers. This point of concern was brought up by Singapore businessmen during the Indian Prime Minister's visit to Singapore in September 1994.

Tax Laws

As of 31 March 1994, India has double taxation agreements with 39 countries, of which the most favourable agreement is with Mauritius.[4] Singapore is in the process of concluding a revised double taxation agreement with India which will grant more favourable terms, especially in the area of repatriation of profits, interest earnings and royalties.

With the 1994 budget, the standard applicable tax rate for domestic companies (companies incorporated under Indian company law) is 46%, and for foreign companies (companies incorporated under foreign laws) it is 55%.

The Government offers a wide range of tax incentives to encourage foreign investment. These include tax holidays for export-oriented units (EOUs) and enterprises in export processing zones (EPZs).

Intellectual Property Laws

The Indian government realises the need to tighten up laws on the protection of intellectual property in order to lure foreign investors into the country. As it stands now, the laws pertaining to intellectual property are as follows:

(i) *Copyright Act:* The *Copyright Act* provides protection for 60 years after the first publication, or for 60 years after the author's death.
(ii) *Patents Act:* In line with the requirements of the World Trade Organisation (WTO), the *Patents Act* is undergoing amendment so that only product patents will be granted. The grant will cover a period of 20 years.

---

[3] This was reported in an article in the weekend edition of *Business Times,* September 10–11, 1994.

[4] See footnote 3 above.

(iii) *Trade and Merchandise Marks Act:* This *Act* provides protection for trade marks and merchandise marks for seven years after which applications can be made for renewals.

DISPUTE RESOLUTION

Rao, the Indian Union Law Secretary, had this to say: "Our (India) economic reforms may remain incomplete if changes aren't made in the law dealing with commercial dispute settlement."[5] Currently, the most common methods of dispute settlement are litigation and arbitration.

Litigation

India has the reputation of having an independent and transparent judiciary which has no reservations about awarding judgements against the government and in favour of the individual. However, litigation is not a viable option for investors because of the extensive wait before a case is eventually heard.

Arbitration

India is a signatory to the New York Convention on the enforcement of foreign arbitral awards. International contracts, in particular, opt for arbitration as the initial means of settling any disputes.

However, despite the option of arbitration, the Indian arbitration system leaves little to be desired. The current Indian *Arbitration Act,* which was enacted in 1940, is outdated and provides for court confirmation of arbitral awards before they can be enforced. In addition, arbitration awards can be challenged in court which causes even more delays. Thus, the original purpose of opting for arbitration, which is to speed up the dispute resolution process and thereby reduce cost, is no longer valid.

These problems will hopefully be solved in the near future when a draft bill which will repeal the existing Indian *Arbitration Act* clears Parliament during the 1996 budget session. Under the draft bill, the arbitrator will have court power to issue a decree, and the appellant to an arbitration award must then deposit the awarded amount in court.

---

5 "Judging a Problem", *India Today,* 15 December 1994, p. 163.

CONCLUSION

India has a long legal history. However, because of years of neglecting to update their laws, much spring cleaning needs to be carried out; old laws need to be repealed, or amended, to be in line with the economic reforms. The Indian legal system has been compared to an iceberg where the tip of the iceberg contains the statutes, and beneath it is a plethora of rules and regulations.

In order for investors to feel secure about entering a foreign country, it is necessary to ensure that the laws are transparent so that they can be seen at a glance. Investors cannot afford to be surprised. India has started making entry into the country easier for investors. Now, she needs to concentrate on ensuring that the laws are favourable enough to enable investors to remain.

REFERENCES

Babu V. V., "Economy and Trade", *Trade and Technology Directory of India,* Vol. 1, 1994.

Hotchkiss C., *International Law for Business*, McGraw Hill, 1994.

"India May Revise Tax Pact to Boost Investment from S'pore", *Business Times*, 10–11 September 1994.

Irani P. K., "Doing Business in India — The Current Climate", *Asia Business Law Review*, No. 5, July 1994, pp. 3–8.

Joseph A., "Towards a New Patent Regime", *India Economic Update*, Vol. 1, No. 3, November 1994, p. 20.

Mitta M., "Judging a Problem", *India Today*, 15 December 1994, pp. 163–4.

Penna L. R., "Singapore and India: Gearing up for the 21st Century — Legal Environment for Facilitating Foreign Investment in India", Conference organised by Centre for Advanced Studies, Faculty of Arts and Social Sciences, National University of Singapore on 27–28 July 1994.

Singapore–India Chamber of Commerce and Industry, *Doing Business with India*, Singapore, 1994.

Singh A., "India — Red Tape to Red Carpet", *Global Law and Business*, June 1994, pp. 14–17.

Tan–Nguyen F., "Investing in India — Corporate Tax Regime", Conference organised by Longman Singapore Publishers Pte. Ltd. on 21 September 1994.

LOCATION

Chapter 6

Regional Growth Opportunities in Southern India

BY
LIN Ling
Oswaldo ACOSTA-RUIZ

INTRODUCTION

INDIA IS OPENING up and embarking on large scale economic liberalisation. Except for manufacturing for the defence industry, all other industrial sectors are now open for investment by both domestic and foreign investors. Vast opportunities exist in infrastructure development, food processing, hotel and tourism related activities, financial services, engineering and technical consultancy services, computers and information technologies, petroleum exploration, construction works, automotive parts, chemicals and pharmaceuticals.

Abundance of natural and human resources and the availability of a huge potential market are attractive considerations for the foreign investor. Already foreign direct investment in the last three years has reached US$4 billion. Foreign corporations with a stake in the economy include IBM, Motorola, AT&T, Honda, GM, and General Electric.

In contrast with India, Singapore is a small country. It faces constraints of labour and natural resources, and opportunities for investment. The Singapore government is actively encouraging companies to go regional and invest abroad under its strategic economic plans.

Business and political relationships between Singapore and India have been very cordial and there has been renewed business interest in this vast market. The purpose of this chapter is to identify growth opportunities for investors in southern India. We provide some information about the geographical, social, cultural and economical aspects of India in general, and southern India in particular. A SWOT analysis is also used to evaluate the investment opportunities in southern India. Information was obtained using a combination of literature search, seminars, interviews and visits to plants and companies, and academic institutes during our Business Study Mission.

A SWOT analysis gave us the technical framework to process the data collected. Southern India is treated as a market. Its strengths are the internal capabilities that make it attractive in a competitive world environment. Its weaknesses are the internal factors that detract from its attractiveness and restrict its economic development. The opportunities are external circumstances, events, or situations that offer this market the chance to achieve or exceed its objectives (i.e., economic development). The threats are the external forces, factors, or situations that might create problems, or do harm to the market, or endanger its ability to improve the economic conditions. The SWOT analysis enables us to evaluate the advantages and disadvantages of the investing environment in southern India. Finally, some recommendations are presented.

BACKGROUND

Geographical Features

India is a diamond-shaped country of 3,287,580 square kilometres in area, bordered in the north-east by Nepal and the Himalayas, and in the north-west by Pakistan and the Valley of the Indus. It is bisected by the Tropic of Cancer, and extends south into the Indian Ocean almost to a latitude of 8 degrees north.

Geographically, India can be divided into three parts; the mountainous north, the great alluvial plain of the Brahamaputra and Ganga (Ganges), and the plateaux and lowlands that occupy the southern area, including most of the peninsula. Each provides an astonishing range of scenery, intensified by a diversity of people, culture and activities.

Social and Cultural Features

India is the second most populous country in the world ranking next to China with a population of nearly 899 million.[1] The population is growing at a rate of 2% per annum. Nearly 70% of the population live in the rural areas.

India is also a country with enormous racial diversity. It has over a dozen major languages, each with a rich literature, and many minor languages. Hindi is the national language. English is extensively taught and spoken throughout the country.

Christian influences come from Catholic churches and shrines remaining from Portuguese and French settlements, and schools and colleges set up by Christian denominations. Small Jewish minorities can also be found.

The constitution provides for a parliamentary form of government. Legislative powers are distributed between parliament and state legislatures. The decentralised decision-making process, and variations in natural resources, climatic zones and terrains, have resulted in some states developing faster than others.

Economy

India has the twelfth largest economy in terms of GDP measured in U.S. dollars, and the sixth largest on the basis of purchasing power parity.[2] Nearly three-quarters of her GDP originates from the private sector. India uses the International Finance Corporation (IFC) and the Asian Development Bank (ADB) to finance large scale projects. By April 1994, India was the largest recipient of such IFC project financing with committed funds of US$933 million to 68 companies.

Since July 1991, the government has launched a programme of economic stabilisation and reforms. The positive impact of the economic reforms can be seen in the growth of GDP from 1.1% in 1991–92 to 3.8% in 1993–94. The growth rate for 1994–95 was 6.3%. Industrial production and exports/imports have improved during the same period. The inflation rate has dropped sharply from 13.6% in 1991–92 to 8.2% in 1993–94. These trends are summarised in Figures 6–1, 6–2, 6–3 and 6–4 respectively.

---

1 "Wide World Atlas," *Readers Digest,* 1987.

2 IMF study, 1992.

FIGURE 6–1
Inflation (%)

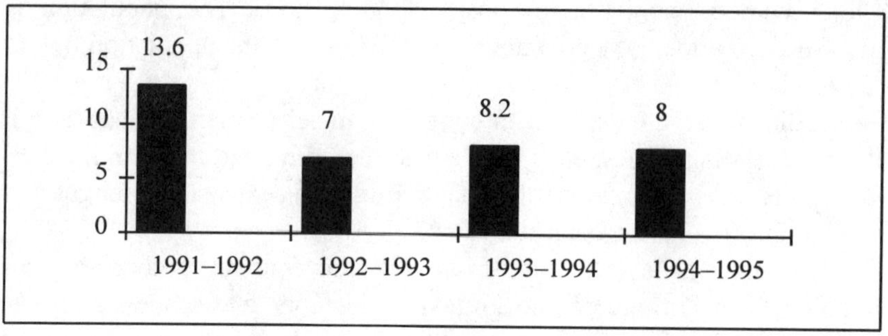

FIGURE 6–2
Growth in GDP (%)

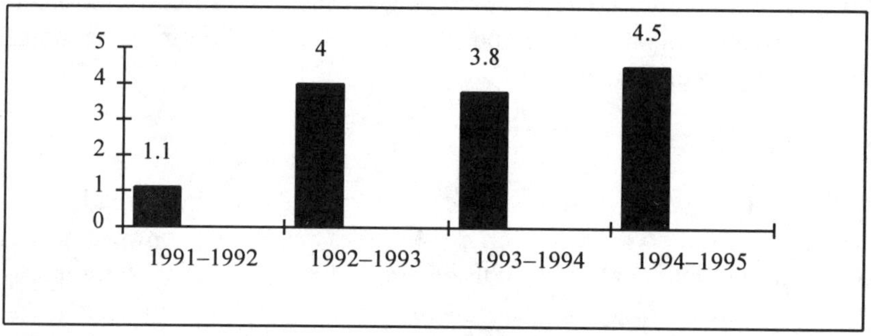

FIGURE 6–3
Growth in Industrial Production (%)

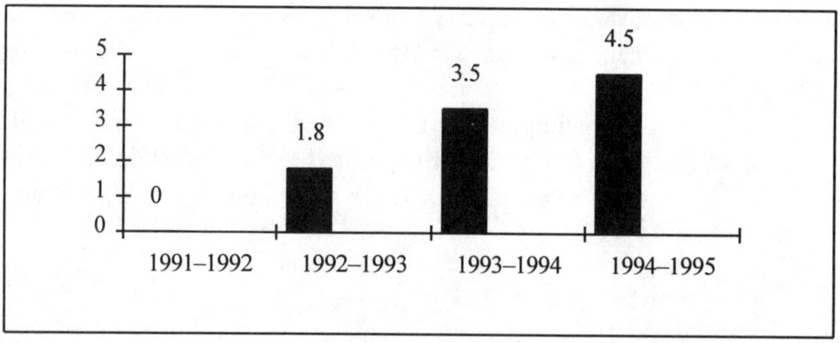

FIGURE 6–4
Exports/Imports (Rs billion)

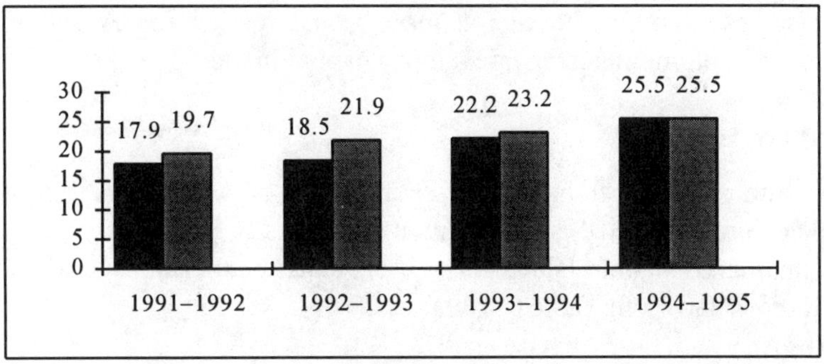

The economic reforms undertaken by the Indian government attempt to ease both local and foreign investment. As a result of the reform programme, Indian industry is now substantially deregulated. Entry regulations were abolished for all projects except for those in the defence industry, which has to take cognisance of security, strategic, environmental and social concerns. For instance, a new mineral policy was announced recently allowing 13 minerals, which had earlier been reserved for exclusive exploitation by the public sector, to be available for investment by both domestic and foreign investors.

Along with industrial deregulation, the government has substantially liberalised the provisions relating to foreign investment. A substantial segment of industry is now open for foreign direct investment up to 51% foreign equity ownership on an automatic approval basis. Service industries such as the establishment of trading houses, hotels, other tourism related industries and computer software, also fall into this category.

The exchange rate is now market determined. Controls on the import of consumer goods are almost eliminated. Machinery and intermediate goods can be imported freely at deregulated tariffs. The maximum tariff now is 65% as compared to over 300% in 1991. Import duties on capital goods and intermediate products are much lower than the peak rate of 65%. The process of tariff reductions will continue over the next two or three years in order to ensure that tariffs are brought in line with those of other East and South-east Asian countries.

Interest rates are largely free from administrative control. There is a single administered deposit rate of 10% to act as a ceiling. The number of administered borrowing rates are limited to three. Companies are free to raise resources in the capital market, and market forces determine prices and volumes as in any developed capital market.

Southern India

The south region of India comprises the states of Andhra Pradesh, Karnataka, Kerala, Tamil Nadu, the union territories of Pondicherry, and the Andaman and Nicobar Islands. The basic data about each state in southern India is shown in Table 6–1 below.

TABLE 6–1
Data on Four Southern Indian States

	Tamil Nadu	Karnataka	Kerala	Andhra Pradesh
Population (mil)	55.9	45	29.1	66.5
Literacy rate (%)	62.7	56	89.8	44.1
Technical parks	5 (Madras, Salem)	4 (Bangalore)	2 (Trivandrum)	3 (Hyderabad)
Capital	Madras	Bangalore	Trivandrum	Hyderabad
Major sea port	Madras	Mangalore	Cochin, Tuticorin	Visakhapatnam
International airport	Madras	-	Trivandrum	-
Per capita income (Rs)	4,619	4,631	4,032	4,731
Mineral deposits	Gold, Manganese	Iron, Copper	-	Copper, Diamond

The total population in southern India is 202 million which is about 23% of the whole country. This region accounts for 23% of India's total exports. Growing at 33% per annum, as compared to the national average of 31%, the south region has enormous export potential which has not been adequately exploited. Tables 6–2 and 6–3 show the export growth trend of southern India *vis-à-vis* India as a whole, and the individual export growth trend for other states, respectively.

TABLE 6–2
Export Growth Trend of Southern India Versus India
(Rupees in crores)

	1991–1992	1992–1993	1993–1994
India's Exports	43,828	53,350	69,547
India's Growth Rate		22%	31%
Southern Region's Exports	8,772	10,350	15,892
Southern Region's Growth Rate		18%	54%
% Share of Southern Region in India's Total Exports	20.01%	19.40%	22.85%

TABLE 6–3
Export Growth Trend by State

	1991–1992	1992–1993	1993–1994
Tamil Nadu	5,437	6,808	9,082
Growth Rate	25%	33%	
Kerala	1,861	1,774	2,482
Growth Rate	-5%	29%	
Karnataka	668	628	1,237
Growth rate	6%	97%	
Andhra Pradesh	806	1,140	3,081
Growth Rate	41%	170%	
Southern Region's Exports	8,772	10,350	15,892
Growth Rate	18%	54%	

SWOT ANALYSIS

Strengths

Compared with other regions in India, the southern part is well equipped in terms of infrastructure, power and transportation. The power tariffs in Kerala are the lowest in the country and the government has frozen power tariffs for all new units for the next five years. It has 31.5% of road kilometres in India, 23.6% of railway route kilometres and 41% of the port traffic. More importantly, this region has five out of ten major ports in the whole country. These five ports are in Madras, Bangalore, Cochin, Tuticorin, and Visakhapatnam. Of the five international airports in India, two are in the southern region; one is in Madras and the other is in Trivandrum. A source from Air India said that "business traffic is expected to grow between Bangalore and Singapore. Once the Singapore-Tata joint venture for an information technology park is in place, we want to be there first to tap the growing market". The Bombay-Bangalore-Singapore flight will be bi-weekly initially.

The region has also performed well on welfare indices such as education, literacy and urbanisation. Compared with the average literacy rate in India (52.5%), Karnataka (56%), Kerala (89.8%), and Tamil Nadu (62.7%) have done well.[3] Kerala not only has the highest literacy rate in the country, but also has the highest density of science and technology personnel at 5.87 per thousand population as against 2.4 at the national level. It has 30% of the entire newspaper and magazine circulation in India. If the urbanisation in towns of over 10,000 population is compared, then the region has a 42% urbanisation rate as against the national average of 24%.

The region also dominates in the production of several commodities: rubber (99% of all India's production), cocoa (100%), coconut (90%), silk (90%), tobacco (52%), fruit (40%), fish (37%), and eggs (44%). Southern India has plenty of metallic and non-metallic mineral resources such as gold, copper, iron, manganese, diamonds, and bauxite.

Compared with other regions in India, southern India possesses strong industrial bases. Karnataka and Tamil Nadu are among the most industrially advanced states in the country. Major industries in these two states are textile, cotton, electronic equipment, sugar, coaches, cement, etc. Bangalore has been host to many high-tech industries such as electronics, computers, telecommunications and information. It is also popularly known as the "silicon valley" of India. The Bangalore-Singapore Information Technology Park aims at creating a one-stop IT park that integrates advanced manufacturing, design and development, training, showroom, office, recreational, and residential activities in to a single location. The park has received approval from the state government to have its own separate power supply cable to solve the power shortage problem in the state.

---

[3] This data is from the 1991 census.

A memorandum of understanding (MOU) has been signed to set up a permanent exhibition and trade promotion centre in the outskirts of Madras city where the state government is also establishing the Madras Industrial Park, formerly called the Singapore Corridor. The centre will promote southern India and its technological capabilities overseas in an effort to attract more foreign investment.

Kerala was the first state in India to set up a state electronics development corporation in 1973. It was also the first state in India to have a fully automated telephone network. Today, Kerala is a pioneer in the provision of state support for the electronics industry and has advanced technological environments such as the electronics technology parks.

Southern India has three export processing zones (EPZs). They are located in Madras (Tamil Nadu), Cochin (Kerala) and Visakhapatnam (Andhra Pradesh). These EPZs provide an internationally competitive, duty free environment at low cost for export production and export-oriented units (EOUs). Each of these zones provides basic infrastructure and customs clearance facilities.

State governments in southern India have been offering incentives to attract investment into their territories. Table 6–4 presents a brief description of some of the incentives in each state.

TABLE 6–4
State Government Incentives

Andhra Pradesh	a) Investment grant ranging from 15% to 20% of the capital cost of the project up to a maximum of Rs 9 million. b) Sales tax deferment varying between 50% to 100% of the fixed capital up to a period of 10 years.
Karnataka	a) Single window clearance facility. b) Investment grant at graded rates of 15% to 25% subject to a maximum of Rs 2.5 million. c) Additional investment grant at graded rates of 15% to 25% subject to a maximum of Rs 1 million for export-oriented units. d) Special assistance up to Rs 0.5 million for installation of pollution control. e) Sales tax exemption for a period of 3 to 5 years for selected zones and thrust areas such as electronics, telecommunications, leather, pollution control equipment etc. f) Exemption from sales tax up to 6 years to units in electronics cities of Mysore and Dharwar.

TABLE 6–4 (cont'd)

	g) Exemption from entry toll on raw materials going into 100% export-oriented units.
Kerala	a) Green channel scheme for expeditious clearance of projects. b) Investment grant at the rate of 15% of the fixed capitals cost. Additional assistance for thrust areas like rubber, electronics, pharmaceuticals, leather, light engineering, etc. c) Cash incentives for setting up quality control laboratories. d) Grant for installations of power generating sets. e) Exemption/deferment of sales tax for 7 to 10 years up to 100% of fixed capital. f) Concessional power tariff. g) Escort services for investment over Rs 500 million.
Tamil Nadu	a) Special grant up to Rs 10 million for mega projects. b) Higher grant for electronic industry up to Rs 3.5 million. c) Special assistance at the rate of 100% up to a maximum of Rs 1.5 million for thrust areas such as auto ancillaries, drugs and pharmaceuticals, food processing, non-conventional energy devices, gold jewellery, etc. d) Financial assistance for purchase of power generating sets. e) Exemption/deferment of sales tax for the full value of investment for a period of 5 to 14 years. f) Concessional power tariff.

Weaknesses

The mere supply of natural resources and an educated workforce is not sufficient for worldwide competition. The power crisis in southern India has discouraged investments. For example, in 1994–95, the estimated energy requirement in Karnataka was 24,272 million units compared to energy available of 20,023 million units. Such serious power shortages forces an increase in the prices of utilities. It also causes inconvenience to industries.

Although the shortage of power and the inadequacy of transport and telecommunications are serious problems in southern India, or for that matter India as a whole, improvements are unlikely in the foreseeable future. Infrastructure projects require hefty financing, and India's poor image with international credit rating agencies (i.e., Standard & Poor's BB plus rating) makes it difficult to raise commercial debt.

Although labour and material costs are lower, communication costs and worker training costs are much higher than in Singapore. While the government has reduced import duties from 300% to 65%, they are still too high, and customs clearance is time consuming. Compared with Singapore's top income tax rate of 27%, the current income tax rate of 48% in India is higher. Moreover, multi-point taxation, where tax is levied on the first sale and at the point of second sale, applies for many commodities in south Indian states. Commodities such as shampoos, soft drinks, furniture, suitcases, audio, video cassettes, vegetable oil, timber, etc., all fall in the double tax net. Traders from 1800 trade associations observed a three-day *bandh* in the last week of November 1994, in Tamil Nadu, to complain about the various taxes imposed on them by the state government. The more contentious complaints are issues relating to the profession tax and multi-point tax. Even local companies complain about the taxes. How, then, can the government convince foreign investors to come to the region?

Personnel at the lower levels of the bureaucracy in India do not share the urgency of economic reforms. For instance, it may take several months to process a licence. Other factors impairing the attractiveness of investing in southern India are the strong labour unions, the lack of an exit policy, and poor labour productivity. These drawbacks inhibit the flow of capital.

Opportunities

The opportunities for investments in southern India can be analysed from two perspectives: the internal and the external economic factors. Since economic reforms commenced in 1991, the federal government has adopted various policies aimed at stimulating economic growth and encouraging both domestic and foreign private investments. GDP growth increased from 1.1% in 1991–92 to 3.8% in 1993–94. The expected growth rate for 1994–95 is 4.5%. The local economy is booming. The living standards of the Indian people are rising. Huge opportunities exist in areas such as construction, electronics and services. Southern India, with its strengths in infrastructure, industrial bases, human, and natural resources, leads the way in economic development. Southern India has proven to be an attractive draw.

External environment refers to the international economic climate. For most developed countries, the major threats faced are higher production costs because of shortages in labour and materials, fierce competition, and limited market share. The solution is to relocate labour intensive industries to the developing countries. Production costs can be reduced dramatically. At the same time, companies can enjoy less competitive markets and explore new markets for their products.

The inflow of foreign investments can stimulate the economic growth of southern India, leading to higher productivity and incomes. Their demand for imports will rise substantially. In this way, the world economic growth rate can also be accelerated.

Threats

The growth of opportunities in southern India depends on its ability to compete effectively in the international market. It encounters competition in both the goods and capital markets from other developing countries such as Mexico, Indonesia and China. In the capital market, international investors will direct their investments to the countries where they can obtain higher returns with lower risks. In the goods markets, the winners will be those who can provide high quality products with low prices. If southern India is to banish poverty, then there must be steady economic growth and continued investments in power, telecommunication, ports, railways, roads, oil exploration, refineries, housing and related urban infrastructure.

Standard & Poor's, a leading American credit rating agency, has said that it will not upgrade its BB plus rating of India's foreign currency debt. It believes that India's current balance of payments position is vulnerable to import growth and sustained high fiscal deficits. It also believes that India's net external debt burden, estimated at 200% of exports in 1994, remains high for similarly rated sovereigns.[4] This rating may make it difficult for India, as well as southern India, to attract foreign capital. To some extent, this may impact its economic growth negatively.

CONCLUSION

Overall, southern India has experienced rapid economic growth since the economic reforms in 1991. The investment environment has improved significantly. Vast opportunities exist in areas like infrastructure, manufacturing, agriculture and services.

Singapore has strengths in information technology, electronics, food

---

4 *The Economic Times,* 14 December 1994.

processing, mass public housing, as well as in various banking and financial services which can complement India.

With its abundant human and natural resources, as well as the strong industrial bases in electronic engineering and software development, southern India can become an ideal place for the relocation or offloading of manpower-intensive manufacturing, and commercialised technology from Singapore. Singapore companies can enter into joint ventures with Indian companies in the form of financial collaborations, joint manufacturing and technology transfers, to achieve mutual benefits.

Although vast opportunities are emerging in southern India, there are still some weaknesses investors should consider. The following are some recommendations for potential investors:

(i) Choose a partner with good political connections, one who can navigate the bureaucratic maze. Good candidates are a relatively efficient state enterprise or a large industrial group.
(ii) Prepare mentally to work in a challenging, not-so-streamlined environment in which certain inefficiencies such as low productivity, poor transport, and power shortages exist.
(iii) Hire only essential staff due to the lack of an exit policy, and take full advantage of automation on the production line, and in the office, if possible.

REFERENCES

Abdoolcarim Zoher, "Investing in India: The Rules", *Asian Business*, February 1994.

Business Opportunities in Kerala Technopark, Address by K. M. Chandrasekhar in Singapore, November 1994.

Deepa Balasubramanyan, "Taxation Double Trouble", *Business India*, 19 December 1994.

"India's Economic Relation With East and South-east Asia", Address by Dr. Manmohan Singh, Finance Minister of India, at a meeting of the World Economic Forum, Singapore, 14 October 1994.

"India Means Business: An Economic Profile — Opportunities in Specific Sectors", Published by the Director, Economic Coordination Unit, 1994.

Sikes Jonathan, "Making the India Connection", *Asia Business*, May 1993.

Singapore-Indian Chamber of Commerce and Industry, *Doing Business With India*, Singapore, 1994.

The Economic Times, Madras, 14, 19, and 29 December 1994.

Vaish Associates, "Doing Business in India — Policies and Procedures". Published by M. K. Bhargava, 1994.

Chapter 7

Investment, Industry Structures and Strategic Alliances in the Economic Zones of New Delhi, Bangalore and Madras

BY
THIA Boon Har
WOON Hin Yong

INTRODUCTION

THE OBJECTIVE OF this chapter is to analyse the investment and industry structures in the economic zones of New Delhi, Bangalore and Madras, and then identify industries of potential strategic alliances in these zones. First, we characterise the strengths of these economic zones for establishing suitable industries. Some of the factors considered are availability of skilled workers, infrastructure, transportation network, and market opportunities. The "suitable industry" focus is discussed to highlight key areas that may be important for Singapore investors. The search is for complementary strengths. Although Singapore is only a city state, with limited experience and exposure in some industrial sectors, it may be able to use its administrative and process skills in India. Complementary needs, which are those that are upstream and downstream of the industries in Singapore, may be possible areas of greater interest.

Tapping engineering skills is another area

that may be considered. This is manifested in the form of product development in India, or the hiring of manpower for relocation to Singapore. One of the core competencies of Singapore is in the area of administration. Therefore, another form of collaboration is the participation in the planning and execution of infrastructure projects on a government-to-government basis. This may help to support the extension of local construction companies into India. One example is the establishment of the IT park in Bangalore using a joint venture framework.

Secondly, we discuss the various ways of investing or forming strategic alliances in identified industrial sectors, or a specific industry. The various alliances that are promoted or encouraged by the Indian government are highlighted. Examples of such alliances include, but are not limited to, licensing, franchising, management contracts, turnkey projects, shared ownership and private labels. The motivation for such alliances lies in the creation of global brand associations, accessing low cost labour/materials, cross subsidisation, dodging of trade barriers and attaining economies of scale. The Indian industrial environment for such alliances is discussed.

The difficulties of managing and controlling these alliances in an emerging economy needs to be evaluated carefully. Industry structure and alliances are important because of the economic and political risks in each situation. Local businessmen must be aware of the difficulties before embarking on any business venture. When the alliance structure is ill-defined, it may be the beginning of the failure of the venture.

Thirdly, we investigate the special promotion zones, and compare these to the planned development of these zones to determine the feasibility for Singapore investors. The continual support of the Indian government is necessary for the long term viability of these zones.

We conclude by recommending alternative investment opportunities in the various zones that would be complementary to the Singapore business climate. These recommendations are based on the discussion pertaining to the three economic zones.

BACKGROUND

After decades of rigid government controls, the Narasimha Rao Government, which came into power in June 1991, introduced aggressive and extensive economic reforms in July 1991. Deregulation is the central feature of the reform strategy. According to the Joint Business Council in New Delhi, the broad medium term objectives of the reform are:

(i) to remove the sharp macroeconomic imbalances that characterise the fiscal and external sectors of the economy; and
(ii) to facilitate the progressive integration of the Indian economy into the global economy.

The economic reforms have been comprehensive and encompass the industrial, trade, and finance sectors, including relaxation of the industrial regulatory environment, liberalising international trade, easing of exchange controls, encouraging foreign investment, reforms in the financial sector and in taxation, as well as cuts in government subsidies and divestment in private sector enterprises.[1]

India is a vast country. It is therefore more appropriate to discuss economic opportunities in India in a regional context. India may be considered as consisting of several economic centres. The opportunities in these centres vary according to their specific strengths which have been derived from factors such as historical, political and social backgrounds. It is important that these factors be considered in conjunction with any investment decision. The main focus in this paper is investment opportunities in the industrial sector, particularly in manufacturing concerns.

Prior to the economic reforms, the Indian industrial policy framework was characterised by extensive bureaucratic control over choices which should ideally be left to entrepreneurial decision-making. A substantial area of industrial activities was reserved for the public sector, thus making it impossible for the private sector to contribute in key areas. Access to foreign technology by domestic entrepreneurs also requires government permission (SICCI, 1994).

The years following July 1991 witnessed a massive infusion of private capital through both direct investment in joint ventures and portfolio investment in stock markets. A large number of well known foreign companies have begun to invest in joint ventures in India and some of those who withdrew in the past have started returning to the country (SICCI, 1994).

Recently, the liberalised foreign investment policy identified 35 in-

1 Singapore-Indian Chamber of Commerce and Industry (SICCI), 1994.

dustries in which foreign investment would be permitted up to 51% automatically. It also permits 100% foreign equity participation for businesses set up in export processing zones (EPZs), or businesses which are 100% export-oriented units (EOUs).

With the new policy of liberalisation, it is believed that substantial strategic alliance opportunities exist for foreign investors in the economic zones of New Delhi, Bangalore and Madras. A good knowledge of the industrial structure in these areas will offer future investors an understanding of the business potential and help in the process of investment decisions.

There appears to be some political uncertainty which may eventually lead to the question of the continuity of policies in the Indian government because the ruling party has lost elections in all the states of Andhra Pradesh, Karnataka, Sikkim and Goa.[2] The loss by the ruling Congress(I) party has caused concern about the fate of the economic reforms that were put in place. These sentiments were echoed in various newspaper reports[3] immediately following the release of the results of the polls.

The message that was given by the various political parties was mixed, with some quarters asking that the reforms be slowed down while others pledged for the continual support of such policies. The politically democratic structure of India will not allow a precise forecast of what will be the future trend, or the fate, of the economic reforms in India .

Since its independence in 1947, India has followed a policy of self-reliant economic progress by utilising a mixed economic model. This has allowed it to advance in agriculture, and in setting up a large industrial and services sector. Nearly three-quarters of its GDP originates in the private sector.[4] The self-reliant policy, which had included active public sector involvement, regulation of industry and restrictions on imports and foreign investment, had caused severe macroeconomic imbalances. There were fiscal and external debts, excessive liquidity and inflationary pressures, depreciation in the external value of the rupee and a squeeze on development expenditure. These problems have led to the current programme of economic stabilisation and restructuring.

The economic reforms are intended to convert India's closed and protected economy to one which is integrated into the global economy, or

---

2 Editorial, *The Sunday Times,* 11 December 1994.

3 Editorial, *The Sunday Times,* 11 December 1994.

4 *Doing Business with India*, Singapore-Indian Chamber of Commerce and Industry, Singapore, 1994.

what is commonly referred to as the globalisation of the Indian economy. Country-wide communication will further reduce the uncertainty of these reform policies. The reforms in India, therefore, have roots in fundamental economic structural problems. This suggests that the reform path would be independent of the political party in power. Popular support of the reform policy will be assured if the benefits of the economic reforms, which are well understood and desired by the industrial sector, are communicated to the masses.

If the reforms had started from a purely ideological battle, then we would not be so enthusiastic about their continuity based on the outcome of the recent polls. Mr. Salman Khursid, former Minister of State for External Affairs, gave these views during his address to the MBA delegation at the FICCI house. The same views were echoed by many of the industrial leaders during the course of this mission. Therefore, there is an upbeat feeling about the reforms that are taking place in India.

The commerce and industry alliance, such as FICCI, seem to have considerable negotiating power in the process of pushing for reforms. Because these organisations are pro-reform, this underscores the confidence that the policies will have continuity. However, these may also be the same organisations that would have pushed for the self-reliant policy in the pre-reform period as well. In other words, the reform process, in the end, must benefit Indian industry for it to have continuity. Otherwise, there will always be opposing forces that make the process unstable. In considering any venture into the India economy, the local interest must be taken into consideration. The publicity push by the Indian authorities for foreign investment has this message. Shared equity investments are thus strongly promoted over 100% of foreign equity.

The Competitive Advantage of India

The competitive advantage position of India may be analysed in terms of the framework developed by Porter in his book "The Competitive Advantage of Nations", which is illustrated in Figure 7–1. The four determinants of factor advantages set up by Porter are factor conditions, demand conditions, related and supporting industry, and firm strategy. This model can be used to analyse the competitiveness of firms in India relative to others in the global context. The strategy of individual firms must compliment the strengths of the Indian economy to achieve competitiveness.

Factor Conditions

India has a large abundance of natural resources. Since 1947, it is this base which has made India successful in pursuing a policy of self-sufficiency. There is also a huge supply of labour with varying skill levels. With a population of over 900 million, India has a large pool of workers, though presently, most of them are in the agriculture sector which could be described as unskilled in industrial terms. Another important factor is the presence of a large consumer market in India mainly fueled by the large population. However, this market is largely untapped for consumerism for historical reasons. India has had a reputation in the past for being a closed economy filled with monopolies that flooded the market with sub-standard goods. Therefore, consumers may not be able to appreciate high quality products since these goods will not be able to compete with the lower quality goods in terms of price, and consumers will not be able to differentiate between them.

FIGURE 7–1
The Complete System

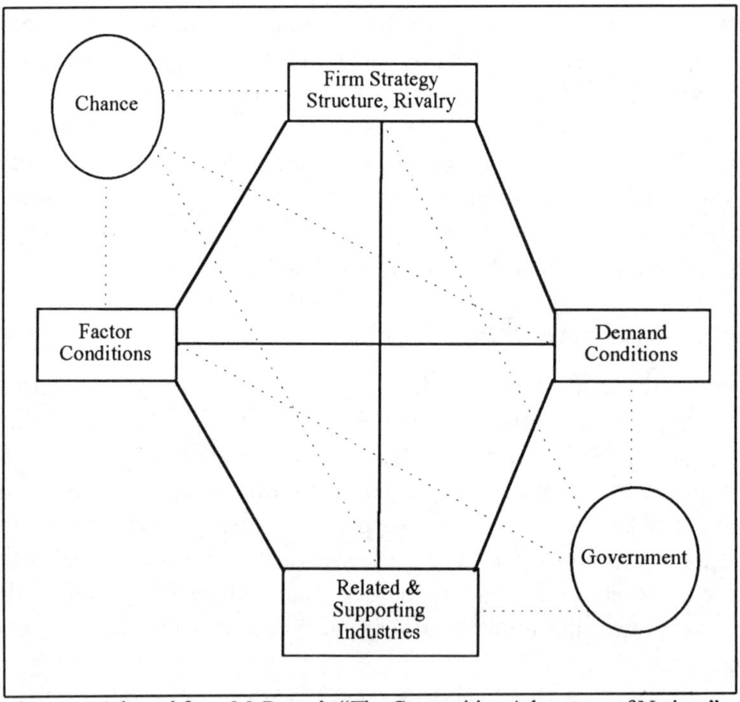

Source: Adapted from M. Porter's "The Competitive Advantage of Nations". The Free Press, New York, 1990.

The democratic form of government is largely stable. This form of government has been in place since independence. In the last few years, although there has been a change of power, the continuity of the political structure has been maintained. Factor creation is relatively weak in India. Although it has established educational institutions, the number of trained personnel is low in comparison to the size of the country. With the reforms, there is also an outflow of talent, especially skilled and educated managerial personnel. This structure has led to problems in turnover of staff in some Indian companies. Turnover management was a major strategy in these companies. Clearly, management has to be innovative in the actions needed to retain their staff.

Infrastructure is a problem in India. However, the problem is not evenly distributed. Many states suffer from a shortage of power and communication facilities. At the other extreme, some states enjoy an abundance of such services. The appropriate selection of investment location, therefore, becomes an important factor. Benefits such as investment incentives, subsidies, and low cost labour may have to be sacrificed in the selection of an appropriate location.

The transportation network is another weak factor. This can cause bottlenecks in the supply and distribution chain. Although the railway network has been established for many years, it has a reputation for being slow. For some industries, transportation will be a determining factor in site selection.

Unlike China, India enjoys a reliable and established legal system which was inherited from the British. The English language is widely used throughout the country. Arising from many years of being self-reliant, entrepreneurial culture is widespread, especially in the small and medium industries.

Demand Conditions

Indian industry has been regulated for decades through a licensing scheme. In a way, the market was protected and there was little rivalry in the market place. Competition was minimal as the bureaucrats decided the nature of competition in the market. As a result, Indian industry may not be globally competitive. The strength in their products and services are those sectors where they have a distinct cost advantage and where resources are abundant in relative terms. For example, the number of Indian software engineers is among the highest in the world. Coupled with the low wage situation, India has an advantage to compete in this sector. Because of the nature of competition in the Indian market, partner selection is an important factor in any joint venture activity.

Related and Supporting Industries

Many industrial sectors are situated all over the Indian subcontinent. The particular strengths of each sector in the respective regions have to be assessed. For example, Madras has a high concentration of support industries for automobile manufacturing while Bangalore has a huge concentration of information technology-related industries. Similar comments are appropriate for Bombay and Calcutta. In assessing this criterion, investors must consider each particular state and compare the strengths and weaknesses. It is not possible to generalise the discussion in this respect because India is a large subcontinent.

Firm Strategy and Rivalry

Historically, markets have been heavily regulated. One could expect that Indian firms are not accustomed to competition in the international sense. Any firm wishing to participate in the Indian market should consider this factor when selecting their Indian counterparts. Firms must review their own intentions and interest in the market *vis-a-vis* the above-mentioned factors.

The competitive position of India is largely dependent upon the success of the reforms. Timeliness is an important element in deciding to participate in India. Competitiveness, of course, will vary from sector to sector. Thus, careful analysis and a well-managed excursion could prove to be advantageous in the longer term as the reform programme begins to unfold greater opportunities for investors.

INVESTMENT AND INDUSTRY STRUCTURE

Manufacturing, construction and utilities account for about 27% of GDP, and they provided a 9% growth rate during 1994–95. The new industrial policy was introduced in 1991 to focus on a free market oriented, competitive and global environment.[5] The tax rate in India was very high in pre-reform periods. Although the tax rate has been reduced substantially, it is still comparatively higher than those in developed countries and the East Asian developing countries. Potential investors need to take advantage of any incentives offered by the Indian government to reduce the effective tax rate. It would be prudent to understand the incentive criteria before deciding to invest in India. It should be noted that there are numerous incentives, especially for non-resident Indians (NCI). Perhaps investors can use this structure to advantage.

Four sets of policies relating to trade, industrial, foreign investment and export-imports are important in considering the manufacturing sector in India. The salient points of these policies are as follows:

(i) ***Trade Policy:***
  - (a) Elimination of discretionary controls by reduction in quantitative restrictions on imports.
  - (b) Reduction in import tariffs across industry sectors.
  - (c) Duties on raw materials and components are lower than on finished goods.

(ii) ***Industrial Policy:***
  - (a) Narrow the areas reserved for the public sector by allowing private sector investment in the power sector, oil exploration and refining.
  - (b) Streamlining its procedures for delicensed industries.

(iii) ***Foreign Investment Policy:***
  - (a) Liberalisation of foreign investment policy by removal of dividend-balancing for non-consumer goods.
  - (b) *Foreign Exchange Regulation Act* (FERA) amended, and investment restrictions on FERA companies substantially removed.
  - (c) Foreign companies allowed to use their trade marks for domestic sales.
  - (d) Foreign direct investment allowed in exploration, production and refining of oil, and marketing of gas.
  - (e) Signing of Multilateral Investment Guarantee Agency (MIGA)

---

5 D. Ravishankar, "A premium offering", *The Smart Investor*, Annual Issue 1993–94.

protocol for protection of foreign investments.

(f) Liberalised guidelines for Indian joint ventures abroad by providing for automatic approval in 30 days for all cases involving an equity of up to S$2 million with a cash remittance of up to S$0.5 million.

(iv) ***Export-Import Policy:***

(a) EOU/EPZ units in the agro sector to get the benefit of duty-free imports if 50% of production is exported.

(b) Export Promotion Capital Goods (EPCG) scheme extended to cover services sector.

(c) 144 items removed from the negative list of exports.

As part of the reform process, the government has implemented various schemes to attract investments in particular export related activities. There are special schemes for the development of extensive free trade zones (FTZ), export processing zones (EPZ) and export-oriented units (100% EOU).

As India moves to be an export-oriented country, the individual states are aggressively competing to get a piece of the action. State governments also give incentives for setting up such entities. EPZs/FTZs are now being set up in the various states that are actively promoting foreign investments.

Each FTZ/EPZ provides basic infrastructure facilities such as developed land for construction of factory buildings, standard designed factory buildings (SDFs), ready-built sheds, road, power and water, drainage system, and a whole range of fiscal incentives. Customs clearance facilities are offered within the zone premises at no extra charge. In addition, facilities for banking, post office, clearing agents, etc., are arranged in the service centres provided in each zone. There are certain incentives to site factories in these zones based on the success of similarly structured zones in Singapore and Malaysia.

EOUs, and units in FTZ/EPZs, offer the foreign investors potential for growth and profitability. These units are allowed to be set up with foreign equity participation of up to 100%. Available concessions also include liberal import facilities. Duty free import of capital equipment,[6] raw materials, etc., is allowed for 100% EOUs and those in the FTZ/EPZs. Central excise and other levies are not applicable to products

---

[6] Investors must be aware that restrictions exist for certain categories.

manufactured in these units. There are special criteria for the automatic approval of EOU/EPZ Units.

Companies wishing to invest should familiarise themselves with these criteria so that they may identify a shorter route to obtain approval for their venture. As FTZ/EPZs are actively promoted by the Indian government, many concerns have indicated interest in setting up such areas. In most states there are activities in progress to set up such industrial areas. The concept is not unlike those of Singapore industrial estates and the FTZ in Malaysia.

NEW DELHI

New Delhi, the capital of India, has recently been accorded the status of a state. Industrial activity in New Delhi seems to be limited. This is not unexpected of a capital city. Related supporting industry in New Delhi seems to be absent. One factory which was visited indicated that most of their supplies come either from overseas or are obtained from Madras.

Old Delhi seems to be bustling with trading activities. One has to visit the place to appreciate the traffic congestion and intensity of activities relating to trade practices. There may be advantages for a trading business to be located in Delhi. The main advantage of a business in New Delhi is the proximity to the international airport. The northern state of Punjab holds some promise for activities in the precision trade. The distance from New Delhi to Punjab is not far, easily accessible within a day.

BANGALORE

Bangalore, also known as the silicon valley of India, is the capital of Karnataka which is the eighth largest state in India. The state has a long coast line with rich marine resources and, also, all-weather ports at Mangalore and Karwar.

It has a strong industrial and infrastructure base for high technology industries in electronics, telecommunications, and informatics. The Karnataka state has become the base for several multinationals and Fortune 500 companies, such as Texas Instruments, IBM, Hewlett

Packard, Digital, Motorola, AT&T, General Electric and others.

Bangalore has grown to be an important industrial centre, particularly for high technology industries. It is also rapidly diversifying into a financial centre in the southern region. Bangalore is also expected to be the future hi-tech commercial and business capital of the southern region.

The state government of Karnataka has identified thrust areas in information technology, electronics, telecommunications, value-added telecommunications services and 100% export-oriented enterprises. Infrastructure projects such as power generation, road construction, urban transportation and telecommunication services are also being sought.

In Bangalore, one may be able to recruit talent for the IT industry. A huge cluster of major international players in the IT industry can be found there. The city, however, suffers from acute shortages in power and telecommunication facilities. Companies need to provide for their own reserve power supply and microwave communication links. With the liberalisation in the power sector, the power problem may eventually be solved. However, at the present moment, industries are subject to power rationing.

MADRAS

Madras is the capital city of the southern state of Tamil Nadu. It is the eleventh largest state with a land area of nearly 130,000 square kilometres. Madras has a population of 5.4 million. It is strategically located midway between the Far-east and Middle-east. It is also one of the most industrially advanced states in India and it accounts for 13% of India's exports. The state has an international airport at Madras and six domestic airports connecting the state to the rest of India. It has two major all-weather ports at Madras and Tuticorin, two intermediate ports and six minor ports. Tamil Nadu does not suffer from acute power shortages.

According to Tamil Nadu Industrial Development Corporation Ltd. (TIDCO), Tamil Nadu has a population (1991 census) of 56 million with a literacy rate of 64%. An export processing zone encompassing 100 hectares, with good infrastructure facilities, is located 10 kilometres south of Madras International Airport. Wage levels in Tamil Nadu are still modest by world standards. Supervisory staff earn around US$5,000 per annum, and skilled workers earn about US$3,000.

Tamil Nadu has inherent strength in a number of industries. It has a long tradition in leather, ready-made garments, cotton textiles, engineering products, marine products, handlooms and granite. The bulk of the exports are mainly from these seven industries which account for 79% of exports from Tamil Nadu. Engineering industries in Tamil Nadu manufacture everything from turbines to castings. The automobile industry also has been developed extensively. Today, the state produces 27% of the commercial vehicles, 26% of the mopeds and 13% of the motor cycles produced in all of India. Industrial units located in Madras, and its satellites, are responsible for nearly 45% of Tamil Nadu's total industrial output.

The main driver of industrial activity in Tamil Nadu is the auto industry. This state also has the necessary infrastructure to support the engineering products industry. Castings factories, printed circuit boards, test jigs, and fixtures suppliers, for example, have their offices in and around Madras.

The Indian culture in Madras is very similar to that in Singapore, and it should not be alien to any Singapore investor. Being familiar with the culture is a great advantage when handling human resources issues.

STRATEGIC ALLIANCES

Visits were made to businesses in three economic zones. The companies visited were publicly listed, and one business was an equity joint venture involving three separate countries.

Prior to the reforms, foreign joint venture partners were not allowed more than a 40% share of a company. With the introduction of reforms, foreign interests are allowed automatic approvals up to 51% in foreign equity in trading companies and priority industries. There is still a small list of industries which require licensing approval from the government. Several products are permitted to be manufactured only by small-scale industrial units and they are not open to large industries unless for export. There are 35 industries in which foreign investment will be permitted automatically up to 51%. This relaxation by the Indian government has made the approval process simple and transparent.

Up to 100% foreign equity participation may be permitted for units set up in EPZs, or units that are 100% EOUs subject to specific norms. Foreign interests are also allowed to submit applications to the Foreign Investment Board if they desire greater than a 51% share in those industries identified. It seems that this latter choice is preferred. About 90% of all foreign investments use the Foreign Investment Board route when entering into a joint venture in India.

Joint ventures with 51% foreign participation are not restricted in their production volumes and they are allowed to freely select the location to build their factories. India allows for equity in perpetuity. Foreigners have no obligation to dilute their investment. This is an advantage that is not offered in many East Asian developing countries.

There are many forms of alliance that foreign participants in India can choose as an entry strategy. Some examples are supplier relationships, licensing, franchising, management contracts, turnkey projects, or equity share ownership in a joint venture company. The limitations of these entry strategies are governed by the regulations on foreign investment and interest in the Indian economy.

Consideration of the need for strategic alliances is important for any company wishing to invest in the Indian economy. Firstly, the company may not have enough knowledge about the problems in India and, therefore, an Indian partner's more intimate knowledge of the environment would moderate the risk to an acceptable level. Secondly, the investor may be interested in an industrial sector where the Indian government may not allow 100% participation. Thirdly, the investor may want to limit risk by learning from the Indian partner. The mode of strategic alliance selected should fit the strategic objectives of the investor.

India has an established legal system which the investor may rely upon. Therefore, the drafting of the alliance agreement has to be carefully reviewed. Alliance with an Indian partner may help the investor to overcome trade barriers, access low cost labour/materials and establish a foothold in the Indian market. Incentives, in terms of subsidies from some state governments, may also be obtained. Investors wishing to enter into an alliance must pay attention to the protection of assets and the duration of the alliance. However, investors should not rely excessively on legal documents to preserve the health of the alliance. Such practices may be detrimental to the survival of the alliance in the longer term. A balanced approach must be taken.

Supplier Partnership

This form of alliance is useful if the investor wants to gain more knowledge about the quality of manufactured components from India. The investment risks are limited by the value purchased. This relationship could be used to assess the management skills of the Indian counterpart. When the investor has gained more knowledge about the environment and the capability and commitment of the supplier, a closer alliance can then be formulated. This method of entry carries a low risk and allows the potential investor to learn the important aspects of managing an alliance with the Indian counterpart. The disadvantages of such a move include missing out on opportunities in the Indian market. Timeliness of investments is always an important factor.

Licensing

This method of alliance could be a quick way to enter the Indian market. A licensing agreement grants rights on intangible property to another firm for a specified period of time and the partner or licensee ordinarily pays a royalty to the licensor in exchange. However, by transferring rights to another firm, the owner undoubtedly loses some control over the asset. There are numerous potential problems with a lack of control that should be settled in the original licensing agreement. Provisions should be made for the termination of the agreement if the parties do not adhere to the directives. Licensing is now possible in India with the relaxation of regulations that limited the use of foreign brands in India. In such cases, the investor must take precaution to ensure that the quality level of goods and services is maintained to protect the image of the brand. This quality aspect was not a forte of Indian businesses in the past. However, there have been improvements in recent times.

Management Contracts

This form of alliance is the most attractive when an investor has distinctive competencies in specific administration and management skills which could be used to improve the operational efficiency of some Indian firms. Management contracts may be combined with equity participation where the foreign firm provides equipment and managerial skills to the Indian partner. Singapore companies who have proficiency in high productivity areas may want to use this expertise to gain benefits from the low-cost labour situation in India. An example of a viable venture is when a foreign investor uses its management capability to produce a high volume printed circuit board assembly in India for export. In this instance, equity participation is also desirable.

The procedures for royalty payments in India have been liberalised. Automatic permission is allowed for lump sum payments up to Rs 10 million for foreign technology agreements in selected industries. However, investors who desire technology agreements that do not fall under the automatic route may apply for approval through the Secretariat of Industrial Approval.

Joint Ventures

This is the most common form of alliance found in India. In the past, foreign participation was limited to 40%. However, with reforms, many of the foreign partners have applied to increase their stake to 100%. Allen-Bradley and AEG are examples of such companies. In most cases, 100% equity owned companies are the desired strategy. No doubt, this preference has resulted from operating in a heavily regulated environment which caused inefficiencies beyond their control. It may be useful for foreign participants to bring in management expertise to train the Indian managers.

INVESTMENT OPPORTUNITY

Despite current problems, India nevertheless is an attractive location for investment. The political structure in the country has been one of stable democracy since 1947. Although there has been a shift of power from one party to another, in recent years there is no instability in the political situation. The whole country is now focused on reform because it arises from fundamental macroeconomic imbalances.

India offers abundant natural resources and, thus, for many Singaporean firms it offers opportunity to gain control over the supply of raw materials. Companies wishing to have more control of sourcing upstream materials should consider India as an investment opportunity.

India has a supply of skilled manpower. Many companies in Singapore have already hired skilled Indian machinists for deployment in Singapore. The labour force is conversant with the English language.

This is an important consideration. The quality of Indian professionals, especially in the IT sector, is well known. The creative nature of the labour force has spawned a large research and development network and an entrepreneurial culture.

Industrial reforms have opened up the Indian economy in stages. Slowly, but surely, the Indian economy will be integrated into the world economy. This offers investors an opportunity to reach out to other parts of the world through India. For example, India has a special trade arrangement with Russia. The industrial base is large, with activities in diversified manufacturing areas. The reforms will also bring about an expanded local market which will be attractive.

India is recommended for investors who have a ready product and who wish to exploit opportunities in the India market; require some control in upstream materials; need to leverage on a low cost labour force; and have the technology and management skills that are relevant to the Indian market. The entry strategy could either be a 100% owned venture or a strategic alliance with carefully selected partners.

CONCLUSION

This paper has reviewed the strengths and weaknesses of the three economic zones visited. Each of the states has its specific strengths in certain industrial bases. We observed that all the states are actively pursuing investors in all areas. The advantages and disadvantages for investors vary in each of the states. Each investor must review the strengths and weaknesses in the light of their own business interests.

There are sufficient reasons and opportunities for Singapore investors to consider India as there are upstream and downstream compatibilities for Singapore industries. Some management problems have been highlighted that need to be resolved but they are not sufficient reasons for by-passing India as a favourable investment location.

The precision industrial base in Madras, for example, offers opportunities for Singapore companies to source their parts and components such as machine and precision die-casting parts. The machine tools industry also may be an attractive market for Singapore because the technology level generally is lower than that in Singapore. Finally, the IT centre in Bangalore may offer Singapore companies opportunities for research and development work since this sector is more advanced.

REFERENCES

Abraham George, *Doing Business in India*, A presentation to the MBA class of the School of Business and Accountancy, Nanyang Technological University, November 1994.

Balaraman V., *An Analysis of Exports from Tamil Nadu*, Chairman, FIEO(SR) , 1994.

Business India, 5 to 18 December 1994.

"Business Standard", *The Smart Investor*, Annual Issue 1993–94.

Doing Business with India, Singapore-Indian Chamber of Commerce and Industry, 1994.

Economic Bulletin, High Commission of India in Singapore, September 1994.

Economic Bulletin, High Commission of India in Singapore, October 1994.

Economic Reforms in India, Highlights and Update, Joint Business Councils, FICCI and ASSOCHAM, October 1994.

Economic Trends, Federation of Indian Chambers of Commerce and Industry, 1994.

Editorial, *The Sunday Times,* 11 December 1994.

India Means Business, Ministry of External Affairs, Government of India, 1994.

Indo-Singapore Bilateral Relations: Trade and Economic, High Commission of India in Singapore, 1994.

India — A Business Destination, Confederation of Indian Industries, August 1994.

Macro Economic Policy Changes in India and its Impact on Singapore-India Economic Relations, High Commission of India in Singapore, 1994.

Sankaran Laxam, *Business Environment and Investment Opportunities — A Post Reform Scenario*, President, GMCI.

Singh Manmohan, *India's Economic Relations with East and South-east Asia*, Address by Finance Minister of India at a meeting of the World Economic Forum, Singapore, 14 October 1994.

INDUSTRY ANALYSES

Chapter 8

Opportunities in the Indian Tourism Industry[1]

BY
Paul TEO Choon Boh
LIEW Kian Heng

INTRODUCTION

INDIA, THE LARGEST democracy in the world, is making great strides and placing great importance on tourism. Tourism is already the country's third largest foreign exchange earner, bringing in Rs 46 billion (S$2.3 billion) in 1993–94 (*Country Report*, p. 22). Recognising the socio-economic importance of tourism, the Indian government is giving high priority to the development of the tourism industry.

According to one of its documents, the Indian government acknowledges the beneficial characteristics of tourism in the following words:

> Tourism is now recognised as an activity generating a number of social and economic benefits. It promotes national integration and international understanding, creates employment opportunities and augments foreign exchange earnings. Tourism also gives support to local handicrafts and cultural activities. Expenditure by tourists has a multiplier effect and also generates consid-

[1] See Appendix 8–1 for acknowledgements.

erable tax revenue. All these benefits are achieved with a relatively low level of investment (Seventh Five-Year Plan, p. 234).

The Singapore government also recognises the potential for tourism investment in India as reflected in recent milestone events including:

(i) the signing of the Memorandum of Understanding (MOU) on Tourism Cooperation with India on 24 January 1994, which marks a formal agreement for tourism cooperation;
(ii) the submission of a tourism plan for India from Singapore's Prime Minister to India's Prime Minister in August 1994, which shows the areas in which the Singapore government thinks it would be able to contribute in terms of tourism investment in India; and
(iii) the visit of Prime Minister Goh Chok Tong, with tourism officials and potential investors to India, from 3 to 6 January 1995, which shows the public and private sector interest in tourism projects.

The objective of this chapter is to analyse and highlight potential areas of tourism investment in India. This is achieved by analysing domestic and international demand, and various components of supply, such as attractions, information/promotion, transportation and services. The scope is kept broad and gives insights into each of the demand and supply components.

METHOD

Data Collection

Information on tourist attractions, hotels and travel agencies were collected from the Government of India tourist office in Singapore. Information on doing business in India was collected from the Singapore-Indian Chamber of Commerce and Industry. Secondary search was conducted using reports, journals, books and CD-ROMs at Nanyang Technological University (NTU), National University of Singapore (NUS) and Singapore Tourist Promotion Board. A country profile of India was also obtained through internet. In India, interviews and discussions were held with officials from the Department of Tourism in Delhi, Bangalore (Karnataka state) and Madras (Tamil Nadu state). Discussions were also held with private sector tour operators, hotel consultants and the British Tourist Authority representative in India. The opportunities identified, and the recommendations put forth, are based on our judgement after these interviews and discussions, and after studying the extensive materials collected.

Data Analysis

In order to obtain a macro view of issues facing potential investors, a demand/supply analysis was used based on a model of a functioning tourism system (Gunn, 1988, pp. 68–73). The model incorporates a demand (market) and a supply component. The demand component refers to domestic and international tourists. The four components of supply are attractions, information/promotion, transportation and services.

Tourist arrivals, both domestic and international, are vital to the success of a tourist destination. A diversity of attractions must be available and information about this, and the destination itself, needs to be promoted. Transportation is required to bring tourists to a destination. Upon arrival, tourists need various services including accommodation, food, beverages, entertainment and tours .

Domestic tourists are hidden residents. Domestic demand is analysed in terms of income classes and their likelihood of participating in domestic tourism. International tourists are visitors from overseas. International demand is analysed in terms of the cost involved, volume, season, sensitivity to negative media exposure, purpose of trip, length of stay and nationalities. For each of the supply components, the current situation is presented, followed by a description of opportunities for investment.

DEMAND ANALYSIS

Domestic Demand

Official estimates of the volume of domestic tourists in India were not obtainable. However, the income distribution in Indian households indicates the potential for domestic tourism as shown in Table 8–1.

Within the income categories of above Rs 25,000 per year (approximately S$1,250), there are estimated to be 100 million people in 20.2 million households. It is assumed that households in the lower-middle, middle-middle, and upper-middle and above income classes, would be more likely to participate in domestic tourism than those in the other income classes.

TABLE 8–1
Income Distribution in Indian Households: 1989 to 1990

Income Class	Annual Income (Rupees)	Number of Households (Million)		
		Rural	Urban	Total
Lower-Lower	Up to 12,000	68.9	14.8	83.7
Lower	12,001–25,000	24.4	13.9	38.3
Lower-Middle	25,001–40,000	7.2	7.1	14.3
Middle-Middle	40,001–56,000	1.2	2.6	3.8
Upper-Middle and Above	Above 56,000	0.6	1.5	2.1
Total Households				**142.2**

Source: Economist Intelligence Unit, No. 6, 1993, *Travel & Tourism Analyst,* p. 21.

International Demand

(i) ***Cost of Items:*** One of the most attractive aspects for international tourists travelling to India is the low cost of various items including food, beverages, transportation, and souvenirs. A survey of the cost of various items was conducted by Thomas Cook and reported in the *Western Morning News*, Plymouth, 3 January 1992. India is the cheapest place to purchase a three-course dinner, a one week car hire, and a bottle of wine (see Appendix 8–2).

(ii) ***Number of International Arrivals:*** Despite the low cost, the number of international tourist arrivals is still low as compared to, say, Singapore which is a more expensive and much smaller country. These differences are shown in Figure 8–1.

(iii) ***Season of Arrivals:*** International tourism arrivals into India tend to be seasonal, with the high season from October through March and the low season from April through July (see Appendix 8–3). The high season coincides with the period during which most of India tends to be pleasantly cool while the low season is during the warmer period.

(iv) ***Sensitivity to Negative Media Exposure:*** The volume of international tourist arrivals into India is very sensitive to media reports about violence and unrest. For example, 1991 was promoted as "Visit India Year", but political uncertainty and thousands of deaths in sectarian and caste violence, led to widespread tourist cancellations and jeopardised plans (*International Herald Tribune*, 17 January 1992).

FIGURE 8–1
Number of International Tourist Arrivals: Singapore Versus India (1987 to 1993)

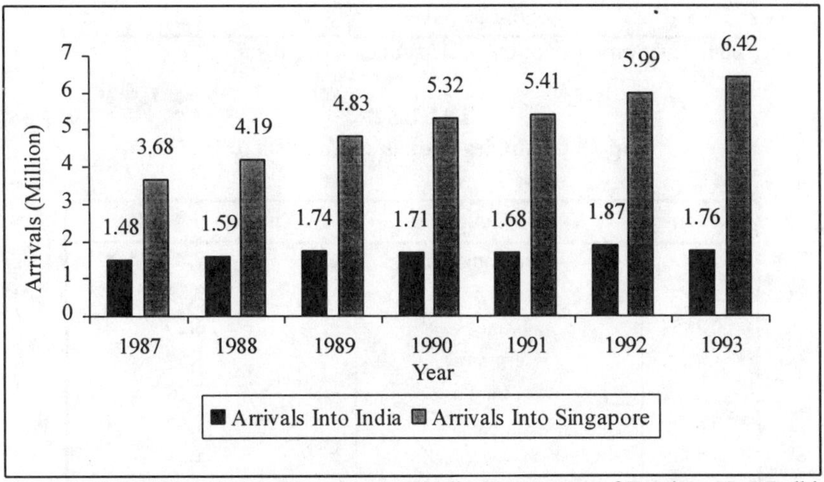

Source: Arrivals into India: Government of India, Department of Tourism, New Delhi, 1993.
Arrivals into Singapore: Singapore Tourist Promotion Board, Singapore Annual Report on Tourism Statistics, 1993.

In 1992–93, a wave of violence swept across India in response to a Hindu mob's destruction of a mosque in the northern city of Ayodhya. This was followed with a strike by Indian Airlines pilots in the middle of the peak tourist season. The impact of these events caused as much as 30% cancellations for many hotels (*Travel Trade Gazette*, 15–21 January 1993).

(v) ***Nationalities of International Tourists:*** Based on figures of international arrivals in 1989–90 (excluding tourists from Pakistan and Bangladesh), the top five regions and the top 15 countries providing the greatest number of tourists to India are listed in Tables 8–2 and 8–3, respectively. A detailed breakdown of tourist arrivals into India by region, and nationality, are given in Appendix 8–4.

TABLE 8–2
Top Five Regions Providing Tourists to India

Rank	Top 5 Regions	Total Arrivals %
1	Western Europe	42.34
2	North America	12.55
3	South Asia	11.02
4	West Asia	8.92
5	South-east Asia	6.33

Source: Government of India, Department of Tourism.

TABLE 8–3
Top 15 Countries Providing Tourists to India

Rank	Top 15 Countries	Total Arrivals %
1	United Kingdom	17.83
2	U.S.A.	9.39
3	France	6.39
4	Germany	5.59
5	Sri Lanka	5.16
6	Japan	4.57
7	U.S.S.R.	3.31
8	Italy	3.16
9	Canada	3.16
10	Switzerland	2.47
11	Malaysia	2.41
12	Singapore	2.27
13	Australia	2.12
14	United Arab Emirates	1.95
15	Iran	1.86

Source: Government of India, Department of Tourism.

As can be seen from these two tables, the markets that India currently serves are mostly Western, particularly the United Kingdom due to past colonial links. However, Asian countries like Japan, Malaysia, and Singapore, also provide substantial tourist arrivals. It can be noted from Table 8–3 that Singaporean tourists into

India represent a fairly important market, the 12th most important source for India. Currently, there are about 25 travel agents in Singapore selling tour packages to India.

Tourists from Pakistan and Bangladesh arriving in India have been substantial. For example, in 1989, 23% (about 400,000) of the 1.74 million international tourist arrivals into India were from Pakistan and Bangladesh.

(vi) ***Characteristics of International Tourists:*** Official figures indicate that international visitors are predominantly male (66.5%), come for a holiday (70%), and are mainly middle-aged (54% are aged 25 to 44, 15% are aged 45 to 54). Furthermore, they tend to come in groups (69%), as opposed to coming as free independent travellers (FIT 31%). Average length of stay is said to be 30.1 days, though it is believed that this figure is skewed by backpackers and business people who stay several months (*Asia Travel Trade*; June 1991, p. 53).

Implications for Foreign Investor

One of the basic decisions that faces an investor is whether to invest in facilities and services that cater to the international tourist market, the domestic market, or both. Given the apparently large domestic tourist market, and the seasonal, sensitive nature of international tourist arrivals into India, an investor should consider facilities and services that could serve both markets. This would help to smooth cash flows and ensure greater viability. On the other hand, the expectations and budgets of the domestic and international markets could differ. Thus, servicing both markets would require careful positioning of the product/service, and differentiating levels of product/service for the different price levels. For example, a hotel might attempt to fill its rooms during the low international tourist season by offering more basic accommodation packages at prices affordable to the domestic market.

SUPPLY ANALYSIS

Attractions

Arguably, there are few countries in the world that can match the geographic, cultural, traditional and religious diversity of India. From the lush green vales of the south, to the ice-capped Himalayan peaks, from the wettest spots on earth in the dense forest in the north-east, to the deserts in the north-west, there is good reason to label India as the "land of all seasons and for all reasons". It is a land of all climates, rarely found in any other single country in the world. The diversity is amazingly attractive, especially with the geography wrapped around the world's oldest civilisation. International chess was invented in India, and the oldest language, Sanskrit, which is still spoken today, goes back to the dawn of history in India. The caste system, the Maharajas, and the convolution of ethnicities and religions, are all contained in thc melting-pot of India.

Opportunities exist for Singaporean investors in both the development and management of attractions. Singapore has over the years developed and managed several high quality attractions like the Jurong Bird Park, the Singapore Zoological Gardens and Sentosa. With such expertise, Singapore could conceivably provide consultancy for developing and managing attractions in India. In fact, the government of India has asked the Singapore government to consider the development of a Fossil Park at Kala Amb, in Himachal Pradesh, as a theme-cum-amusement park (Indo-Singapore Cooperation on Tourism Development Proposals, 1994, p. 17).

Information/Promotion

(i) ***Dissemination of Information to Tourists:*** The Department of Tourism under the Ministry of Civil Aviation and Tourism is responsible for the formulation, and implementation, of policies and programmes for the development of tourism within the country. It also deals with attracting tourists to India by way of publicity and promotion overseas, and disseminating information for tourist interests. It operates through 20 tourist offices in India, and 18 overseas offices. We obtained from Indian tourist offices in Singapore and New Delhi, 60 different pamphlets, brochures, maps and directories promoting the various cities, attractions and tourist circuits of India. The materials have been found to be interesting and of good quality. However, such materials for tourists are not easy to locate while in India, as they are not prominently displayed at major airports and hotels. Copies of such brochures appear to be scarce, and information officers at the Government of India tourist office appear reluctant to give them away.

Besides the dissemination of information, the projection of an attractive image is also important. In this respect, India is perceived as an unsafe and dirty destination. As S. Ramachandran, a senior executive at Thomas Cook said "Our major hurdle is the image of India. Because of a few troublemakers, our image is spoiled" (*Business Times*, 11 January 1991).

(ii) ***Dissemination of Information to Potential Tourism Investors:*** The dissemination of information about potential areas for tourism investment for foreigners is complicated by the fact that India possesses a federal structure which divides the vast subcontinent into 32 states and union territories, each with its own local government. Tourism is a state subject which means that the national centre cannot legislate on tourism for an all-India application. Thus, each state and union territory sets their own incentives and guidelines for tourism investment. While in India, we discovered that there is no one-stop information centre where a potential investor might obtain comprehensive information on investment opportunities, incentives, tourism statistics and so forth. Each state tends to maintain its own information.

(iii) ***Inconsistent Tourism Policies:*** The tourism industry is susceptible to the vagaries of political instability and change, resulting in inconsistency in the efforts by the former three governments headed by three different prime ministers (Rajiv Gandhi, 1989; Vishwanath Singh, 1990; Chandra Shekhar, 1991). In 1989, Gandhi's government drafted the concept of the "Visit India Year" to be launched in 1991. Vishwanath Singh's government ordered the slashing of the tourism department budget in 1990 as part of austerity measures. And when Chandra Shekhar's government took office, it directed that some of the 20 overseas tourism offices be closed. These inconsistent actions have created uncertainty for potential investors (Ahmed, 1991, p. 79).

(iv) ***Information/Promotion Opportunities:*** The Singapore Tourist Promotion Board, since its inception in 1964, has been actively involved in the collection, compilation, analysis, and publication of tourism research. The Department of Statistics, in the Ministry of Trade and Industry, also has considerable expertise and experience in statistical research at the national level. In Singapore's private sector, there are also various reputable research companies like Survey Research Singapore and Frank Small & Associates. These public and private sector companies could offer their expertise in providing consultancy in the collection, compilation, analysis and publication of tourism research.

Transportation

(i) ***International Access:*** There are about 43 international airlines which fly into India with an estimated 90,000 seats per week, or about 4.68 million seats per year (90,000 seats per week × 52 weeks per year). Figures for 1993 indicate that Indian nationals travelling abroad exceeded the 2.2 million mark while the corresponding inbound tourism figure was around 1.7 million. To realise the target of five million arrivals set by the National Committee on Tourism in 1989, and subsequently by the Minister of Tourism, Madhavrao Scindia, an estimated ten million international air seats need to be available annually (*Asia Travel Trade*, May 1994, p. 31). This target was originally planned for the year 1997, but it has been pushed back to the year 2000 because of the 1994 plague, and delays in implementing the plan (*Asian Wall Street Journal*, 17 January 1995, pp. 1 and 4).

In theory, the Indian government appears to support the concept of an "open-sky" policy in order to increase the number of air seats into India. Implementation of such a concept in practice, however, has not been smooth. For instance, Lufthansa German Airlines struggled for almost two years before winning approval late in 1994 to serve the southern city of Madras, a bustling leather and electronics centre. Only one carrier, Air India, connects New Delhi and Hong Kong, though Hong Kong-based Cathay Pacific Airways has been negotiating for more than five years to serve the Indian capital (*Asian Wall Street Journal*, 17 January 1995, p. 4).

India has only four major international gateway cities, namely Bombay, New Delhi, Madras, and Calcutta. The percentages of international tourists that use these cities as ports of entries are Bombay 42.2%, Delhi 39.7%, Madras 7.4%, and Calcutta 3.2 % (*Asia Travel Trade*, June 1991, p. 53). Other geographically vast countries with high tourism traffic, such as Australia, China and Japan, have at least six gateway cities each.

In addition, India lacks frequent and convenient air connections to key international points. As an illustration, India is connected by only seven weekly flights from the U.S.A., six from Japan and none from Australia. In contrast, Singapore has 48 weekly flight connections with the U.S.A., 66 with Japan and 75 with Australia.

(ii) ***Domestic Access:*** Domestic air services are operated by Indian Airlines and Vayudoot, with a network connecting more than 70 major cities. However, this network can be improved further to link key cities of interest to tourists. As an illustration, Agra has the country's top tourist attraction, the Taj Mahal, but it still lacks air links with the cultural city of Jaipur in Rajasthan, the next biggest tourist draw. Instead, it takes five tiring hours of driving, or sitting in a coach, along 190 kilometres of dusty, potholed roads, to connect the two cities (*Asian Wall Street Journal*, 17 January 1995, p. 4).

(iii) ***Ground Transport:*** Train travel is operated by the Indian Railway System, which is Asia's largest, and the world's second largest railway system. More than 11 million commuters a day use the railway service in 11,000 trains, criss-crossing 62,000 kilometres of railway lines which connect 7,021 stations. The Indrail pass ticket, which is available to foreigners, can offer unlimited rail travel with substantial savings. Next to railways, motor transport is the chief means of travel on paved roads and highways. There is a growing need for expansion, particularly of the interstate highways (India: The Destination of the 90's, 1994).

(iv) ***Transportation Opportunities:*** Given the inadequate transportation infrastructure in India, opportunities exist for Singaporean large scale investors to enhance this aspect. However, most opportunities would be more suitable for consortiums made up of Singapore government companies, government-linked companies, or private-sector organisations and Indian partners.

The Indian government has proposed to the Singapore government that it consider developing airports on a "build and operate" basis in various locations, including an international airport at Sindhudurg (State of Maharashtra), a domestic airport at Spiti (State of Himachal Pradesh), an international airport at Bodhgaya (State of Bihar), and a domestic airport at Diu in Western India.

Ground handling operations are restricted by law to national/international carriers. National carriers can do ground handling for any party while international carriers, like SIA, can do ground handling only for their own flights. The International Airports Authority of India (IAAI) and the Department of Civil Aviation are seeking amendments to the law by which private parties can form joint ventures for providing ground handling at international airports.

In the area of flight kitchen operations, IAAI offers land on a competitive bidding basis for flight kitchen operations near international airports. SIA could bid either on their own, or through joint venture partners, for flight kitchen land as, and when, it is offered by the IAAI.

Apart from the above-mentioned large scale projects, smaller investors might consider investing in air-conditioned cars and coaches under the liberalised economic policy. The government of India has allowed the import of 1500 air-conditioned cars and 250 air-conditioned coaches with concession customs duties of 110% and 50%, respectively (Indo-Singapore Cooperation on Tourism Development Proposals, 1994, pp. 4–7).

Services

The most important functional components of tourism from an economic perspective are facilities and services, such as hotels, motels, restaurants, bars, retail outlets, and other services. Tourist spending on facilities and services accounts for the largest share of economic input in most destination regions (Gunn, 1988, p. 71). In view of space limitations, the analysis here is restricted to the accommodation sector:

(i) ***Three-Star and Four-Star Hotels:*** Currently in India, there are about 45,000 rooms in approved hotels, and about 45,000 rooms in hotels outside the approved category. The breakdown of the 45,000 rooms in the approved category are: 33% (15,000 rooms) in 5-star/5-star deluxe hotels, 9% (4,000 rooms) in 4-star hotels, 13% (6,000 rooms) in 3-star hotels, and 45% (20,000 rooms) in 2-star and 1-star hotels.[2]

From the figures above, it can be seen that the fewest number of rooms in approved hotels are in the 4-star and 3-star categories. From conversations with tourism officials and hotel consultants in India, it appears that there is considerable demand for 4-star and 3-star hotels. They offer price categories that are affordable to both

---

2 R. Subramaniam, Managing Director of Tourism Finance Corporation of India Ltd., Speech at Management Development Institute on 10 December 1994.

international tourists and middle-income domestic tourists.

Non-resident investment in India's hotel industry is encouraged on an attractive non-repatriable as well as repatriable basis. In the non-repatriable scheme, non-resident Indians (NRIs) can invest up to 100% equity without obligation to include resident Indian participation. Capital investment and profits can be fully repatriated under two schemes for 40% or 74% equity as in the case of hotel projects in the 3, 4, and 5-star categories.

To attract more foreign collaboration with Indian hotels and convention centres, liberalised guidelines are identified both for franchises and management contract operations. A foreign collaborator can invest foreign exchange equity capital in hotels or convention centres for up to 51% of the equity. The investor is allowed to repatriate dividends freely. Moreover, hotels are granted priority consideration in the allotment of essential facilities such as connection for telephones, telex and cooking gas (Fong *et al.*, 1993–94, p. 33).

(ii) ***Heritage Hotels:*** As means of preserving old buildings, particularly palaces, forts and havelis, the Indian government has encouraged the conversion of such privately held properties into heritage hotels. The incentives offered by the State governments are 20% of the eligible capital up to 20 lakhs. Apart from this, investors would also be eligible for other incentives given by the central government, such as a capital subsidy up to five lakhs. Investors are also eligible for income tax benefits under Section 80-HHD and 80-IA of the *Income Tax Act* in which 50% of income in foreign exchange is exempt from tax. The balance of 50% can also be exempted from tax if it is reinvested in the tourism industry (Indo-Singapore Cooperation on Tourism Development Proposals, 1994, pp. 9–10).

According to Jayanta Sanyal, Additional Director-General of Tourism, the challenge of heritage hotels is to modernise them without losing their basic charm as palaces and castles (*Travel News Asia,* 6–19 July 1992, p. 11).

(iii) ***Beach resorts:*** Peninsula India, bounded by the Arabian Sea, Bay of Bengal, and Indian Ocean, has a long coast line of around 7,500 kilometres. Opportunities for resort development exist along various beaches, for example, at the Bekal Beach in Kerala, and Diu in Western India. Sinhudurg, in Maharashtra, has been identified as a special tourism area because of its many beautiful beaches and its proximity to the internationally known beach of Goa (Indo-Singapore Cooperation on Tourism Development, 1994, pp. 4, 7, 16).

(iv) ***Camps:*** The tented camps set up by the India Tourism Development Corporation's Tourism Task Force have been a success. More camps are being planned at Diu, in Goa, and the Andamans, after the success of Narwar, Bir and Jaisalmer. Setting up of camping sites, together with the provision of recreational vehicles, is an area that small/medium-sized Singaporean investors could consider. This is a good way to increase and augment accommodation in a novel way and at low cost (*Travel News Asia,* 12–25 October 1992).

CONCLUSION

A one-paragraph recommendation to any potential investor for investment in the tourism industry would be incomplete and inadequate. The opportunities for tourism investment in India are tremendous and wide-ranging. Some are very rewarding while some may be risky. Potential investors should seek out investment opportunities that are within their budget and scope of experience. Therefore, in this section, we have segregated the various groups of potential investors so as to broadly match the types of investments available. A strategic positioning matrix matching the type of potential investors to the estimated investment size is shown in Table 8–4.

TABLE 8–4
Strategic Positioning Matrix

Investment Size	Up to S$10 million	Up to S$50 million	S$50 million and above
Multinational Corporations (MNCs)	Speciality expertise	Golf courses, airline cargo services, and domestic services	Roads, highways, airports, and public amenities
Government-Linked Companies (GLCs)	Transfer of expertise, and government related resources	Golf courses, airline cargo services, and domestic services	Roads, highways, airports, and public amenities

TABLE 8–4 (cont'd)

Investment Size	Up to S$10 million	Up to S$50 million	S$50 million and above
Public-listed and multi-subsidiary corporations	Institutional collaborations, tour agencies, coaches, and car rentals	Cargo/baggage handling arrangement, hill resorts, public transport and taxi services	3–5 star convention centres
Small and Medium Enterprises (SMEs)	Institutional collaborations, tour agencies, coaches, and car rentals	Hotels (e.g. 3–4 star hotels, heritage hotels, beach resort hotels)	Integrated resorts
Individuals	Consultancies, retail, restaurants, and handicrafts	Franchises	

Generally, the type of investments are associated with the location due to the intrinsic factors of each location. For example, as many privately owned palaces and forts are located in Rajasthan, investments in Heritage Hotels may be more easily located in Rajasthan than in other states. Similarly, for investments in beach resorts, the identified localities along the beautiful stretches of beaches fronting the Arabian sea, Bay of Bengal, or the outlying islands, would be more attractive.

Admittedly, it may not be easy to identify exactly the size, location, and/or indicate the returns on investment, without relying on further feasibility studies. Every state or city has different sets of incentives and procedures which may change one's judgement and decision. Each investment will thrive on strengths and opportunities, while eliminating as much weakness as possible through the transfer of technologies and joint ventures. Reliable partners are important, though hard to identify.

The strategic positioning is intended to provide a strong intuitive correlation. The matrix is not intended to be exact nor final. Certain investments may overlap across the matrix horizontally or vertically. Nevertheless, smaller entities would be better suited to smaller scale investments while the larger investors could exercise their might in larger projects. For example, the niche of providing tourism related consultancy services could be feasible for individual investors while it would be more sensible for GLCs to undertake airport development projects.

Finally, the timing for making any investments must be carefully and logically determined. Time is required to feel the environment, to understand potential partners, to evaluate, and to assess the financial and non-financial aspects of the investments. In India, time is critical to many investments since factors beyond the control of the investors can cause serious delays affecting the profitability of the project. However, with the Singapore government's drive to sprout our second wing, and with the Indian government's reforms opening up the Indian economy, the timing for investment is more opportune than ever before. Opportunities may come knocking on the door only once.

In closing, we wish to leave the following parting words as food for thought:

When You Miss an Opportunity,
You Miss a Chance for Success

APPENDIX 8–1
Acknowledgements

We would like to express our sincere appreciation to the following persons whose valuable assistance made the completion of this report possible: Mr. Ivan Polunin for accompanying us on several interviews with government officials in India, and for arranging an interview for us with Mr. Prem Subramaniam from the British Tourist Authority in India. Dr. Ravi Zutshi for organising the various site visits and presentations in India, and for providing us contacts for our tourism research. Associate Professor, Toh Thian Ser, for his valuable feedback and advice on the presentation and report. Associate Professor, J.J. Williams, for explaining the format requirements for the report and for keeping the Business Study Mission fun and lively. The following persons from SITA World Travel (India) Pte. Ltd. for sharing with us their experience with tour operations and their views on the interests of international tourists: Mr. V. Jayaraman, Deputy Manager — Tours; Mr. Ayappa Somaiah, Senior Executive — Tours; and Mr. Samir Madan, Executive — Outbound Tours. Ms. R. Sasi, Government of India Tourist office, Singapore, for providing numerous tourist information, directories and videotapes. Also, Mr. R. Raghu, Assistant General Manager, Karnataka State Industrial Investment and Development Corporation Limited for providing guidelines and incentives offered by the state. M. Thangavelu, General Manager, State Industries Promotion Corporation of Tamil Nadu Ltd. for sharing information with us on tourism investment projects and attractions within the state. Ms. Chuden Tshering Misra, Joint Secretary, Ministry of Tourism, Government of India, New Delhi, for providing us with her insights into investment opportunities for beach resorts, heritage hotels, and three and four-star hotels. Mr. A. K. Sood, Under Secretary, Department of Tourism, New Delhi for providing information on heritage hotels. Mr. Roshan Lal, Director, Department of Tourism, New Delhi for providing the latest publications on tourism investments and incentives. Mr. Gangesh Tewari, Director, Department of Tourism, New Delhi for sharing with us his views about amusements centres and cable car developments in India. Mr. Narendra Kothiyal, Tourist officer, Government of India Tourist office, New Delhi for sharing with us his views on potential food and beverage investments, and for providing insights from his direct experience with tourists. Mr. J. R. Bangera, Managing Director, Premier Starch Products Pte. Ltd., and Mr Dennis T. Basil, from Dam Den for sharing with us their concept and experience with plantation resorts. Dr. Nisha Sahai Achuthan, Commissioner Tourism & Hill Development and Advisor, Cultural Affairs, Uttar Pradesh Government for sharing with us her thoughts about the potential for hill resorts, camp grounds and trailers. Mr. R. Subramaniam, Managing Director, Tourism Finance Corporation of India Ltd. for providing statistics about various categories of hotels in India. Mr. Avinash Narula, Hotel Consultant, for providing his insights on the potential for investment in three and four-star hotels. Our spouses Karen and Sandra for accompanying us on the Business Study Mission to India, and for their encouragement and patience when we were writing the reports and Karen for her invaluable assistance in doing several of the charts and tables. Last but not least, all those who have helped and contributed in one way or another to this project.

APPENDIX 8–2
Panel A: Cost of Three-course Dinner

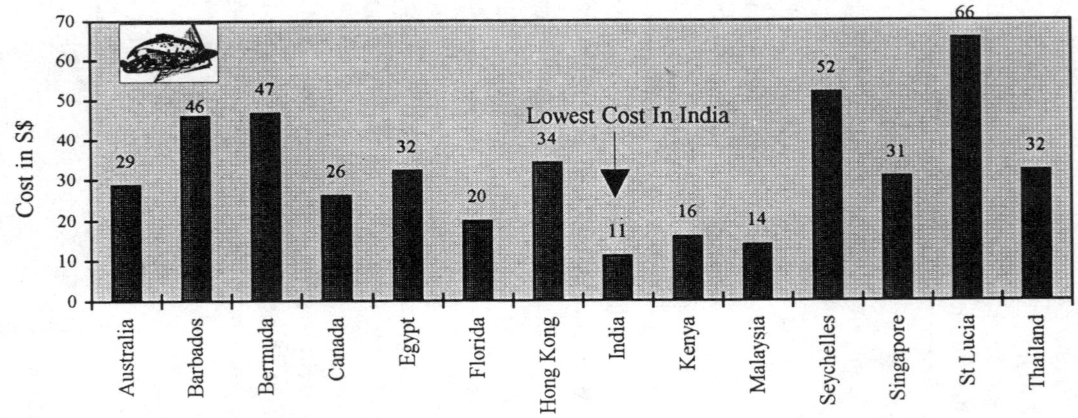

Source: Thomas Cook Survey as reported in the *Western Morning News*, Plymouth, 3 January 1992.

APPENDIX 8–2 (cont'd)
Panel B: Cost of One Week Car Hire

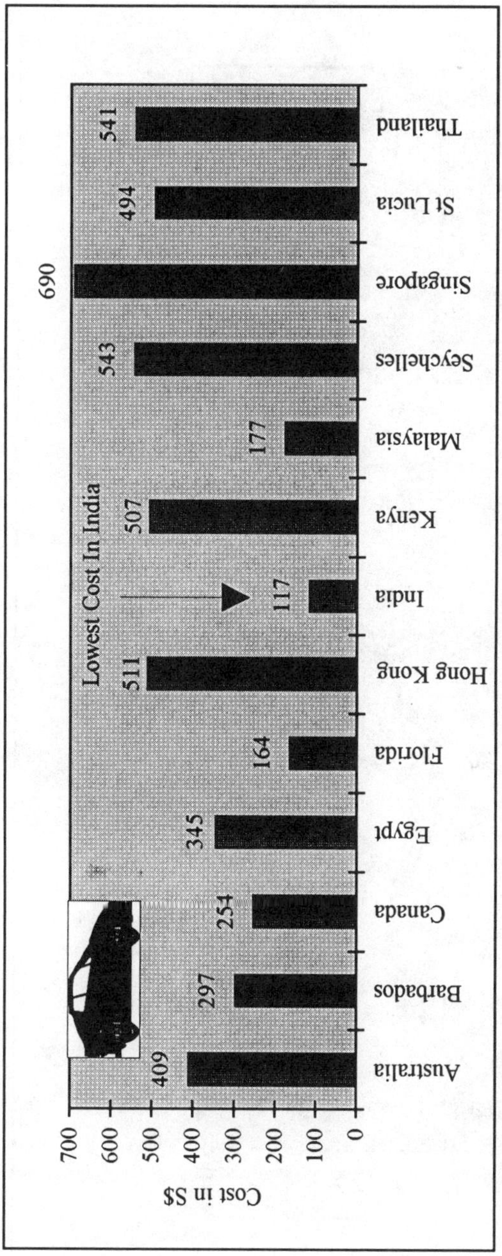

Source: Thomas Cook Survey as reported in the *Western Morning News*, Plymouth, 3 January 1992.

APPENDIX 8–2 (cont'd)
Panel C: Cost of One Bottle of Wine

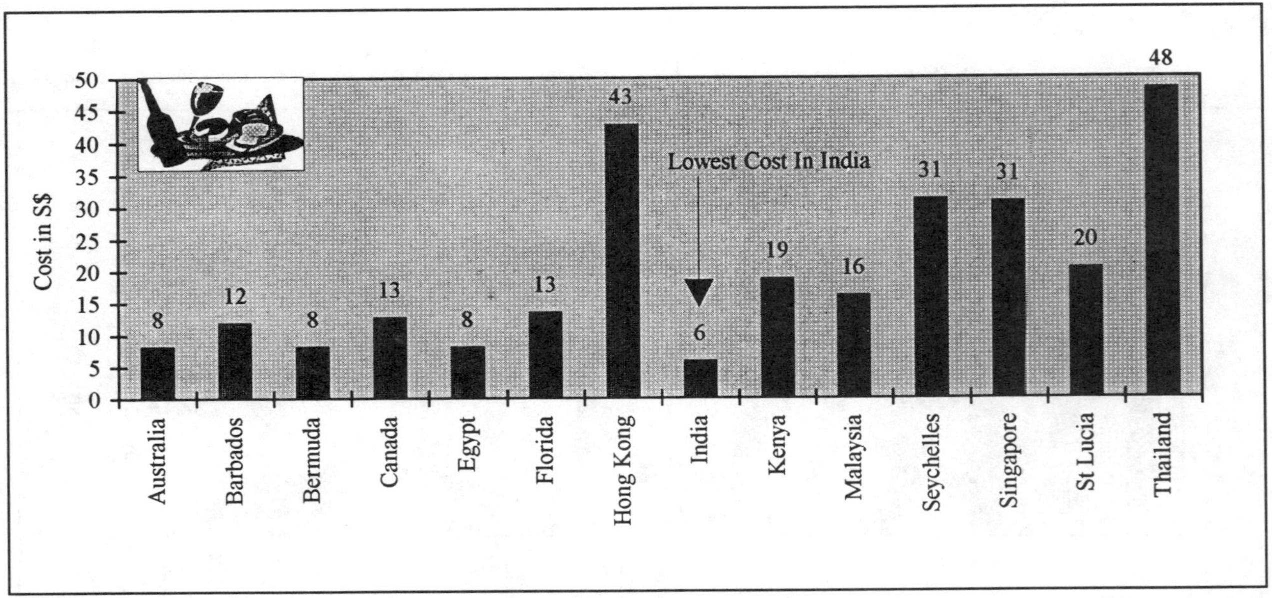

Source: Thomas Cook Survey as reported in the *Western Morning News*, Plymouth, 3 January 1992.

APPENDIX 8–3
International Arrivals into India in 1993

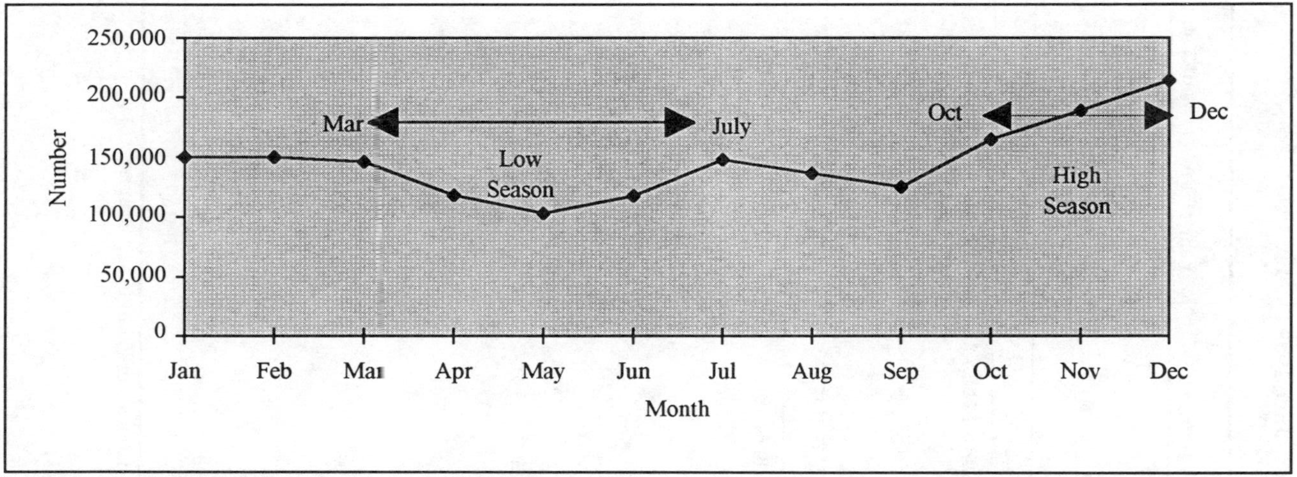

Source: Government of India, Department of Tourism.

APPENDIX 8–4
Tourist Arrivals into India by Country or Nationality*
June 1989 to June 1990

Country or Nationality	Year 1990	% of Total
North America		
Canada	20,169	3.16%
U.S.A.	59,942	9.39%
Others	4	0.00%
Total	80,115	12.55%
Central and South America		
Argentina	545	0.09%
Brazil	1,506	0.24%
Mexico	713	0.11%
Others	1,884	0.30%
Total	4,648	0.74%
Western Europe		
Austria	4,654	0.73%
Belgium	5,393	0.85%
Denmark	3,724	0.58%
Finland	1,590	0.25%
France	40,753	6.39%
Germany	35,694	5.59%
Greece	962	0.15%
Ireland	1,296	0.20%
Italy	21,058	3.30%
Netherlands	9,944	1.56%
Norway	2,202	0.35%
Portugal	1,571	0.25%
Spain	4,875	0.76%
Sweden	6,514	1.02%
Switzerland	15,747	2.47%
U.K.	113,764	17.83%
Others	448	0.07%
Total	270,189	42.35%

* (excluding the nationals of Pakistan and Bangladesh)

APPENDIX 8–4 (cont'd)

Country or Nationality	Year 1990	% of Total
Eastern Europe		
Czechoslovakia	1,872	0.29%
Hungary	725	0.11%
Poland	5,959	0.93%
U.S.S.R.	21,090	3.31%
Yugoslavia	899	0.14%
Others	1,274	0.20%
Total	31,819	4.98%
Africa		
Egypt	1,413	0.22%
Ethiopia	2,671	0.42%
Kenya	4,990	0.78%
Mauritius	2,451	0.38%
Nigeria	2,264	0.35%
Somalia	1,359	0.21%
S. Africa	3,890	0.61%
Sudan	1,568	0.25%
Tanzania	1,952	0.31%
Zambia	889	0.14%
Others	2,040	0.32%
Total	25,487	3.99%
West Asia		
Bahrain	6,345	0.99%
Iraq	3,044	0.48%
Israel	2,344	0.37%
Jordan	1,715	0.27%
Kuwait	4,823	0.76%
Oman	7,196	1.13%
Qatar	2,230	0.35%
S. Arabia	8,878	1.39%
Syria	1,823	0.29%
Turkey	1,297	0.20%
United Arab Emirates	12,413	1.95%
Yemen Arab Republic	3,905	0.61%
Others	851	0.13%
Total	56,864	8.92%

APPENDIX 8–4 (cont'd)

Country or Nationality	Year 1990	% of Total
South Asia		
Afghanistan	11,158	1.75%
Iran	11,846	1.86%
Maldives	3,854	0.60%
Nepal	9,629	1.51%
Sri Lanka	32,912	5.16%
Bhutan	908	0.14%
Total	70,307	11.02%
South-east Asia		
Indonesia	1,800	0.28%
Malaysia	15,382	2.41%
Philippines	1,950	0.31%
Singapore	14,474	2.27%
Thailand	6,100	0.96%
Others	678	0.11%
Total	40,384	6.34%
East Asia		
China (Main)	1,386	0.22%
China (Taiwan)	961	0.15%
Hong Kong	4,719	0.74%
Japan	29,169	4.57%
Korea (South)	2,319	0.36%
Korea (North)	884	0.14%
Others	48	0.00%
Total	39,486	6.18%
Australasia		
Australia	13,532	2.12%
Fiji	547	0.09%
New Zealand	3,834	0.60%
Others	178	0.03%
Total	18,091	2.84%
Stateless	674	0.11%
Grand Total	**638,124**	100.00%

Source: Government of India, Department of Tourism, 1994.

REFERENCES

Abdoolcarim Zoher, "India's Power Unleased: The World's Second Most Populous Country is Open for Business", *Asian Business,* February 1994, p. 19.

Ahmed Zafar U., "India Tourism: A Victim of Mismanagement", *Cornell H.R.A. Quarterly,* October 1991, pp. 75–83.

Asia Travel Trade, June 1991, p. 53.

Asia Travel Trade, May 1994, p. 31.

Asian Wall Street Journal, 7 July 1992.

Asian Wall Street Journal, 17 January 1995, pp. 1 and 4.

Beaches of India, Government of India, Department of Tourism, Visual Communication: New Delhi, India, June 1992.

Business Times, 11 January 1991.

Business Times, 4 July 1991.

Business Times, 30 March 1992.

Business Times, 17–18 October 1992.

Business Times, 21 January 1993.

Chopra P.N., *The India You Do Not Know*, Prabha Chopra. Editors. Sterling Publishers: New Delhi, India, 1993.

Chopra Suhita, *Tourism and Development in India*, Ashish Publishing House: New Delhi, India, 1991.

Colourful Rajasthan for All Seasons, Government of Rajasthan, Department of Tourism, Art and Culture, India Tourism Development Corporation Ltd: New Delhi, India, February 1994.

Country Report: India, Economist Intelligence Unit, 4th Quarter 1994, p. 22.

Das Manoj, *India: A Tourist's Paradise*, Facet Books International: New York, New York, U.S.A., 1985.

Doing Business With India, Singapore-Indian Chamber of Commerce and Industry, September 1994.

Fong Nien Shen, Lim Swee Sing and Toh Guat Chin, *Business Opportunities in India*, Nanyang Technological University, School of Accountancy and Business, Final Year Project, 1993–94.

Fudor Eugene and William Curtis, *Fudor's Guide to India*, MacGibbon and Kee: London, 1962.

Government of India, *India 1990: A Reference Annual*, Ministry of Information and Broadcasting, 1990.

Gunn Clare A., *Tourism Planning*, Taylor and Francis Ltd: New York, U.S.A., 1988, pp. 68–73.

India: A Golfing Guide, Government of India, Department of Tourism. Cross Section Publications: New Delhi, India, June 1993.

India: Destination of the '90s, Government of India, Department of Tourism, Cross Section Publications: New Delhi, India, March 1994.

India: Little Known Treasures, Government of India, Department of Tourism, Cross Section Publications: New Delhi, India, July 1994.

India: The Destination of the 90's, Government of India Tourist Office, Kuala Lumpur, Malaysia.

India: The Enchanted Circuits, Government of India, Department of Tourism, Cross Section Publications: New Delhi, India, December 1993.

Indo-Singapore Cooperation on Tourism Development Proposals, Government of India, Department of Tourism, 1994.

International Herald Tribune, 17 January 1991.

International Herald Tribune, 2 July 1992.

National Action Plan for Tourism, Government of India, Ministry of Civil Aviation and Tourism, May 1992, p. 15.

Nyrop Richard F., *Area Handbook For India*, Third Edition. Superintendent of Documents, U.S. Government Printing office: Washington, U.S.A., 1975.

PATA Country Report: India 1994, Pacific Asia Travel Association, 1994.

Schettler, Margaret and Rolf, *Kashmir, Ladakh and Zanskar*, Lonely Planet Publications: Victoria, Australia, 1981.

Seth P.N., *Successful Tourism Management*, Sterling Publishers: New Delhi, India, 1985.

Seventh Five-Year Plan, Government of India.

Subramaniam R., Managing Director of Tourism Finance Corporation of India Ltd, Speech at the Management Development Institute, 10 December 1994.

The Straits Times, 12 November 1991.

The Straits Times, 7 June 1994.

The Sunday Times, 15 August 1993.

Tourism Telephone Directory, Government of India, Department of Tourism, India Tourism Development Corporation: New Delhi, India, 1 March 1993, pp. 14–18.

Travel and Tourism Analyst, Economist Intelligence Unit, No. 6, 1993, p. 21.
Travel News Asia, 6–19 July 1992, p. 11.
Travel News Asia, 12–25 October 1992.
Travel Trade Gazette, 15–21 January 1993.
Western Morning News, Plymouth, 3 January 1992.

Chapter 9

The Telecommunications Sector

BY
LING Hui Mei
Timothy WEE
Kek Chong

INTRODUCTION

INDIA'S TELECOMMUNICATIONS network has experienced impressive growth since independence. The number of telephone lines has risen from a mere 86,000 to about eight million today. The number of exchanges has also gone up from 321 to more than 18,620. Despite this frenetic pace of growth, India's telecommunication sector has the highest proportion of unfulfilled demand among all service sectors. India's burgeoning middle class has kept demand for telephones far ahead of availability.

The Indian government was quick to realise that, for the new economic reforms to succeed in improving India's competitiveness in the global market, its telecommunications infrastructure must improve. Therefore, in the Eighth Plan, development of the telecommunications sector was given high priority. The government's approach to the telecommunications sector has undergone a metamorphosis since 1984, when the Department of Telecommunications (DoT) prepared its first perspective plan. This envisaged total telephone line demand reaching 20 million by the year 2000, and aimed at providing telephone and telex connections practically on demand. All of these spell opportunities for foreign investors particularly since the government has announced plans to privatise the basic telecommunications services.

This chapter provides potential investors with some background information about telecommunications in India today and summarises the government initiatives taken to attract foreign direct investments into this sector. It also discusses some of the issues which potential investors may want to consider before entering the lucrative telecommunications business.

BACKGROUND

Traditionally, telecommunications has been regarded as a relatively straightforward public utility. Over the last quarter century, the importance of telecommunications as a vital channel for economic and social development has become evident. Telecommunications is now widely considered as a strategic investment to maintain and develop competitive advantage at all levels — national, regional and firm.[1] Telecommunications constitutes a core infrastructure for any economy characterised by a growing information intensity. In addition to providing basic services, telecommunications is being increasingly used in connection with a broad range of economic, production and distribution activities, delivery of social services and government administration. It also contributes to the quality of life, and the attainment of various social, political and security-related objectives.

In many countries, telecommunications services traditionally have been provided by government departments or state-owned enterprises. These entities build and operate country-wide infrastructures, meet the demand for basic telephone service, and introduce other advanced services. In the eighties, however, driven by the twin forces of technological innovation and increasing demand, a wave of liberalisation and privatisation have introduced major changes to the structure of the telecommunications sector in many industrial nations. For example, there was the divestiture of AT&T in 1984; the establishment of facilities-based duopoly, privatisation of British Telecom and Cable & Wireless in the United Kingdom in 1981 and 1984, respectively; and the introduction of competition and privatisation of NTT in Japan in 1985.[2]

---

1 "Background Report", December 1994.

2 See footnote 1.

The drive to telecommunications reform, beginning in industrial economies, has quickly spread to developing countries. This was exemplified by the privatisation of Singapore Telecom, a statutory board for more than 40 years, in 1992. Needless to say, India realises that for the new economic reforms to succeed in improving its competitiveness in the global market, its telecommunications services must be developed to be of world class standard. There is a pressing need for India to overhaul its telecommunciations sector. This has begun with the liberalisation of the telecommunications sector in 1992, followed by a series of government policies and guidelines to attract foreign direct investment in basic telecommunication services in 1994.

TELECOMMUNICATIONS IN INDIA TODAY[3]

Networks and Density

India has a network comprising over 18,620 exchanges, with a capacity of 8.4 million lines and seven million working telephones. The number of telephone connections grew at 8.3% annually in the eighties. The telephone density in India is only 0.8% as compared to the world average of 10%.

A total of 2,491 subscriber trunk dialling (STD) stations were in operation at the beginning of 1994. The international telephone service (ITS) is provided through four gateway switching systems located in four metropolitan cities. Fully automatic international subscriber dialling (ISD) service is available for 235 countries and trunk manual service is available for all countries. Around 140,000 villages are provided with telephone connections, and there are over 100,000 public call offices (PCO) in the urban areas.

The network has been growing at the rate of 15% to 17% per annum for the past two years. The demand for telecommunication services has far outstripped the availability. There was still a backlog of 2.85 million telephone connections at the beginning of 1993. Meanwhile, an excess capacity has been built up in tele-instruments production, which is roughly three times the actual demand.

There is, therefore, an urgent need to augment the production of

---

3 The following sections are adapted from "Background Report", December 1994, and "Telecommunication Industry — A Profile", *FICCI,* 1994.

switching equipment so as to eliminate the mismatch. The government has opened these sectors to private investment. Joint ventures, in collaboration with leading foreign companies and domestic companies, have been permitted to manufacture electronic switches. The old strowger and cross bar exchanges will be phased out of production and replaced by digital switching equipment. Some key data on the Indian telecom service sector is presented in Table 9–1.

TABLE 9–1
Key Data on Indian Telecom Service Sector

	Unit	1990–91	1991–92	1992–93
Direct exchange lines (DELs)	'000	5,074.7	5,809.9	6,796.7
Telephone waiting list	'000	1,961.0	2,287.0	2,845.9
Registered demand	'000	7,035.7	8,096.9	9,642.6
DELs added annually	'000	485.2	735.2	986.8
Number of telex working lines	'000	46.7	48.6	48.9
Telex waiting list	'000	2.8	3.3	2.4
Registered demand	'000	49.5	51.9	51.3

Source: Background Paper, India-Japan Telecommunications Roundtable.

Government Organisations in the Telecom Sector

Telecom services in India continue to be the sole monopoly of the central government. Recent privatisation notwithstanding, government shareholding in two highly profitable telecom corporations, the Mahanagar Telephone Nigam Limited (MTNL) and the Videsh Sanchar Nigam Limited (VSNL), is around 75%.

The VSNL is responsible for providing and maintaining international switching and transmission facilities to Indian subscribers. VSNL operates four main gateway centres at Bombay, Calcutta, New Delhi, and Madras. MTNL handles the telephone systems of Bombay and Delhi. Telephone services in the rest of the country are handled by the DoT.

Production facilities have also, until recently, been the sole preserve of the public sector. The Indian Telephone Industries (ITI) produces switching systems and telephone instruments.

Private Sectors and MNCs

The major international companies coming to India in this sector are telecom giants AT&T of the U.S.A., CIT Alcatel of France, Siemens of Germany, Fujitsu of Japan, Ericsson of Sweden, and Australian Telecom. Asian companies, like Singapore Telecom, Telecom Malaysia, and Hutchinson of Hong Kong, are also becoming involved.

AT&T and Australian Telecom are vying for the prestigious network management centres to manage the long distance telecom service in India. AT&T is already offering real value products, like U.S. direct, world connect, and namaskarseva, for the consumer and the global business communication systems featuring products like key telephone systems (KTS), video conferencing and voice processing for the domestic upmarket. Singapore Telecom has already tied up with an Indian agent of Alcatel for cellular and paging services. Australian Telecom has offered a loan to the DoT to set up network management centres. It has also joined an Indian company for cellular phone service.

In the manufacturing sector, CIT Alcatel of France enjoys a dominant position in the Indian market with its E-10 exchanges. It has also signed a pact promising to transfer its latest technology in switching systems OCB-283 to ITI free of charge. Siemens has offered DM500 million to meet DoT's foreign exchange needs for imports. Ericsson, too, has proposed to manufacture switches, transmission gear and cellular radio based stations apart from setting up a large software development centre. The Japanese giant, Fujitsu, has a proposal to set up a joint venture to produce digital exchanges.

GOVERNMENT INITIATIVES

The new economic policy adopted by the government aims at improving India's competitiveness in the global market and rapid growth of exports. The new economic policy also aims at attracting foreign direct investment to boost the economy of the country. To ensure the success of this policy, the telecommunications services must be developed to be of world class quality. The Indian government was quick to recognise this and has given the highest priority to the development of the telecommunications services in the Eighth Plan.

The Eighth Plan

This plan on telecommunication services is based on a long term objective of a gradual building up of the telephone density to 60–70 phones for every 1,000 persons. Currently, the density is eight phones per 1,000 as compared to 20 per 1,000 in developing countries and 400 per 1,000 in developed nations. The short term objective is to double this density to 14 phones per 1,000 persons.

The eighth plan endeavours to reduce the waiting period by installing additional switching capacity of 9.3 million lines (11 million including replacement) in order to provide 7.5 million new telephone connections. The principal physical targets of the telecommunications sector for the eighth plan (1992–1997) are presented in Table 9–2.

TABLE 9–2
Physical Targets for the Telecom Sector in the Eighth Plan

	Unit	Status as at 31.3.92	Target during 1992–97	Likely status at 31.3.97
Local telephone system:				
Switching capacity	million	6.8	9.3	16.1
Direct exchange lines	million	5.8	7.5	13.3
Long distance switching:				
TAX capacity	lines	196,600	272,000	468,600
Long distance transmission:				
Coaxial cable systems	R km	27,420	3,000	30,420
Microwave systems	R km	36,786	20,000	56,786
UHF systems	R km	21,157	150,000	171,157
Optical fibre systems	R km	8,810	20,000	28,810
Others:				
LDPTs	Nos.	38,952	338,000	377,000
Telex capacity	Nos.	54,660	31,200	85,860

Source: Telecommunications Industry — A Profile, Federation of Indian Chamber of Commerce and Industry, Biznet.

New Telecom Policy

In view of the country's new growth path, and the reassessed demand, some of the targets in the eighth plan have been revised in the national telecommunications policy of 1994. The focus of the new policy is telecommunications for everyone and within the reach of everyone. The target is telephones available on demand and in all villages by 1997. In the urban areas, a PCO will be provided for every 500 persons. All value-added services available internationally will be introduced to raise telecommunication services to international standards well within the eighth plan period and, possibly, by 1996.

The objective of connectivity will be achieved by providing the STD facility to all exchanges by 1 April 1997. There will be a similar facility for all the industrial growth centres, and tourist and pilgrim centres. Besides these, all the district headquarters will be linked by digital network.

Highest priority has been assigned to the development of telecommunications services in the country. Private initiatives will be used to complement government efforts. The manufacture of telecommunications equipment has been progressively delicenced with the objective of meeting the telecommunication needs of the country.

In order to achieve standards comparable to international facilities, the sub-sector of value-added services was opened up to private investment in July 1992 for electronic mail, voice mail, data, audio text, video text, video conferencing, radio paging, and cellular mobile telephone services. Companies registered in India are permitted to operate under licence on a non-exclusive basis for all of these services except radio paging and cellular mobile telephone services. This policy will be continued. In view of the constraints on the number of companies that can be allowed to operate in the area of radio paging and cellular mobile telephone service, however, a policy of selection is being followed to grant licences through a system of tendering. This policy will also be continued.

The government has recently allowed the private sector to participate in providing basic telecom services. Foreign equity participation up to 49%, setting up a regulatory body and granting licences on the basis of circles, are the salient features of the guidelines for basic telecom services announced on 17 September 1994.

The set of guidelines for basic telecom services proposes a duopoly of two operators: one is the DoT and the other is a private operator in each of the 18 telecom circles and the MTNL areas of Delhi and Bombay. This ends, for the first time in over 100 years, the monopoly of DoT and, thus, provides a choice between two competing operators for telephone subscribers. A summary of the guidelines on the provision of basic services by the private sector is given in Appendix 9–1.

New Foreign Investment Policy

To attract direct foreign investment in the telecommunications sector, the government proposes to throw open voice communication (telephone services) to multinationals. It is reported that the government will make a provision for a dual rate of return on investment depending on the source of financing. In the case of enterprises borrowing in the Indian market, a higher return has been suggested because high interest rates, excise and custom duties result in higher costs. If the investor is borrowing from the international market where money is cheaper and interest rates are lower, then the rate of return should be lower.

Another major step being considered is to allow companies the freedom of fixing tariffs within the cap determined by the Telecommunications Commission. It will oversee the functioning of multinational companies and act as a correcting agency where imbalances creep into the system. A separate foreign investment policy for telecommunications has been suggested as a number of world giants are keen on large investments in manufacturing facilities.

Another factor forcing the government to liberalise this sector is the lack of adequate communication facilities which is a major hurdle in attracting foreign direct investment. A highly liberal policy is needed in the telecom sector, not only to develop the communications network but, also, to create the basic infrastructure for industrial development. The DoT has accepted, in principle, a new policy to lease digital switching systems to upgrade the country's telecom network. The systems will be leased out to manufacturers and will see a much greater involvement of multinational in the operation and maintenance of the telecommunications network.

OPPORTUNITIES FOR INVESTMENT

It is estimated that the expansion programmes in the telecommunications sector can lead to business worth US$15.7 billion. The attraction of multinational corporations to India is obvious; many aim to make India their base for operations in Asia. Unlike China, which has opened up its economic borders, India's internal market remains largely untapped. Its strategic proximity to Central and West Asian countries also represents a good opportunity for telecommunications equipment manufacturers.

Market Demand

Presently, the penetration level of telephone lines in India is only eight per 1000 people, with about seven million telephone lines in total. At the very minimum, the number of telephone lines must increase threefold to about 20 million lines by the year 2000.[4]

In March 1993, there were 2.8 million applicants waiting for telephone lines. According to analysts, this country-wide gap between the demand and the supply of phone lines will rise from 40 million in 1995 to 54 million in 1999. The rate of growth will taper off from 20% in the first year to 8% in the fourth year. This trend is shown in Figure 9–1.

FIGURE 9–1
The Gap Between the Potential Demand and Supply of Telephone Lines

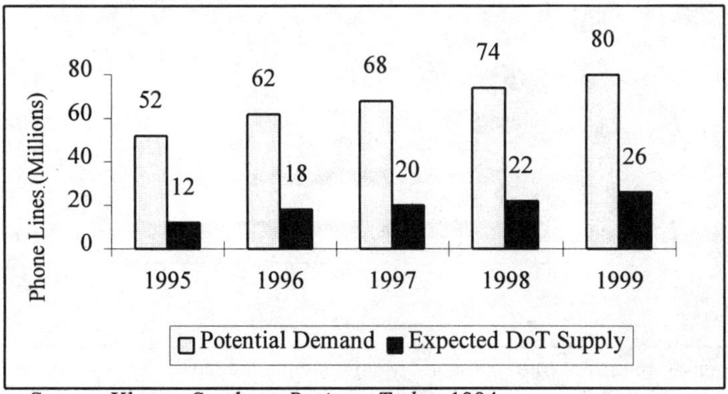

Source: Khanna Sundeep, *Business Today*, 1994.

The penetration level is not uniform across the different states and cities in India. Cities that are commercialised, industrialised, and with large populations, have higher penetration levels than others. For instance, the penetration level in Bombay and Delhi is nearly ten, well ahead of the Asian average of five. The penetration level in both these cities is also higher than Manila in the Philippines and Jakarta in Indonesia. Bombay, Delhi, Calcutta, and Madras are among Asia's 15 most populated cities. By the year 2000, these cities could see population increases of 36.1%, 33.0%, 14.4% and 20.0% respectively. According to

[4] Manmohan Singh, October 1994.

projections made on the basis of demand and industrial growth patterns, analysts have also identified the seven states with the most lucrative telecommunications markets. They are Maharashtra, Gujarat, Andhra Pradesh, Tamil Nadu, Punjab, Karnataka and Delhi. Details are shown in Figure 9–2.

Ironically, 70% of India's population is in rural areas which accounts for only 10% of India's telephones. Clearly, there is room for growth both in the rural and the urban areas.

FIGURE 9–2
High Potential States Identified by Current Demand Level

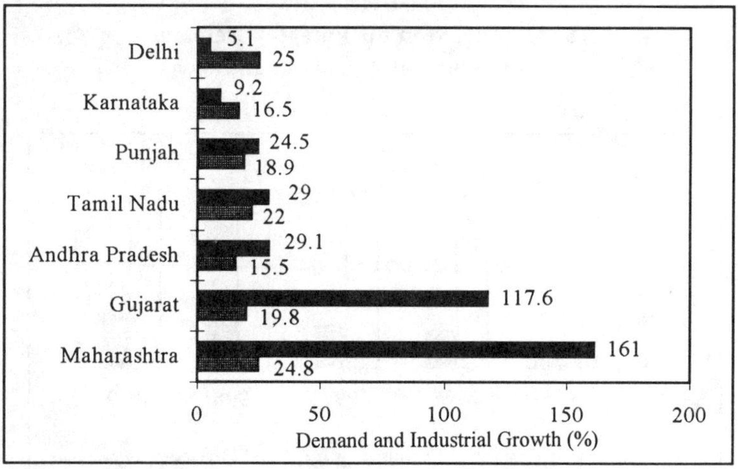

Source: Industrial Entrepreneur's Memorandum and DoT.

Growth Potential

A 1988 study by the International Telecom Union (ITU) revealed the following: the per capital leverage (benefits) from a telephone in a developing country, with a per capita income of US$100, is 300 times more than that in a developed country, with a per capita income of US$20,000.[5] The report also indicated that the percentage of income spent on services like communications continuously rises as a country progresses economically. As India's economy grows, given its vast land area and population (ranked seventh and second, respectively, in the world), its telecommunications market will also boom. With the recent

[5] *Global*, November 1994, pp. 36–38.

announcement by the Indian government to privatise the basic telephone services business, the impressive growth figures must be an attraction to any businessman.

CONSIDERATIONS FOR POTENTIAL INVESTORS

Before a foreign investor invests in the telecommunications business in India, certain factors should be considered. This section, addresses potential concerns in entering this lucrative telecommunications business. The entry strategies, investment, technology, financing, tariff structure and returns are discussed. The primary focus is on the basic telephone service, that is, the plain old telephone service (POTS), even though the telecommunications business normally includes POTS, value-added network services (VANs), and customer premise equipment (CPE).

Entry Strategies

Under the new telecom regulations (September 1994), companies interested in vying for the POTS business (hereafter referred to as the telecorps) will be issued licences by the ministry in a two-phased fashion. First, a pre-qualification round to short-list the potential players on the basis of their financial strengths and past experiences. In the second, and decisive phase, the licences will be auctioned. Here, bidders who offer the highest franchise fees to the DoT will be selected. One licence will be issued for each service area, with each area comprising a specially designed mix of states and cities to include both urban and rural coverage. The successful bidder will only compete with the DoT in that service area. However, there will be no limits on the number of licences each telecorp can be awarded.

The DoT's guidelines stipulate that only companies registered in India will be permitted to participate in providing basic voice telephone services. In the event of a joint venture between an Indian and a foreign company, the latter's equity stake cannot exceed 49%. But joint ventures are unavoidable since only foreign companies can fulfil the experience criteria. Past experiences in the bidding for cellular phone and radio paging licences suggest that bids for licences may bear no relation to revenue potential because the aim is to win the auction. Judging from earlier bids for radio and paging services, the franchise fees offered to the DoT could range anywhere from US$31.3 million, for one of the north-eastern states, to US$156.5 million for Bombay or Delhi (Khanna, 1994).

Besides vying for a new licence, an alternative entry strategy is to join hands with, or acquire, existing licence-holders. For instances, some telecorps can try to acquire a controlling stake in the MTNL (the state-owned telecommunications company providing POTS services in Bombay and Delhi) when the latter is privatised. The MTNL has an infrastructure of US$125.2 million (replacement value is US$5.64 billion) and 2.1 million lines in two cities (accounting for 23% of the country's telephone network). Striking an alliance with the MTNL is, therefore, a smart strategy because it will eliminate competition. Major international telecom giants are contemplating this option. However, a 51% equity stake in the MTNL would cost, at today's market prices, US$1.5 billion.

The demands of financing, as well as the benefits of alliances, dictate that the telecorps must function as a consortia rather than individually. Operational control, by virtue of experience, must rest with the foreign partner. But the choice of consortia will prove crucial. For instance, the convergence of transmission technologies for phone and video signals, which allows both to be distributed over the same network, suggests that a player in the electronics media should be included in every consortium. Other consortia members could include a switch-manufacturer, to reduce the costs of equipment purchase and, perhaps, a state-owned organisation to overcome bureaucratic hurdles.

Significantly, nine state industrial development corporations are planning to enter the POTS business through various consortia. Such partners will help secure clearances for digging, cable-laying and so forth. As explained by Nalin Tikkoo, Executive Director, Usha Martin: "Anything in the public domain involves a plethora of local authorities requiring a gamut of approvals." So, the ideal composition of a consortia should comprise an Indian corporation with a 40% stake, and a foreign phone service provider with a matching stake. The remaining 20% stake can be shared among an environment giant or cable television operator, a switch-manufacturer, or an institutional investor (Indian or foreign) and a state-owned organisation (Khanna, 1994).

Technology

The Indian government is anxious to see the country utilising state-of-the-art technology in the telecommunications business. Hence, it is very strict on the type of telecommunications technology foreign investors can introduce into the country. To be successful in obtaining the licence from the DoT, and to operate profitably thereafter, the potential investor(s) will have to consider carefully the technical platform to adopt.

A good strategy is to use a mix of technologies to ensure an optimum size of network, with the possibility of expanding as demand increases. With their costs fast converging, the use of fixed cellular phones must be combined with that of wired services. Deployment costs for such services are 20% to 25% lower than for mobile cellular networks while the cost per subscriber is 30% lower.

Since the cabling costs of a wired network increase in proportion to the geographical area over which subscribers are dispersed, the cost of setting up a wired local loop to service rural subscribers is almost twice as much as that of a fixed wireless loop where the local exchange transmits the signal to subscribers using radio waves. Consequently, network sizes that are not viable if wired technology is used, will become viable with the use of wireless communication. However, the physical character of the terrain must be factored in when determining the technology.

Fibre optic cables are becoming cost-competitive *vis-à-vis* jelly-filled cables because of their suitability for the digital transmission of signals, lower signal losses, and a call-carrying capacity that is 10,000 times that of jelly-filled cables. A 20-pair cable which services ten lines will cost about US$1,100 per cable kilometre (CK). So if, say, 600 lines are to be serviced in the same area, a 1,200-pair jelly-filled cable will be required which could cost over US$31,290 per CK, versus US$3,760 per CK for fibre optic cables. But in low demand areas, jelly-filled cables will be more cost effective.

In the urban areas, fixed cellular technology will offer the added benefit of starting a POTS business quickly without having to dig up roads or erect pylons. AT&T built a nationwide wireless network in Argentina in under six months. However, the backbone of the network must consist of fibre optics, since it has the additional advantage of being able to carry voice, data, and image signals. A telecommunication expert at Motorola explained, "It is best to use fibre optics as the backbone and start wireless service from there."

Broadly, the best mix will be wireless in sparsely-populated areas, low and medium-paired jelly-filled cables on low volume routes, and fibre optic cables on multimedia networks. Therefore, telecorps should start their services through wireless local loops since they provide small subscriber bases with more cost effective service, installing wired network as they add more subscribers. The optimum switch-over point, of course, is 100,000 subscribers per exchange when cabling becomes cost effective. However, the nature of the last 2,000 to 3,000 feet of cable servicing every subscriber, leading from the network hub to the site of the phone, must be determined by user needs.

Investment

For telecorps which bag licences, franchise fees will account for a proportion of the initial investment. The biggest capital investment will be on the basic infrastructure where cost, at current equipment prices, will be between US$780 to US$940 per line.

Since the minimum capacity of a viable wired exchange is estimated at 100,000 subscribers in India, the initial investment on equipment alone may start at between US$78.2 million to US$93.9 million. If the franchise fees and the operational expenses are added, then the total project cost for a telecorp may run to at least US$156.5 million. Costs could be lowered by using a number of strategies. Typically, costs would be 30% lower for operators who manufacture their own switches.

Administrative and selling costs for efficient operators could approximate 20% to 25% of their revenues. Since lines can be laid by contract labour, a telecorp's personnel costs would be comprised mainly of service staff costs. It is estimated that a private operator will need a workforce of 2,200 for every 100,000 lines. Assuming a mix of four blue-collar employees to every one white-collar employee, the resultant wage bill could add up to US$25 million per annum. This analysis implies that potential investors must be prepared to pump in huge initial sums of capital when they enter this business.

Financing

The emphasis here must be on long term funding. Because of the uncertainties in the initial stages, equity must match debt, in contrast to other core sector projects where debt equity ratios of up to 2:1 are permitted. Mr. D. Sengupta, group leader of ICIC Telecom Working Group, believes that: "The equity component will have to be very high because of the high risk perception." Thanks to the 49% limit on the stake of the foreign partner, Indian promoters must be prepared to invest one-quarter of the project cost themselves, or US$39.1 million.

Since they are new companies, telecorps cannot charge a premium on their initial public offerings either. To spread out their capital expenditure, the telecorps must use innovative financial strategies, like deferred payments, equity against equipment sales and leasing switching equipment. This is another reason why telecorps should include switch manufacturers as equity partners in their consortia. Already, transnationals, like Fujitsu and NEC, have announced their willingness to be involved in POTS projects in India.

Tariff Structure

The tariff bands for at least the first year of operations will be determined by the DoT, possibly at the level charged by the DoT itself. Currently, these tariffs involve a monthly rental of US$10, and a charge of US3.9 cents per call above the free limits of 150 calls per month in the urban areas and one-half that in the rural areas.

The opening up of long distance telephone services to the private sector, which is expected by 1997, will lead to a reworking of revenue prospects. Globally, local calls are priced low while long distance calls are priced high to bring in maximum revenues. Currently, the costs of long distance calls are four times that of a local call but the DoT charges between 30 and 40 times as much. Nearly 80% of MTNL's revenue comes from long distance traffic.

However, it would be prudent for telecorps to structure their tariffs to ensure viability of POTS operations. A representative of U.S. West International commented, "Even at the current tariff levels, it is possible to do viable business." Since at least 20% of the network must service business users who generate high volumes to be viable, higher tariffs should be designed with them in mind.

A representative from Alcatel South Asia Pacific, suggested that: "Even within a tariff band, companies can repackage their services to suit individual customers." In fact, the global trend of bulk discounts for increased usage both in terms of number of lines, and usage per line, must be followed.

Returns

The national average for a telephone bill is US$280 per subscriber, per annum, which adds up to an annual business of US$2.6 billion at present. However, desegregated billing patterns reveal strong urban skews. Accordingly, internal rates of return will be as high as 25% in some areas versus the national average of 15% to 17%. With approval to operate long distance services, returns are likely to increase.

Within three to five years, telecorps can expect to operate at a capacity utilisation of 80%. The only benchmark available is promising: the MTNL's profit before tax in 1993–94 was US$287 million, 38.1% of its revenues of US$752.3 million. With more efficient manpower, better technology, aggressive marketing, and a strong consumer-orientation, new telecorps are bound to find profits in POTS.

CONCLUSION

In a survey conducted by Chiang Hai Ping, a senior diplomat and Senior Visiting Fellow at the Institute of South-east Asian Studies in Singapore, it was revealed that India's huge domestic market attracted Singapore companies the most.[6] The result of the survey was a compilation of responses from 39 companies in Singapore which had invested, or were expected to invest, in India.

Although the POTS business in India looks lucrative, potential investors must be patient when recouping investments. The initial capital investment is large, and there is no guarantee that telecorps can recover its investment within seven years. With the current low tariff structure, telecorps should look to the long term if they intend to enter the market. To be profitable, telecorps must provide value added services on top of basic telephone services. With new services, telecorps can set new tariffs and be more profitable.

A concern that most foreign telecommunications companies have in investing in India's telecommunications infrastructure projects is the lack of transparency in the tender selection process. For instance, one major initiative to provide cellular phones ran aground after unsuccessful bidders took legal action to protest against thc selection process. The decision to award radio paging in 1992 has also been challenged. Observers concede that problems may arise because the tenders were issued

---

6 *Straits Times*, 29 December 1994.

without framing adequate rules or procedures governing the issue of licences.[7]

Telecommunication reforms are initiated and driven by the central government. During the tender phase, telecorps deal with the DoT. However, when the tender is awarded, the successful telecorps must work with the state government which may belong to a different political party. The successful telecorps must then enter into another round of negotiations with the state government to receive favourable terms and conditions to implement the projects. The political situation can be dynamic and can prove to be a stumbling block to telecorps.

Another major concern foreign investors have is that there is no provision for an exit policy for companies doing business in India. The present law stipulates that any company which has set up business in India will not be allowed to fold. It must continue its business operations even if it is making a loss. The potential foreign investor, therefore, must be conservative in human resource recruitment.

Investing in India is the buzz word today. There is no denying that the huge domestic market in India is a very attractive draw to foreign investors. However, the telecorps must persevere to work through the hurdles along the way. The telecorps will have to contend with numerous other questions such as: where will demand levels peak; what is the optimum size of networks; which are the most lucrative areas; will tariff structures be free or regulated; and will long-distance services be opened too? Answers to these questions hold the key to tapping the telephone lines profitably.

Clearly, tomorrow's telephone company must quickly master a fresh set of skills that include not just operational efficiencies but, also, strategic bidding, innovative financing and smart marketing in order to win the game.

APPENDIX 9–1

Summary of Guidelines in respect of Provision of Basic Telecom Services by Private Sector

1) **Licensing Authority:** Companies wishing to enter into the field of

---

7 See India — Opening up for Growth, 1994.

basic telecom services may make an application for the grant of licence to the DoT .

2) **Equity Participation:** Only companies registered in India will be permitted to participate in providing basic voice telephone services. In the event of a joint venture between an Indian and a foreign company, not more than 49% foreign equity would be permitted.
3) **Geographical Area of Operations:** The licensing of private sector will be on a circle basis. Only one licence, in addition to DoT, will be granted for each circle. The private sector will not be licenced for the long distance telecom network (i.e., national and inter-circle long distance lines) in the first instance. This position will be reviewed after five years.
4) **Regulatory Authority:** This will be a Telecom Regulatory Authority of India (TRAI). The TRAI will be an autonomous body. The terms of reference of the authority will include standard setting, price regulation, ensuring technical compatibility among different service providers, revenue sharing arrangement between different service provider, fixation of access charges and the like.
5) **Pilot Projects:** Pilot Projects are those which envisage inflow of new technology and management techniques, and generally involve foreign investment. Projects involving not more than 49% foreign equity will be allowed.

   The pilot projects will be accepted in the areas of low telecom density, but with high growth potential. The technology brought in by the pilot projects should be the latest available internationally which has not been in use in India. The party providing the basic services will be preferred.

   Pilot projects will not be allowed to be used as a back-door entry for providing basic voice services. Proposals for setting up pilot projects will be scrutinised by DoT. The recommendations of the DoT will be referred to the Empowered Committee on Foreign Investment for approval.
6) **Tendering:** The tender documents would be detailed and self contained. While in the technical bids, clarification may be obtained if necessary, there will be no provision for negotiations in the financial bids.
7) **Period of Licence:** The government will be the licensing authority. The period of licence will normally be 15 years.
8) **Network and service obligation:** A standard document will be

prepared to spell out the network and service obligations of the licencee.

9) **Penalties:** In order to protect the interest of consumers in this new situation of a large number of service providers, the service providers will be accountable for providing the prescribed level/quality of service to the consumers and other obligations as may be specified by the government, failing which they will be subject to penalties as are, or may be prescribed, under the law.

REFERENCES

Background Report, India-Japan Telecommunications Roundtable, December 1994.

India — Opening Up for Growth, Euromoney Publications, PLC, 1994.

Khanna Sundeep, "Entering and Operating Basic Telephone Services in India", *Business Today*, 22 November to 6 December 1994, pp. 81–9.

Opportunity in Specific Sectors, Economic Coordination Unit, Ministry of External Affairs, Government of India, September 1994, p. 10.

"Ringing in the New", *Global*, November 1994, pp. 36–8.

Singh Manmohan, Finance Minister of India, Meeting of the World Economic Forum, Singapore, 14 October 1994.

Size of the Market, Economic Coordination Unit, Ministry of External Affairs, Government of India, September 1994, p. 4.

"Telecommunications Industry — A profile", *Biznet*, Federation of Indian Chamber of Commerce and Industries, 1994.

"Telecommunications — New Policy", *Biznet*, Federation of Indian Chamber of Commerce and Industries, 1994.

The Straits Times, 29 December 1994.

Chapter 10

The Software Industry

BY
Mario Alain Gonzalez HERNANDEZ
KUM Kwok Kee

INTRODUCTION

INDIA IS THE world's largest exporter of software outside the U.S.[1] On the home front, the Economic Coordination Unit of India's Ministry of External Affairs reported that the Indian software industry is currently among the fastest growing sectors in the economy.[2] This chapter examines the software industry in India. It provides some general information and identifies trends in the industry. A SWOT (strength, weakness, opportunity, threat) framework is used to analyse the industry. Infosys Technologies Limited then is examined as a specific example in the industry. Finally, the chapter concludes with some implications about India's software industry for Singapore businesses. In particular, should Singapore's software houses view their Indian counterparts as an opportunity (i.e., a partner) or a threat (i.e., a competitor)?

---

1 *Economic Trends*, 1994.

2 "Opportunities in Specific Sectors, India Means Business", Economic Coordination Unit of the Ministry of External Affairs, India, 1994.

BACKGROUND: GENERAL INDUSTRY INFORMATION

The Indian software industry has built up a reputation for its sophistication and technical competence. Skills have been developed in the areas of software design, technical competence of management information, and decision support systems. In recognition of this special advantage, many leading IT players have set up software operations in India, or made offshore software development arrangements with Indian companies.[3] The IT players are global companies such as TI, IBM, AT&T and HP, from the developed Western countries.

Impressive Growth

The Indian software industry has experienced impressive growth in the past decade. During the past ten years, the industry grew at a compounded annual growth rate of 42.35%, with the export segment growing at almost 54.31%.[4] The industry grew 55% from 1991–92 to 1992–93, reaching Rs 11,650 million (US$388 million) as shown in Table 10–1.[5]

Over the last seven years, the software segment has shown a compounded annual growth rate of 35%. Domestic sales have grown at a compounded annual rate of 25% and exports have grown at a compounded annual rate of 45% in the same period.[6]

TABLE 10–1
Performance in Software Industry (US$ million)

Sector	86–87	91–92	92–93	93–94
Domestic	30	108.33	163.33	231.66
Export	39	143.33	225.00	330.00
Total	69	251.66	388.33	561.66

Source: FICCI *Bisnet.*

3 See footnote 2.
4 *Computers and Communication*, August 1993.
5 FICCI *Bisnet*, December 1994.
6 *India Economic Update,* November 1994.

Size of the Industry

Currently, the software industry in India employs more than 80,000 professionals. There are approximately 600 companies in the software sector catering to the domestic and export markets. In 1992–93, there were 150 software exporters.[7]

The *Computer and Communications*'s survey of the Indian infotech industry (1992–93) reported that each of over 70 companies exported more than Rs 1 crore (US$333,333) worth of software. A study conducted by the National Association of Software & Service Companies (Nasscom) highlighted that in 1993–94 each of more than 100 companies exported software worth over US$3,220,000. Five years ago, only five companies were in this category. In 1994, about 15 companies exported over US$5 million each.[8]

However, the Indian software industry is still very small within the global market for software. The global market is estimated to grow to US$213.5 billion in 1995 while Indian software revenues for the same year are expected to be nearly US$800 million which represents only 0.38% of the worldwide market.[9]

Market Composition

India's software industry has two major market components: export and domestic, with the former being more dominant. The export market represents more than 55% of the total revenues of the software industry in India. Table 10–2 shows a comparison between the domestic and export markets in terms of their percentage contributions to the total revenues.

TABLE 10–2
Market Composition of the Software Industry (Percentages)

Sector	86–87	91–92	92–93	93–94
Domestic	43.48	43.05	42.06	41.25
Export	56.52	56.95	57.94	58.75
Total	100	100	100	100

Source: FICCI *Bisnet*.

---

7 See footnote 5.
8 See footnote 1.
9 See footnote 5.

Professional services account for more than 50% of the revenues from exports. The breakdown for the export sector in the year 1992–93 is shown in Figure 10–1.

FIGURE 10–1
Software Exports Break-up: 1992 to 1993

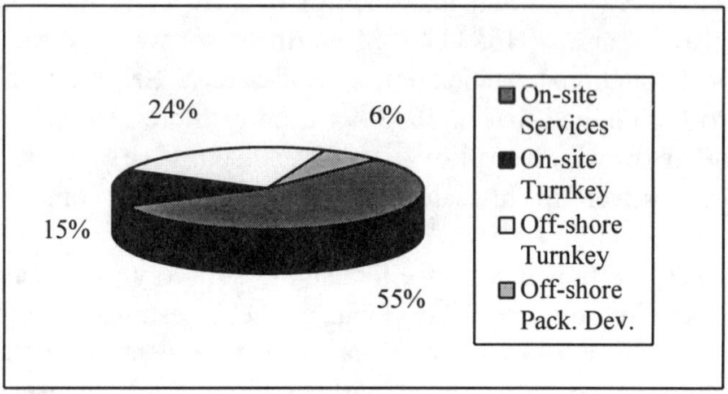

Source: *Computers and Communications.*

The foreign market composition, in terms of world regions served in 1992–93, was 62% U.S., 19% Europe and Japan 5%. The reason for the software industry being Western export-oriented is historical. Western companies, knowing the software development capability of the relatively low cost Indian labour, set up their software development centres in India. At the same time, they engaged Indian software houses with off-shore development expertise for their software projects at home.

Tata Consultancy Services and Tata Unisys Ltd. are the dominant software export companies in India. Both belong to the Tata Group. In 1992–93, the two companies had a 34.41% share of the export market. TCS alone had 25.97% of the total software export revenues in 1992–93.[10]

The domestic market was virtually flooded with numerous software firms thanks to the fact that it does not require huge initial investment (Anto, 1994). The breakdown for the domestic software market is shown in Figure 10–2 for 1992–93.

---

[10] See footnote 4.

Concentration Areas of the Industry

The software industry is mainly concentrated in Bombay and Bangalore. There are a few software companies in the New Delhi area. Southern India, comprising the states of Andhra Pradesh, Karnataka, Kerala, Tamil Nadu, the union territories of Pondicherry, and the Andaman and Nicobar Islands, is home to most of the Indian software companies. This is because it has 23% (202.2 million people) of India's population and it also has an enormous pool of professional talent (i.e., engineers, chartered accountants, MBAs, etc.) which accounts for over 35% of India's share of these professionals.[11]

FIGURE 10–2
The Domestic Software Market: 1992 to 1993

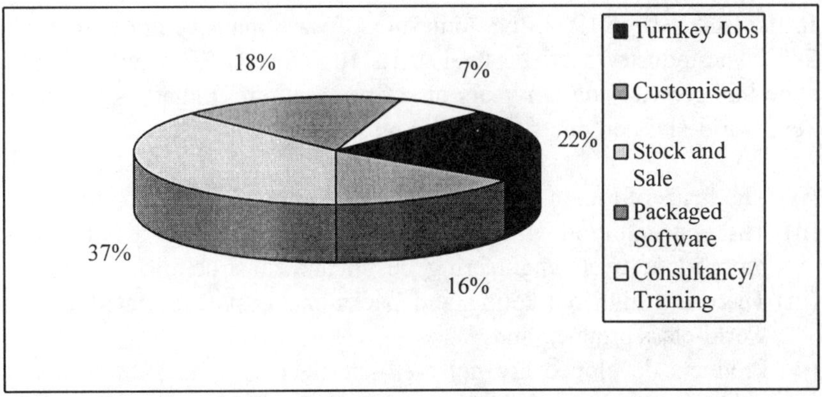

Source: *Computers and Communications.*

TRENDS

Resale Market

The Indian software market mainly resells foreign products particularly from U.S. software giants like Microsoft and Novell. The Indian companies provide value-added services like marketing, distribution, and technical support for these imported software products. The resale nature of the industry is because of the lack of sufficient domestic demand for

[11] See footnote 2.

Indian products, hence, discouraging local companies from designing and developing their own software packages. Another reason for this strategy is that the costs of developing, marketing and packaging software packages for Indian software firms are high.

Mr. Yusuf Lanewala, President of Mafatlal Consultancy Services, Bombay, explained why software is primarily a resellers market. Firstly is the fact that, in the past, Indian companies have not seriously considered software development for inhouse products. Most companies have not effectively utilised inhouse skills to develop customised software. A second reason is the high turnover of software staff and the attraction to the U.S. and other markets abroad. He thinks that the whole effort has been towards export and inhouse development.

Signs of Emerging "Made in India" Software Products

In the first half of 1994, the domestic software industry grew by about 36%. The industry posted a total of Rs 105 crore (US$35 million). Despite this growth, and ten years of software culture, India has yet to invent world-class products. The main reasons are:

(i) The focus of Indian software companies is on niche applications;
(ii) The concentration of IT people is on programming, leaving little room for software engineering, design and construction;
(iii) There are high marketing and packaging costs associated with a world-class product; and
(iv) Products developed are not well-packaged (i.e., lack of manuals, video for training, brochures, hot lines, etc.).[12]

However, there are some companies which have successfully launched India-made software solutions. Examples are Infosys' DMAP (Distribution Management System), Eagle (Warehouse Management System) and Bancs 2000 (SAFE technology for global banking).[13]

Expected Domestic Market and Export Growth

Both the domestic and export markets are growing. However, the export market is expected to grow at a faster rate than the domestic market. In

---

[12] *Software Today,* November 1994.
[13] *Infosys Annual Report* 1993–94 and brochures.

fact, software exports for 1994–95, estimated at US$500 million, are expected to reach the US$1 billion barrier in 1996–97.

The export market will still be targeted at the West but there is increasing interest in developing other markets such as Africa, the Middle East (Syria, Lebanon and Jordan) and the Far East (Japan, Singapore, etc.). In fact, the Far East market approximated 17% of total export revenues[14] in 1994–95.

Government Incentives to Boost Software Exports

The Indian government launched a major initiative to boost the software industry by introducing the Software Technology Park (STP) scheme in 1991. With a 100% export-orientation, the STP scheme is meant for the development and export of computer software using data communication links, or physical media, including the export of professional services.

To implement this scheme, an autonomous organisation, Software Technology Parks of India, was set up by the government under the Department of Electronics (DoE). This organisation established STPs under Gandhinagar (near Ahmedabad), Hyderabad, Noida (near Delhi), Pune and Thiruvananthapuram, to foster the export of computer software. The state governments of Rajasthan and West Bengal also set up STPs at Jaipur and Calcutta, respectively.

The main objectives in setting up the STPs are:

(i) To establish infrastructure resources like data communication, core computer facilities, built-up space, common amenities, etc.;
(ii) To provide services like import certification, software valuation and project approvals;
(iii) To promote the development/export of software services through technology assessments, market analysis, marketing segmentation, marketing support, etc.; and
(iv) To train professionals, and encourage design and development in the field of software engineering.

Some of the benefits are:

(i) 100% foreign equity is permitted.

---

[14] See footnote 6.

(ii) All imports on STP units are completely duty free.
(iii) Sales in the domestic tariff area are permissible (up to 25% of the export in value terms).
(iv) STP units are exempted from corporate income tax for a block of five years in the first eight years of operations.[15]

At present, around 270 companies have been registered under STP. Of these, 131 companies have already started operations and 70 of them have started exporting. The number of foreign investment and technical collaboration approvals from August 1991 to June 1994 was 190 (technical 44; financial 146).

Need for a National IT Vision

There is a growing realisation of the need for a national IT vision. Based on a survey conducted on the status of IT in India, FICCI called for a "comprehensive National Information Technology Strategy and Policy and time-bound action plans". The IT sector is developing rather haphazardly and haltingly, sometimes resulting in the duplication of investment and an increased cost burden to users. The use of IT in India is still parochial with a ratio of more than one thousand people to a computer. Key infrastructure areas, like power, telecom, food supply management and transportation, still use the technology in a minuscule manner.[16]

The IT vision should be one in which government, industry, users and the media work towards promoting the use of IT in a more meaningful way. Even with the question "what could the Indian IT vision be?" still in the air, a few points are obvious. First, a vision should have users as the focal point and it would have to involve private and government IT associations. Second, it would have to select a few highly visible implementable action points, identify key priority areas which IT can address, and suggest where usage can be actively pushed. Third, the vision would have to focus on the continuous development of quality manpower, in addition to integrating computers and communications in its fold. Finally, it would need a medium-term framework for implementation and the capability to raise resources for its implementation.[17]

---

[15] See footnote 12.
[16] See footnote 6.
[17] *Data Quest*, December 1994.

STRENGTHS

Highly Skilled and Low Cost Labour

One comparative advantage of India in the software industry is a large pool of inexpensive and well-trained manpower. Comparing average salaries in 1992, the monthly wage in India was US$225 which is much lower than other South-east Asian nations, like the Philippines (US$450) and Singapore (US$600). At HCL, the programming staff has a monthly salary of US$500 while a fresh software engineer at Infosys gets US$220. In Singapore, a software engineer's monthly salary is about US$1,300.

Indian software professionals produce some of the best work in the world. For example, two Japanese companies have demonstrated their confidence in Indian IT experts. Motorola Japan is launching a plan to make India a "brain centre" for engineering and design work, and DEC's Japanese subsidiary chose Indian software engineers over its own Japanese employees to write the tricky computer programs that translate English code into Japanese characters.[18]

Other traits in favour of Indian professionals are: their English proficiency which has attracted western companies to develop their software in India; their quantitative skills, which are well recognised all over the world; and their ability to be mobilised in large numbers for training.

Global IT giants, such as Motorola and Texas Instruments Inc., have a special interest in India, particularly in the southern region. This is easy to understand. A huge plus point in India's favour is a highly qualified workforce. There is considerable emphasis on disciplines like engineering and computer science because "Indians naturally love intellectual puzzles".[19] The skills of Indian engineers have won high praise and worldwide recognition. Incredibly, these same engineers are employed at a fraction of the cost that foreign MNCs are accustomed to paying. The *Asian Wall Street Journal*, in an interview with a Texas Instrument official, reported that a typical software engineer in Bangalore costs employers just $400 per month in salary and benefits.[20]

India has 1.3 million programmers and 0.19 million software man-

---

[18] *Forbes*, May 1994.

[19] This was a comment by Anand Khandejar during an interview with the *Asian Wall Street Journal* published on 12 January 1995.

[20] *Asian Wall Street Journal,* 12 January 1995, pp. 1, 8.

agers making it the third largest software developer in the world after the U.S. and the former U.S.S.R. However, the parallel growth of the domestic market and exports has put great pressure on the supply of reliable professionals.[21] One estimate shows that there is likely to be a shortage of 15,000 professionals by 1996 and much of it will be top level jobs for export-oriented software.[22]

First in On/Off-Shore Development

A study conducted by the World Bank rated India first in on-shore and off-shore software development as compared with seven newly industrialised countries: Israel, Ireland, Singapore, Philippines, China, Hong Kong and Mexico. In terms of software exports, according to Mr. R. H. Naqvi, Executive Director of the Electronics and Software Export Promotion Council, India ranks first in Asia and second after Ireland among developing countries.[23]

For a market with an export-orientation, and with a wide range of off-shore services, it is crucial to have world-class communication facilities and this is another area where India is competitive. Further, India's data communication is comparable with other developing countries.

Extensive Exposure to IT Giants

Through establishing partnerships with some U.S. and European technology giants, Indian software companies have gained exposure to stringent demands in developing software with international quality standards. One Indian company which has established alliances with occidental partners is Tata Consultancy Services. It provides service and support for IBM products and, more recently, marketing for various internationally renowned software products like Oracle, SAS, Nexpert Object, etc. Also, TCS has established a relationship with Bell-Northern Research (BNR), the R&D arm of Northern Telecom, Canada's largest telecommunications company. The objective here is to set up a world class telecommunications software development laboratory in Borivali, India.[24]

---

[21] *Electronic Review*, June 1992.

[22] See footnote 6.

[23] See footnote 6.

[24] *PC Magazine Index*, December 1994.

Another example is Wipro which has set up a joint venture with America's General Electric to make sophisticated medical diagnostics-imaging equipment. Furthermore, Texas Instruments, in conjunction with Wipro, has a centre in Bangalore for research into computer-aided-design software which it uses to design its own semiconductors.[25]

As a result of this kind of exposure, Indian software companies are in touch with the latest technology and software products. They are motivated to be more efficient and cost effective in producing high-quality standard products.

Readiness for Competition

The economic reforms in 1991 were a big test for the Indian infotech companies. The consequent entry of MNCs following the reforms, negligible government protection and the grey market onslaught were the symptoms that warned the industry to stand on its own feet. Some major local players were not ready to face these changes, but most of them showed that they are nimble to changes in business climate as evidenced by the restructuring they have undertaken in response to the opening of the Indian economy.

Some of the steps taken by the infotech companies include the removal of duplication in operations, slashing of overheads, appropriate product (re)positioning, rationalising distribution channels, cutting the production cycle time to reduce inventories and removing the extra manpower flab. According to business parlance, these actions are termed corporate restructuring.[26]

Time Difference Advantage

The geographical location of India results in a time difference of 12 hours as compared to the United States which is the dominant market for India's software industry. Most companies, like HCL and HP, have capitulated on this advantage and work in conjunction with their North American counterparts to have a virtual 24-hour working day. The American partner works on a normal day scheme and, by the end of the working day, they prepare a brief report on the state of the project which is sent to India. At the same time, the Indian professionals are just start-

[25] *The Economist,* May 1991.

[26] See footnote 17.

ing work. They receive the latest version of the project from their North American counterparts and continue with the same effort. This implies having a more productive day and finishing the projects in a shorter period of time.

WEAKNESS

Infrastructure Problems

India's infrastructure remains poorly developed. Roads and buildings are poorly maintained. There is a shortage of reliable power and blackouts are a common phenomenon. In 1991, Karnataka could supply only one-half of the contracted demand for power to some factories. Like many other companies, Texas Instruments has been forced to buy its own continuous power supply. It has also bought its own satellite earth station which is the first private one in India. The telecommunication demands of the growing software industry are outstripping the supply. Bangalore STP could not take up any more members due to the limit on microwave connectivity. Data communications facilities are available mostly in STP locations.

The India government realises that the infrastructure inadequacies hinders the sustained growth of its industries. It has taken steps, like privatising the power and the telecommunications sectors, which were traditionally public domains to speed up development in these areas.

Piracy

The top software companies have conceded the presence of software piracy in India.[27] Although software piracy is actually a worldwide phenomenon, the problem is more pronounced in India. In 1993, the global software industry was valued at US$190 billion and the market value lost to pirates was estimated at US$12 billion. In India, the domestic industry was worth about Rs 12.5 billion while losses due to piracy were Rs 1.25 billion.[28] The Washington-based Software Publishers Association (SPA) estimated that piracy in both India and Pakistan accounts for US$69 million. Business Software Alliance (BSA) estimates that 79% of

---

[27] See footnote 12.
[28] See footnote 24.

the software marketed in India is illegal.[29]

The main reason for this thriving piracy is because of the huge price differential between the original and its imitation. Table 10–3 illustrates the big gaps between the original market price and the pirated price.

TABLE 10–3
Original and Pirated Software prices: A Comparison

Packages	Market Price (Original) (Approx. US$)	Pirated Price (Approx. US$)
dBase 1.5 & 2.0 for DOS	740	15
Borland Office 2.0 for Windows	643	77
Paradox 4.5 for DOS	1,030	12
Paradox 4.5 for Windows	643	15
Foxpro 2.5	645	15
MS Windows 3.1	190	20
DOS 6.2	109	8
MS Office 4.2	806	77
Excel 5.0	451	20

Source: *Computers Today*, December 1994.

Software piracy hinders the creativity and motivation of software manufacturers by not giving them the appropriate recognition and monetary returns. Checking software piracy is important if India aspires to be a global player. By depriving the software industry of revenue that is their due through lost sales, piracy jeopardises India's leadership in an important high-tech industry in which she has the potential to be globally competitive.[30]

However, anti-piracy measures are under way. One approach is through litigation. The current amendments to the Indian *Copyright Act* has become the severest of instruments available against computer theft. According to section 63B of the *Act*, a deliberate copying of a program by an individual would lead to imprisonment for seven days, extendible for three years, and a fine ranging from Rs 50,000 to Rs 200,000, depending upon the severity of the violation of the *Act*. Government agencies and independent global agencies, like Business Software Alliance

[29] See footnote 6.

[30] See footnote 24.

(BSA), have drawn up plans to rigorously enforce the new copyright law in India.

The other anti-piracy approach is through public awareness. The government has sponsored a high profile campaign against software theft under the banner of Indian Federation Against Software Theft (Infast), the National Association of Software & Services Companies (Nasscom) and the Manufacturers Association Information Technology (Mait). In August 1994, Nasscom launched India's first piracy hot-line. In September 1994, Nasscom's hot-line received 216 calls. A "self-help" kit is being distributed to help users ascertain whether they are using pirated software and how to tackle such problems.[31]

Low Computerisation Level

The level of computerisation in India is relatively low, resulting in a weak domestic base for software products. The number of PC's sold in 1993 in South Korea was 700,000, in Thailand it was 200,000, while in India the figure was 125,000. The growth rate for PC's is 10% per annum.

A large and vibrant domestic base is necessary for the sustained growth of the Indian software industry. In an interview with *Software Today*, Sarit Bose, the Executive President of Birla Consultancy & Software Services, said that any world-class software product needs a certain amount of support from the domestic market because that becomes the ground for beta testing. In India's underdeveloped domestic base, there is no scope for beta testing. Furthermore, the export markets of the West are much more lucrative for Indian software firms than the domestic market. Because of the valve of U.S. dollar *vis-a-vis* the rupee, for the same amount of work an Indian firm puts into software development the returns from abroad are much higher than in India.[32]

Slow Legal Process

This weakness affects the effective tackling of the piracy problem. Though estimates of the extent of software piracy range between 58% to 95%, legal actions taken against pirates have been few. SKW Software Pte. Ltd. is the first company to be taken to court for software piracy. It

---

[31] See footnote 6.

[32] See footnote 12.

was sued by Microsoft Corporation. However, the slow and cumbersome Indian judicial system has deterred many companies from approaching the courts.[33]

THREATS

The main threat for India's software industry is the competition from other developing countries. China, Russia, Israel and South-east Asian countries are jumping onto the off-shore band wagon. They offer comparable software development and service rates to India, but they have a bigger clout than India at higher policy making levels.[34]

OPPORTUNITIES

There is high growth potential on both the domestic and East Asian fronts, in addition to the U.S. and European markets. On the domestic front, many Indian companies are starting to exploit the opportunities of the growing Indian economy. Mafatal is focusing on niche domestic markets like banking, finance and manufacturing. Its vision is to be an IT dominant force in India. If the IT Vision for India is conceptualised and implemented, then the domestic market will boom further as computer usage becomes widespread.

Though India's software exports have traditionally gone to the West, some Indian software firms are looking at East Asia as well. For instance, Unicorp Industries is launching a wholly-owned subsidiary in Singapore to market Unicorp and Compaq computer systems in the East Asian region, including China, Singapore, Thailand, Malaysia, Indonesia and Vietnam. Midpoint Software and Electro System Ltd. has taken up an expansion project to develop 24,000 software packages and to set up new facilities in Maharashtra. It has entered into a marketing tie-up with Frontier Technologies Pte. (Singapore based) to market its product (Auto Crook copy protection system) world-wide.[35]

Generally, Western-oriented export companies are further develop-

---

33 See footnote 6.

34 *Data Quest,* December 1994.

35 *Computer Today*, December 1994.

ing their U.S. and European markets. For example, Wipro is establishing a R&D centre in Silicon Valley, U.S. Infosys still ranks the U.S. as the most preferred foreign market, with Europe as the second preferred foreign market for their products and services. Infosys currently has little interest in developing the domestic East Asian markets.[36]

INFOSYS: AN INDIAN SOFTWARE COMPANY

Operating since 1981, Infosys Technologies Limited today is among the top five information technology consulting companies in India. Located in Bangalore, the "silicon valley" of India, Infosys employs about 920 staff, 95% of whom are graduates. Since its incorporation, the company has experienced a consistent annual growth rate of over 60%. The company went public in February 1993 to raise Rs 13.07 crores (US$4.357 million) to finance its plans to establish its presence in major world markets, to compete on quality and production rather than cost, to compete as a solution provider rather than as a programming resource, and to raise inhouse training to a level that would create world-class software professionals.

Infosys clients include General Electric of the U.S., Nestle, Switzerland, and Holiday Inn, U.S., as well as Reebok, AT&T, and Salomon S. A., among other clients in Canada, U.K., France, Italy, and even Japan. Its main activities are software export (including off-shore design and development, off-shore maintenance and on site consultancy), packaged software solutions, and marketing of software packages. Its installed bases are in the U.S., France, Belgium and Russia. In 1993, Infosys diversified into telecommunication applications with Bell Northern Research (BNR), a Northern Telecom subsidiary, as its first overseas telecommunications customer. To better serve their customers, Infosys has offices in San Francisco, Boston, Cincinnati, Atlanta and the Netherlands.

In 1993, off-shore development constituted 80% of software exports. In 1993–94, exports accounted for 91% of total sales. Distribution of imported software was the main revenue earner in the domestic software market. Its very own "distribution management application pack-

---

[36] Obtained from a questionnaire completed on 16 December during a factory visit to Infosys in Bangalore.

age" earned Rs 4.77 crores (US$1.59 million) in 1993 from implementation in Reebok, U.K. and Reebok, France. Infosys introduced its BANCS-2000 package in 1993 to the domestic banking sector. By mid-1994, the product had already become the industry standard. However, exports are expected to be the main revenue earner.

So far, Infosys has sold its own products but they may be appointing some distributors soon. Figure 10–3 below illustrates Infosys' performance from 1992 to 1994.

FIGURE 10–3
Infosys' Performance

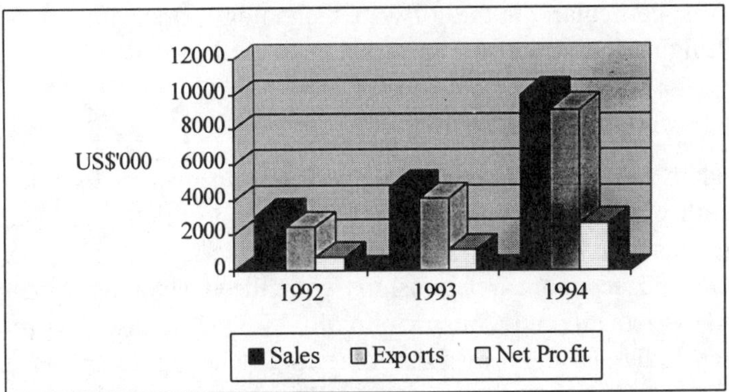

Source: Infosys Annual Report 1993–94.

CONCLUSION FOR SINGAPORE BUSINESS: COLLABORATE OR COMPETE?

From our study of the Indian software industry, it appears that there is scope for Singapore software companies to collaborate and compete with their Indian counterparts.

Strong Competition Expected

Singapore software concerns should expect strong competition from the Indian software companies in both the domestic (Singapore) as well as the regional markets. The competition will come mainly from Indian companies that have set up wholly-owned subsidiaries in Singapore to penetrate the markets in the East Asian countries on their own.

Opportunity to Leverage Indian Software Expertise

The strong Singapore dollar and the high cost of living in Singapore have made software development costs in Singapore relatively high compared to India. Due to the strong Singapore dollar, software imports and services from India are very cost effective alternatives to developing software locally. Singapore software houses can capitalise on the "value for money" Indian software expertise by:

(i) Engaging India's well-developed and proven off-shore software development expertise;
(ii) Setting up a software manufacturing base or centre to exploit incentives, particularly in the software technology parks; and
(iii) Bringing Indian software professionals to Singapore.

Possible Collaboration Strategies

For Indian software businesses, Singapore companies are excellent partners with whom they can gain effective access to the fast growing markets in East Asia for their services and products. Singapore has close political and economic relationships with the developing countries of ASEAN, Vietnam, and China. Culturally, Singapore also acts as a link between India and these markets. Like India, Singapore has an English speaking population and is a former British colony. However, unlike India, 70% of Singapore's population is of Chinese origin, 20% is of Malay origin and 8% is of Indian origin, making it culturally close to East Asia. Therefore, together with its strategic location at the crossroads of the India Ocean and the South China Sea, and its marketing and experience in the region, Singapore is an excellent channel for India's export-oriented software sector to exploit East Asia's growing economies and their corresponding demand for IT services and products. Indian software houses might seek collaboration with Singapore partners where the latter provide marketing and sales support while India provides software development and technical support for local (Singapore) and regional (East Asia) markets.

Good Investment Opportunities

The forecast for the global and Indian IT industry is optimistic. The World Bank predicts that the IT industry will be the largest world-wide at the turn of the century. By 1997, Business Software Alliance estimates that the Asian market for software will reach US$17 billion, up from US$9 billion in 1993.[37] In India, there are many high growth software companies. For example, Infosys had an impressive track record with revenues and profits doubling between 1993 and 1994. These markets constitute good opportunities for Singapore investors.

REFERENCES

An Economic Profile, India Means Business, Economic Coordination Unit of the Ministry of External Affairs, India, 1994.

"Anti-piracy Hot-line Picks Up", *PC Magazine India,* December 1994, p. 150.

Anto Joseph T., "The Software Euphoria", *India Economic Update,* November 1994, pp. 16–18.

"BSA Says Asia is Fastest Growing Software Market, Piracy Highest Too", *Computers Today*, December 1994, p. 69.

Chhaya Urmik and Nitin Chittal, "India's Computer Industry: Yesterday, Today, Tomorrow", *India Economic Update,* November 1994, pp. 4-12.

"FICCI Urges Urgent Need for Comprehensive National Policy on Information Technology", *Economic Trends,* Federation of Indian Chamber of Commerce and Industry, December 1994, p. 18.

Fuhrman Peter and Michael Schuman, "Now We Are Our Own Masters", *Forbes*, 23 May 1994, pp. 128–38.

"India's Electronics Industry: Skills Exporter", *The Economist*, 4 May 1991, pp. 69–70.

Infosys Annual Report, 1993–1994 and brochures.

Kashyap K. R., "The Offshore Advantage", *Data Quest,* December 1994, pp. 160–63.

Lehner Urban C., "India Blossoms to Rival China in Investment Stakes", *The Asian Wall Street Journal,* 12 January 1995, pp. 1 and 8.

Malhotra Shyam, "India Vision", *Data Quest,* December 1994, p. 11.

"Midpoint Software to Expand Business", *Computers Today* (December 1994), p. 155.

---

37 *Computers Today*, December 1994.

"Opportunities in Specific Sectors, India Means Business", Economic Coordination Unit of the Ministry of External Affairs, India, 1994.

Raman Rakesh and L. Subramanyan, "Restructuring to Success in the New Economic Order", *Data Quest*, December 1994, pp. 82–8.

Sharma Ajay, "Behind the Scenes — Interviews", *Software Today*, November 1994, pp. 91–111.

"Software — A Profile", FICCI *Bisnet*, December 1994.

"Software — Growing Designs", *Computers and Communications,* August 1993, pp. 47–50.

"Software Technology Parks and India's Software Industry — Partners in Progress", *Software Today*, November 1994, pp. 67–70.

Subramanyan L., "The Domestic Dilemma", *Data Quest,* December 1994, pp. 63–6.

"TCS, Allies Open World-Class Telecom Lab", *PC Magazine India*, December 1994, p. 144.

"Unicorp Plans Subsidiary in Singapore", *Computers Today,* December 1994, p. 23.

Whiting Rick, "Take the Black Magic out of the Software Development", *Electronic Review*, June 1992, pp. 34–42.

Chapter 11

Technological Policy after Economic Reform

BY
PHAN Thanh Truc
Darren DOWDELL

INTRODUCTION

PARTICIPATION BY FOREIGN companies, particularly with regard to the dissemination of industrial technical knowledge, is of value to the rapid industrialisation of a country. This is particularly so in India. Indian capital needs to be supplemented by foreign capital, not only because national savings are insufficient for the rapid development of the country but, also, because scientific, technical and industrial knowledge, and capital resources are best secured along with foreign capital in most cases.

While the focus was on acquiring improved technology from abroad along with foreign capital, greater reliance was placed on technology imports while less reliance was placed on foreign direct investment (FDI). In view of the importance attached to technology imports, the FDI policy had allowed foreign capital only for joint venture projects where the foreign partner was also the supplier of technology. In other words, foreign investment had to be accompanied by technology transfer.

With economic reforms, foreign investors can now hold up to 100% equity in 100% export-oriented units. In high-tech and sophisticated technology areas, foreign equity may be as high as 74%. Foreign equity of up to 40% is permitted in most other cases. Higher foreign equity encourages import of technology in areas where domestic capabilities are still at an early stage of development, or where large foreign exchange earnings are desired through exports.

According to an article in *Business International* (August 1989, p. 9), technology transfer was diluted in the early 1980s to facilitate the inflow of investment funds from oil-exporting developing countries and non-resident Indians. Investments by oil-exporting developing country investors in the priority industry areas was encouraged even without the accompanying transfer of technology. Non-resident Indians were offered various investment opportunities, including bank deposits and portfolio investments, that were not opened to other categories of foreign investors. The underlying objective of this policy relaxation was to acquire additional resource inflows from abroad for funding development projects as well as to provide support for the country's balance of payments position.

ECONOMIC REFORM

As the reforms initiated by former Indian Prime Minister Narasimha Rao are beginning to affect the economy, closing the technology gap has taken on renewed urgency. India is hoping to bolster exports quickly.

The long awaited economic reforms were announced on 24 July 1991. The new economic policy (NEP) includes welcomed steps to attract higher inflows of technology to revitalise the Indian economy. Apart from allowing majority foreign participation in priority industries, the reforms permit the setting-up of foreign trading companies. A special board promotes foreign investment under the auspices of the Prime Minister's office. As the sequence of the new technological policies unfolds, substantial changes have been effected into law. These relate to research and development, foreign technology transfer, and the relationship between technological knowledge and manufacturing.

Research and Development

India has one of the world's largest technical workforce. However, there is an unusually low level of industrially useful innovation, a by-product of the chasm between Indian industry and the nation's research and scientific establishments (Zorpette, 1994). A stifling bureaucracy and lack of commercially useful innovation are only two of the fundamental problems facing Indian industry. At least as serious, are outmoded labour policies and an archaic, inefficient manufacturing sector. The vast majority of sophisticated manufactured goods sold in India's domestic markets are developed primarily by non-Indian companies, typically Western multinationals. Although the road may be long, and progress often slow, the direction is clear. Nearly all of the major political parties support liberalisation.

India's problem is not a shortage of scientists and engineers. Her problem was self-imposed economic isolation and centralised planning that gave industrialists little incentive to innovate (McDonald, 1992). Companies that produce obsolete goods were protected from competition. Many unprofitable enterprises were bailed out or taken over by the public sector. Improvements in the science sector only began during the 1984–89 period when import controls were relaxed. However, it was the government's balance of payments crisis (caused by a consumer boom) that led to dramatic economic liberalisation in 1991. Both businessmen and scientists believe that a more competitive economy will increase the demand for research and development.

Cost Effects in Manufacturing

Expenditures for R&D, royalties, and technical fees potentially induce both Hicks-neutral efficiency shifts and substitution between capital and labour in an indirect cost function framework. There is an apparent paradox between the large and growing technological effort in India's manufacturing sector and her disappointing performance in terms of efficiency. This implies that either the technological efforts are misdirected or that they take place in firms that are so grossly inefficient that the efforts do not raise productivity above the industry norm. The issue is that the quality of managerial effort in increasing efficiency is more important than any particular pattern of expenditure.

The determinants of inhouse R&D, and the impact of technology transfer on R&D expenditures of firms belonging to India's private sector listed on the stock exchanges in India, have been analysed by Siddharthan (1992). Using the transactions costs framework, modes of technology transfers were considered first through the market, namely arm's length purchases against lump sum payments. Secondly, they were considered through foreign direct investments. The results indicated a complementary relationship between the import of technology and R&D. Indian R&D intensities are very low and they ought to be stepped up considerably. This is because it is not possible to identify and evaluate the technologies to be imported without a good R&D set up.

Technology Transfer

In February 1992, the Indian government's radical budget, aimed at liberalising the economy and opening it up to free trade, ushered in big cuts in tariffs. That has led to a significant increase in imports at competitive prices. Meanwhile, the continuous devaluation of the rupee has maintained and improved the competitiveness of Indian industry. However, the devaluation has also raised production costs. This means that industry can relapse into high cost production if adequate attention is not paid to cost control.

The best way to upgrade products for domestic sales and exports is through the use of technology transfer agreements. The questions raised are: (1) what will be the size of the product's market in the coming years; and (2) what will be the best technology to opt for in order to stay competitive in the market by the turn of the century? The dilemma facing Indian industry, in short, is how much to invest and where to invest. These issues are undoubtedly interrelated. Where to invest subsumes a technological choice which, in turn, has a cost implication associated with it.

The new policy of foreign investment and technology agreements allows firms access to any technological choice. It also provides automatic permission for foreign technology agreements in high priority industries up to a lump sum payment of Rs 10 million. There is a 5% royalty imposed for domestic sales and 8% for exports, subject to a total payment of 8% of sales over a ten-year period from the date of agreement, or seven years from the commencement of production. The new policy also states that no permission is necessary to hire foreign technicians or for foreign testing of indigenously developed technologies. This policy gives India access to raw materials, components, skilled technical manpower and technological choice. However, the weaker Indian currency has increased the cost of machinery, equipment and technology purchased overseas. In turn, the increased availability of imported goods has raised doubts over the need for new plants, investments and joint ventures.

India's capabilities as a host country for technology transfer and foreign investment have also paved the way for its emergence as a supplier of appropriate technologies to the less developed countries of Asia, Africa and Latin America. By April 1992, there were more than 200 Indian joint venture projects in 38 countries. Of these joint ventures, 80% were in production with the remainder under implementation. The initiative taken by Indian firms to operate beyond national boundaries may be viewed in the context of strengthening India's commercial and economic links with those countries, and also to give a boost to her export effort.

As a result of the technology import policy, India has been able to develop domestic capabilities and has attained self-sufficiency in a wide range of industrial products. For 22 broad industry groups, there is no foreign technology requirement. However, the list is subject to constant review. There is also an effort to spell out more clearly the criteria for permitting or rejecting foreign collaborations in these, and other, areas to provide greater transparency and predictability for prospective investors.

The foreign investment and technology transfer policy is fully integrated with the national policy of promoting rapid economic development through successive five-year plans. The available data shows that between 1957 and 1989, nearly 13,000 foreign collaborations were approved by the government. The approved annual level of foreign investment has picked up in subsequent years as a result of liberalisation and the improved investment climate. Starting with a few industries at the time of independence, the country has made rapid progress towards industrialisation by setting up basic and heavy industries as well as consumer goods industries. Since self-reliance was the major plank of development planning, the main thrust of industrialisation was on import substitution industries designed to meet most of the country's requirements through domestic production and to minimise dependence on imports. Industrial growth was supported by technology inflows which is evident from the industry-wide distribution of foreign collaborations.

Recent religious violence and disease in India have damaged the country's reputation but these problems, and the competitiveness of other countries, have forced New Delhi to speed up reform and introduce further investment incentives. The unrest is likely to continue, but it is expected to have little impact on GDP growth in 1995. Incentives for foreign investment include simplification of procedures for the inward and outward flow of funds, and more liberal royalty and technology licensing payment rules. Tax rates for foreign companies will be reduced over the next two years from 65% to 45% or 50%. The partial privatisation programme will gain momentum as the government strives to meet the budget deficit. Price controls will be reduced and further relaxation of trade policies is possible.

Although the changes made to the legal framework have attracted more investments, there are some significant problems to potential investors. Investment in developing nations, and transfers of technology to them by U.S. companies, are heavily influenced by the strength or weakness of a nation's intellectual property protection. This is more pronounced in high technology sectors like the chemical and pharmaceutical industries. The effect of intellectual property protection depends greatly on the type of investment. Protection may not be so important for investments in sales and distribution outlets. However, for investments in rudimentary production and assembly facilities involving base technologies well known to firms in the industry, protection will be more important. More than 30% of U.S. firms believe that intellectual property protection in India is too weak to permit investment in joint ventures (Seltzer, 1994).

THE RELATIONSHIP BETWEEN TECHNOLOGICAL KNOWLEDGE AND MANUFACTURING

Technology is about knowledge. The result of technology is related to the manufacture of a real product. Technological policy helps turn an idea into a mass produced item for the global market. Today's manufacturers face an unforgiving environment of relentless cost pressures and increasingly competitive markets. Flexible manufacturing, started by the Japanese in the late 1970s, is driven by customer preferences. Computer integrated manufacturing was conceived as a single system (from design to delivery) driven by the needs of the market. A company considering investing in advanced manufacturing technology should ask itself three questions: (1) will the investment lead to more business for the company?; (2) will it really reduce costs?; and (3) will it improve response time or improve quality?

Companies are setting up factories in India because of cheap labour and a large readily available labour force, both of which help reduce costs in manufacturing. Therefore, profit can be made on products manufactured in India. Besides the cost issue, quality and value added are also important considerations. The closed economy of the past was extremely insular, almost totally inward looking, with the belief that all forms of technology could be developed locally. However, Indian industries were talented enough to meet the demands of the domestic market alone. Goods were usually in such short supply that anything and everything of barely acceptable standard were immediately snatched up. Demand was so great that the emphasis was on production volumes and not quality. This has to be corrected in today's market. The expectations of the local market have risen dramatically because people are exposed to foreign products, packaging and technology. This exposure is compounded by the advent of satellite TV.

As India's national standards body, the Bureau of Indian Standards (BIS) has undertaken various measures to assist exporters in developing and managing the quality of their goods and services. The aim is to make their products increasingly competitive in the international marketplace. The BIS has adopted internationally accepted practices in the formulation of standards, and operates a third party certification scheme comprising both products and quality systems for the benefit of exporters. In addition, the BIS plays an educational role in promoting the concept of quality and standardisation in the business sector. The BIS has been harmonising Indian standards with international standards to facilitate imports, to promote exports of goods and services, to assist in the transfer of technology, to raise the status of national standards and to optimise the resources of the BIS.

India is still considered to be a high cost economy, as efficiency and productivity have been at low levels in comparison to some other countries of Asia. Poor quality of goods has been another factor responsible for the poor growth and performance of India's exports. The solution to these problems lies in attracting a larger inflow of technology from the developed world to India, particularly Japan and Germany, the top exporters of technology in the world.

THE MARKET FOR TECHNOLOGY

In 1947, when India became a sovereign independent state, most consumer goods were imported and this was the starting point of India's developmental efforts. India's accomplishments in high technology areas, such as nuclear and space science, electronics, and defence research, have been highly commendable. The criteria for selecting challenging areas of technology should be set forth explicitly based on demand from industry and the service sectors, while at the same time, taking into account that industries are gradually shifting from high-technology to multi-technology. Various opportunities where cross-technology interactions are fast developing include micro-electronics, fibre optics, lasers, bio-technology, computer-integrated manufacturing and new materials.

There is a need for the export of value-added products through technological upgrading. A tremendous market exists if investors have the will to go for it. There is potential for small and medium investments in technology. The products that can be marketed abroad can be either a whole product, and/or the components and spare parts. A suitable market-niche should be identified, i.e., a suitable country, and an appropriately demanded product. For instance, India is the second largest producer of bicycles. It should not be too difficult for Indians to manufacture and export bicycles abroad in large numbers. Bicycle makers only need to upgrade the quality, and make suitable changes to the product such as a lighter, streamlined body. There is a vast market in Europe, the Americas and other developed countries. The total export market for bicycles and motorcycles to the EC alone is worth about US$6 billion. India has a very negligible share of that market, about 0.2%, which includes mostly bicycle parts. The current exporters are mainly small to medium size businesses.

In the engineering goods sector, there is a tremendous opportunity to export items such as hand-tools and builder's hardware (screws, fasteners, etc.) if technology investments are made in these sectors. A study of the Western European market has shown that this geographical area imports about US$10 billion worth of such goods, of which only 0.7% has been contributed by India (McDonald, 1992). Automotive parts is another sector for opportunity.

India is the world's second largest consumer market and its commercial potential in electronics is huge. The country's electronics industry annually generates about US$4 billion. Advanced technology industries could translate India's low wage structure into commercial advantages for supplying radar, specialised communications gear, and similar equipment, at costs far below the international price level.

In the past two years, the food processing sector in India has become the third largest recipient of foreign investment. India is keen to expand food processing because it benefits incomes and employment in the politically important farm sector and it increases foreign exchange earnings. In addition, India is the second largest producer of fruits and vegetables in the world with an estimated production of 79 million tonnes. Despite the positive aspects of Indian agriculture, the potential for the processing industry has remained largely untapped. This sector has been limited by several factors, such as poor infrastructure and high hidden costs. The food processing industry in India requires a further infusion of technology in packaging and methods for extending product shelf-life.

The list of potential investment areas could be extended to show that the need for technology transfer is not only for government projects and big companies but, also, for small and medium size firms to produce value-added products. Granted, the power and infrastructure sectors require large investments. For these sectors, the concept of build, operate and transfer may be adopted whereby the foreign investor puts up the money to build roads, bridges or power stations. The investor builds these infrastructure facilities and operates them for an agreed period. To recoup the investment plus an acceptable profit, appropriate toll charges may be levied. However, there are several opportunities where there are miles of open field but small and medium investors have acquired only a few square feet.

CONCLUSION

Until recently, the people of developing countries, like India, China, and Vietnam, were separated from the global economy because of their political systems or lack of technology and capital. Today, all that has changed; political systems have been transformed, technology can be transferred anywhere in the world, and capital is free to be invested wherever the anticipated yields are greatest. Investors with large resources in developed countries should look for investment opportunities in the developing world which could offer higher rates of return at lower risk.

If India were to redefine her policies so as to make investments more attractive, then it would be easier to position the country in a competitive world. After all, it has other attractions like size, a growing middle class, a legal system, democracy, etc.

Return on investment is determined by, among other things, the cost of capital and productivity of both capital and labour. Cost of capital can be reduced through an imaginative tax policy. India's import tax is still rather high at 50%. Productivity improvements would depend upon technological inputs. Hence, an all out effort must be made to encourage Indian companies to access state-of-the-art technology. To make Indian industry efficient and competitive in the world market, high quality technologies are necessary. The conditions for technology transfer have been improved through technical collaborations, agreements, and joint ventures by offering higher royalties, lump sum payments and longer agreements.

India sees herself as a world power in the making and has conducted her regional and international relations on this basis. The result has been insignificance abroad, suspicion in the region and turbulence at home (Thakur, 1992). It would be better to reverse this process. Stability and prosperity at home, and in the region, would enhance her international status, and give credibility to her claims of global leadership. India needs Western capital and technology. Western countries should exploit the vast Indian market potential which has a consumer ethic and an infrastructure well-poised to take-off quickly. Given her size and resources, the integration of India into the world financial markets would be a major boost to international capitalism. India has made significant strides in industrialising her economy but there is a need to widen the production base, enlarge the basket of goods being produced, and improve their quality through modernisation and technological upgrading. Technology transfer can be effected through technical collaboration agreements (i.e., licensing arrangements) and joint ventures with minority/majority equity participation.

A number of Indian companies have reported that the nature of technology transferred is related to the level of equity that foreign companies are permitted. Potential foreign investors have expressed the view that minority participation places them at a disadvantage; royalty payments are low taking into account the tax element, and there is inadequate intellectual property rights protection (Indian Investment Centre, 1985). These apprehensions may or may not be exaggerated. It cannot be denied that the quality of technology introduced into Indian industry, by and large, has been "narrow and shallow". This situation will be remedied by the new government policy for liberalising the economy and simplifying procedures.

Despite a number of advantages that India has to offer, foreign investment has been relatively small. It has been estimated that India receives 2% to 3% of the world's foreign direct investment (FDI). Not only is this a paltry showing, but India does not compare favourably with other Asian countries. Many developing countries adopted restrictive FDI policies in the past to regulate the entry and operation of foreign investors. This earlier reluctance, a result of the colonial fears that direct investment would influence internal decision-making, is now yielding to an awareness of the benefits that accrue to host countries, including technology transfer, employment generation, bridging the foreign exchange gap, raising the level of investment and boosting exports. This has been brought about by opening up more sectors to FDI, simplifying screening procedures, changing the limits on foreign equity ownership restrictions and providing greater freedom in the repatriation of profits.

REFERENCES

"ILT: India", *Business International,* August 1989, p. 9.

Indian Investment Centre, *Partners in Progress 1960–1985*, Silver Jubilee Brochure, New Delhi, 1985.

McDonald Hamish, "Time to Catch Up: India Tries to Bring Science Closer to Business", *Far Eastern Economic Review*, Vol. 155, No. 49, 10 December 1992, pp. 45–8.

Richard Seltzer, "Intellectual Property Rights: Risk Cuts Flow of Investment, Technology", *Chemical & Engineering News*, Vol. 72, No. 11, 14 March 1994, pp. 6–7.

Siddharthan N.S, "Transaction Costs, Technology Transfer, and In-House R&D: A Study of the Indian Private Corporate Sector", *Journal of Economic Behaviour & Organisation*, Vol. 18, No. 2, July 1992, pp. 265–71.

Thakur Ramesh, "India After Nonalignment", *Foreign Affairs*, Vol. 71, No. 2, Spring 1992, pp. 165–82.

Zorpette Glenn, "Technology in India", *IEEE Spectrum* (SPC), Vol. 31, No. 3, March 1994, pp. 24–32.